WorkLife Book Club

WorkLife Book Club

Volume One: Shoreditch

Carmel O'Reilly

ISBN 978-1-914278-04-4

Cover, book design & editing by Albarrojo
Drawings (interior and cover) © Ian Remedios
Photographs (interior and back cover) © Carmel O'Reilly
Photograph (front cover) © DrimaFilm

Published by Amaurea Press
Amaurea Press is an imprint of Amaurea Creative Productions Ltd.
London, United Kingdom
www.amaurea.co.uk

In memory of my dear friend

Norma Rafferty

our WorkLife Book Club of two

and our many book discussions over a glass and a plate

Contents

Preface

WorkLife is our life both in and out of work and the impact each has on the other. I believe WorkLife needs to be considered holistically because all areas of our life are so intrinsically linked, they cannot be separated.

A word about language I use throughout this book. I have connected the words Work and Life to express the meaning they hold for me. I capitalise the first letter of each word to highlight their importance and relationship.

As a WorkLife learning practitioner and writer, I create learning programmes and resources to help people manage, develop and transition their WorkLives in good, challenging and bad times. The focus of my work begins by helping people identify a WorkLife path that's true to their core values, purpose, and motivation. This is followed through by creating meaningful short- and long-term WorkLife plans while enabling self-coaching, self-directing and self-leadership to drive these plans.

My inspiration in creating my work comes from a lifelong passion for learning. My work has taught me that the one thing in life that can never be taken away from you is your learning.

I love reading as much as I love learning about people's amazing WorkLife stories. I wanted to find a way to combine people's stories of their WorkLife experiences in which they share their dreams and ambitions, along with the challenges and obstacles, failures and successes they encountered along the road of their WorkLife journey. Together with how they used the power of book wisdom to help them navigate their path to live their WorkLife with purpose, passion and pride. This led me to create a weekly blog and podcast called *WorkLife Book Wisdom* (later incorporated into *WorkLife Stories*).

But what if this could be taken further? What if people who enjoy learning through reading and who also enjoy discussing books and interesting stories could come together to share their experiences?

I thought about my love of reading and how it has always been my go-to place for learning. In my WorkLife, reading helps me to understand people and situations. That's because it draws me into imagining a character's circumstances, which can help me relate at a deeper level to people in real life. When I read a story, I connect it to personal experiences. I find myself having thoughts and emotions that correlate with the storyline. This leads me to reflect on my past social interactions and real-life situations that I've encountered. From there, I begin to imagine future interactions. All of this helps me gain insight into things that have happened in the past by relating them to a character or situation in a story. This gives me different perspectives on things. Reading allows me to appreciate and understand my own emotional responses, as well as giving me an insight into what might be going on emotionally for other people.

This is what has led me to the idea of the WorkLife Book Club.

The premise behind the idea is that experiences that we have in our WorkLife shape our understanding of the world, and experiences we have through reading can also shape or change us. Stories help to communicate truths about human behaviours and relationships.

This provides an opportunity for change and development from a place of deeper understanding. Books help to anchor WorkLife conversations through characters, plots and settings. This can enable working through a range of issues in an open and honest manner. Because when people come together to discuss stories and engaging texts, they are presented with characters with competing yet often equally valid viewpoints.

My stated mission is to guide people's WorkLife learning through reading. I also have a secret mission, which is to draw attention to stories of change and active decision making, people standing up and saying they want to do something different with their WorkLife. I want to highlight stories, books and discussions that focus on in-depth portrayals of the subjects' inner feelings, thoughts and motivations. While readers will not encounter the exact scenarios they read about, they will be able to use an increasingly finely tuned ability to understand and respond to multiple competing viewpoints.

The stories I write are based on real WorkLife dreams and ambitions, challenges and obstacles, failures and successes. The characters in the stories, including the character of the restaurants, are not based on real people or entities. The restaurants described in the book are fictional, but they are representative of those that you really can find in Shoreditch.

It is my hope that the Shoreditch WorkLife Book Club, and the stories, books and discussions featured here, will inspire others elsewhere, anywhere in the world, to follow their example, and establish their own WorkLife Book Club. If that is something you are interested in doing or have already done, I would love to hear from you. I can be contacted through my website schoolofworklife.com where you can also find other WorkLife-related learning resources.

Acknowledgements

Writing this book was hard at times and also more rewarding than I could have ever imagined. I want to thank my friend, editor and publisher, Jonathan Curry-Machado, for his consistent support in helping me to push through and bring my concept to life. From reading early drafts and sharing his thoughts on ways to strengthen the book, to his ideas and attention to detail in creating a book that looks great on the page.

I would also like to think my friend, Ian Remedios, for the wonderful sketches throughout the book. A fellow learning and development professional, Ian is also passionate about connecting learning and the arts. His collection of ink sketches depicting buildings, streetscapes and community life truly capture the essence of Shoreditch and its unique character, which is both rich in cultural heritage and the vibrancy of everyday cultural scenes.

A very special thanks, too, to my neighbourhood, Shoreditch, where all aspects of my WorkLife take place. Whether I'm having conversations, talking or listening, or alone with my thoughts, I draw inspiration daily from the people I meet or observe, the places I eat and drink, and the streets I walk. Shoreditch truly is a place of wondrousness. Some time ago, I began a photo project, 'Capturing the Beauty in Everyday WorkLife'. Throughout the book, I include a few images captured in Shoreditch.

WorkLife Book Club

Introduction

The neighbourhood I live in is full of people with different WorkLife experiences. Located in the East End of London, Shoreditch is where banking, law, design and tech all converge. Vibrant by day and night, it's rich in history, art, music and culture, with museums, art galleries, live music and performing arts aplenty. It has an eclectic dining scene featuring great restaurants, pub food, global street food, artisan coffee shops and bars. Independent shops are popular, from vintage to modern design, and much, much more in between. It is also home to a number of colourful street markets, including Brick Lane, Columbia Road and Spitalfields. I believe that what makes Shoreditch such a special place to be, is the incredible diversity of life paths that comes together here, spanning the whole globe and many walks of life.

It was in Shoreditch that I met my dear friend Florian, owner of a steakhouse and bar. He also owns a café, which I discovered for the first time two years ago, with its wonderful communal space, bordered by benches and with a library vibe. It quickly became a regular haunt for me when looking for some quiet time with a cup and a book. Our friendship was formed over a shared love of coffee and reading.

Before opening his restaurant, Florian had worked as a sommelier, and now despite his day job keeping him busy, he also finds time to make his own wines at his winery in Spain, where he loves to escape to when he can and relax with his wife. For now, together with their team, his children are managing both the day-to-day operations and future growth plans. One day his intention is to retire there. One day.

Florian has a genuine interest in people and loves to learn more about them. His natural ability to connect with people allows him to do this in an engaging yet non-intrusive way. He loves the power of asking simple questions, which often brings about quite profound answers.

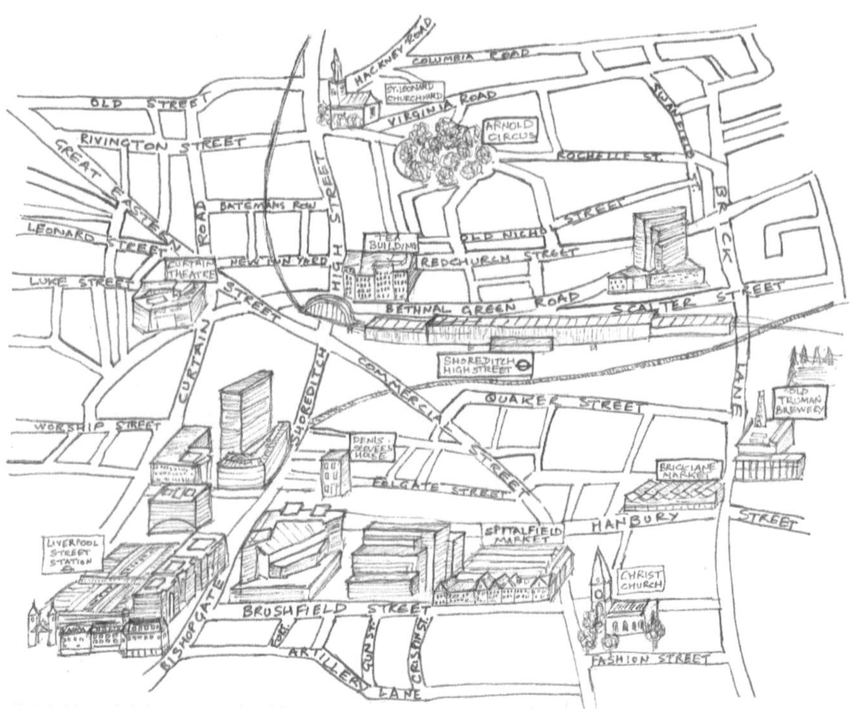

On one visit to Florian's restaurant, I chatted with him about my idea for the WorkLife Book Clubs. I also mentioned how I intended to research and develop a *Learning Through Reading* series, creating stories inspired by real WorkLife stories and events that would be made available to the Book Clubs. The stories that would be presented as cases for group discussion and the accompanying recommended book would be required reading for each meeting and would help to frame the subsequent discussion.

Florian was immediately drawn to the idea and said he knew a few people who he believed would be interested. He shared the idea behind the series I had created with five acquaintances, asking if it was something they would like to explore as a group. He also suggested taking them on a tour of his favourite places to eat, introducing them to great food and drinks – to satisfy their tastebuds over stimulating conversation while supporting local businesses and his fellow restaurateurs. All of them agreed, and so the monthly Monday night Shoreditch WorkLife Book Club was formed.

As the mutual connection who had brought everyone together, Florian had gotten to know each of the group when they stopped by to sit and read awhile over a coffee, drink or meal. He began by simply asking them: "What do you enjoy about reading?"

He then went on to share what he enjoyed about it.

Florian: Books have always kept me connected to and curious about the world of yesterday, today and tomorrow. From a young age, I sought out books that illuminated the world to me – books of history and rebellion, art and poetry, society and culture. Not only do I love reading itself, but I also love to watch people absorbed in the act of reading, and I'll often ask what they're reading. More often than not, it begins a conversation about favourite writers and a great recommendation.

The relationships grew from there, and that was how on hearing about my idea about a WorkLife Book Club, Florian immediately knew who he wanted to invite.

Saoirse is a freelance reporter and journalist. She covers local news and human interests features. Having travelled the world covering breaking news stories, in the last year she has established a base in London. She also writes a popular blog, which comes from her love of live music, craft beer and gin. At first, it was simply a way of sharing the adventures her passions took her on, and the experiences she encountered along the way. Over time she began to share the stories of the people behind the music, the breweries and the distilleries, appreciating the impact they have on the community and neighbourhood that supports them.

Saoirse: I think of reading as creative problem-solving: identifying with the characters, plots and settings, and trying to resolve the challenges unlocks my creativity. I like books that tell stories of full human experiences, happy and sad moments, because that's how real life is. All these moments and the emotions that go with them co-exist, and I like to experience that full spectrum of life and humanity.

Benny is creative director of a brand-strategy company. He leads a team of designers, writers and planners, and is always quick to call out words, phrases or anything he considers to be meaningless – that includes 'salt-free potato chips', which he has to be reminded are called 'crisps' in the UK. He is a New Yorker through and through, which he claims means he's tough and can survive any situation. This also means tough-talking – the ability to tell it like it is. Benny's truth, however, is that in reality, his soft or 'fluffy' side regularly pokes through his tough act, and when it does, someone is sure to call out 'California Dreamer', the nickname this had earned Benny.

Benny: Reading supports my power of observation: to put myself in the shoes of other people grows my capacity to be attuned to what's going on around me. 'Imagining' stories gives me an understanding of others because they require me to see the world from a new perspective. In particular, interactions in which I'm trying to figure out people's thoughts and feelings. Stories offer me a unique way to engage in this capacity, as I identify with characters' challenges and problems. I love authors who have the ability to make fiction read as though it is reality. To paraphrase Salman Rushdie, by being untrue, stories can make you feel and know truths that the truth can not.

Annie is an information and security analyst. She transitioned from being a software engineer, where she had started out as part of a team at a small tech startup. She now works within government at Whitehall, managing defence planning against cyberattacks. When it comes to technology, Annie is a self-professed geek and loves nothing better than exploring ways to use technology to help solve problems and make a positive impact to the world around her. She's an avid fan of superhero films – something else she likes to geek out on.

Annie: Reading for me is about continuously fine-tuning my learning agility. It's about seeking out and learning from unfamiliar experiences and then applying them to new situations. I'm encouraging my brain to imagine the unimaginable. My mind has no limits while reading. I can attribute this to my love of comic books, which began as a child. I can still remember clearly Fridays were comic-book days – the day my mum would pick up the newly released weekly comic book for me. I would run home from school eager to discover the new plot twists and turns the characters were going to encounter, and how they were going to navigate through these.

Pascal is a management consultant. One of the nattiest dressers in management consultancy, he is rarely seen without a bespoke tailored suit, pocket square and his signature Clark Kent styled spectacles in a variety of shades. As a management consultant, he has endured many jokes that hint at the sense of confusement that encircles his profession: what does a management consultant really do? Are they really worth their exorbitant fees? Jokes and questions that both amuse and bemuse Pascal, to which he usually responds in a good-natured way. Usually.

Pascal: Reading enhances my reasoning skills. Reading can give me insights that help my work beyond logic. In situations that may be impacted by emotion or past experience, it helps me keep an open mind while processing information – a necessary skill for effective decision making. I find reading fiction helpful to understand other people's emotions. I particularly like stories that are set in foreign locations, that give cultural insights to the characters and plots because they help to anchor difficult discussions in the global workforce that we as a company operate within today.

Maggie is a police officer. Following in the footsteps of her father, she joined the police force straight out of university. A life-long love of dogs led her to apply to work with the dog-support unit. She completed her training and now provides police and dog-handler support across the Metropolitan Police. Maggie has excellent observational skills and thrives on attention to detail. She can be pretty obsessive about tying up loose ends both in and out of work, which can serve to both entertain and bewilder her family and friends in equal measure. A keen runner, she is also quite skilled in hand-to-hand combat.

Maggie: Reading benefits my wellbeing. By losing myself in a thoroughly

> engrossing book, I can escape from the worries and stresses of everyday society and spend a while exploring the world of the author's imagination. Suspense fiction – thrillers and mysteries are my favourite night-time read. They help me to switch off. It seems contradictory, but they help to relax my mind and unwind and feel ready for sleep. I couldn't understand why this was at first, and as with all paradoxes, I had to figure it out. What I figured was that in the same way we need physical exercise to maintain good health and wellbeing, we also need to work out our brain to keep it in peak condition. Thrillers and mysteries help achieve this because they provide puzzles to work through. A good workout – physical and mental – aids better sleep.

Florian's idea behind the restaurant tour was to create a unique setting for each encounter of the WorkLife Book Club. He believes that food is an expression of individuals, communities and cultures. He wanted to take the group on a journey through the old and the new. His intention was to create an experience that is less like venue visiting and more like dropping in for a catch-up with a series of food-loving old friends. He wanted the experience to be as convivial as it is culinary – and it's not about just the food either, as importantly, for Florian, it's also about the drinks.

Each chapter details a meeting of the Shoreditch WorkLife Book Club, each of which is held at a different location as Florian takes the members on a tour of the neighbourhood culinary art cuisine. Every meeting has an overarching theme, reflected in the choice of WorkLife story and featured book, which they take turns to choose. The person who chooses is also the person who reads the case at the beginning of the meeting. Each case tells the protagonist's story and introduces the book from which they gleaned wisdom and found help in navigating their situation. The WorkLife Book Club then discusses the case. At the end of the meeting, they each summarise the WorkLife lessons they took from this.

1

January

The Case of the Short-Term and Long-Term WorkLife Plans

Featuring *Lean In*, by Sheryl Sandberg, accompanied by Spanish cuisine

Florian welcomed the group to his restaurant for the first meeting of the monthly Monday-night WorkLife Book Club, Shoreditch Chapter. They all arrived together and precisely on time. That was the great thing about Florian's promise to take them on a tour of the wonderful places to eat in Shoreditch – they all lived nearby, which meant there was no need to navigate London transport. Instead, they were able to time their journey perfectly, partaking in a leisurely walk, lost in their thoughts while breathing in the evening air.

It had been November when Florian had first suggested the idea of the Book Club to each of them individually. Since then, they had met once for a drink in his bar, when he brought them all together by way of introduction to each other. That was early December, which marked the beginning of the festive season. In keeping with the drink that was traditional throughout Europe at this time of year, Florian had welcomed them with a Spanish hot spiced wine – known as mulled wine in the UK.

Florian's ability to bring people together helped to connect the group with a natural ease. They agreed January was the perfect month to begin the Shoreditch Chapter of the WorkLife Book Club. With the holidays over, they were ready to start something new. The fact that this involved reading was just perfect because with it came a sense of time to reflect, rest and recuperate, and be gently eased back into social activities through a relaxed social outing.

Florian's restaurant was already abuzz with diners, many of whom had come straight from work. His steakhouse and tapas bar has wooed much of London since opening; word of mouth and of social media has served to create a buzz around the restaurant and its food. Great steaks and vegan burgers, great tapas inspired by the Mediterranean foods in Spain, a great wine and drinks menu, a warm and welcoming atmosphere, together with its rugged, traditional Spanish look and feel, adds to the charm and makes it a popular meeting place that families and friends, colleagues from nearby businesses and local residents, restaurateurs and chefs from near and far come to eat and relax.

Florian led them to their table. When they were seated, Gael arrived, introducing himself and letting them know he would be their waiter for the evening. He had brought water for the table together with the first wines Florian had selected.

Florian: If you permit, I'd like to introduce you to some of Spain's newly popular and older, more traditional wines this evening. It's a little indulgence on my part to show off my heritage and my passion for good wines.

Everyone expressed their appreciation and agreement.

Florian: I've also taken the liberty to ask Chef Pérez, our tapas chef, to choose a selection of tapas, both traditional and new dishes, to demonstrate the quality, variety and creativity of Spanish cuisine. I hope that's OK.

Again everyone expressed their appreciation and agreement.

Florian: And finally, if I may suggest our house steak, which is our speciality. Annie, we serve a plant-based burger, which is very popular for vegetarians, if I may suggest that for you.

And again, the group expressed their appreciation and agreement. Florian had conveyed a wonderful warmth, pride and humility in his words. The group felt they were being welcomed into his home, which in a sense, they were. Florian treated all his guests as though he was welcoming them into his home. That was who Florian was; and who he was played into the ambience of the restaurant.

With all of that agreed, Florian poured Benny a glass of wine.

Florian: In choosing your wines, Benny, I chose three different wines to accompany the different courses we're having this evening. In Spain, in producing alcohol-free wines, we use a process which is known as de-alcoholising. The wine is fermented in a French oak barrel before the alcohol is removed. This means there is plenty of flavour left behind. This first wine is from my winery. It's rich with notes of blackcurrant, and there's also a lingering toastiness which comes from the wood.

He then poured everyone else a glass of Manzanilla sherry.

Florian: There are two things I need to say about sherry. One: it is held in very low regard by anyone under sixty, and that's because most people have never tasted real sherry. Two: sherry is a wine, not a spirit. Manzanilla is one of the most refreshing drinks on the earth and one of my favourite white wines. It is a variety of fino sherry made around the port of Sanlúcar de Barrameda, in the province of Cádiz, Andalusia. Being matured so close to the sea gives it a unique and subtle tangy, salty finish.

And with that, he invited them to raise their glasses in a toast to the first meeting of the Shoreditch WorkLife Book Club.

Florian had chosen the first case: The Case of the Short-Term and

Long-Term WorkLife Plan, to which the accompanying book was *Lean In* by Sheryl Sandberg.

Florian suggested he read the case while they enjoyed their first drinks. Everyone agreed, and so he began to read the story.

The Case of the Short-Term and Long-Term Worklife Plans

It was the Spring of 2009 when as a teenager, Petra visited London from Poland on a school trip. Staying at YHA London, St Paul's, she met people who were visiting the city to take part in a march, demanding action against poverty. A representative from BOND (formally known as British Overseas NGO's for Development), who were involved in coordinating the Put People First campaign, was at the hostel rallying people for what turned out to be a 35,000 strong march. Joining the march with her friends, she was deeply touched by the people she spoke to and the speakers who called on the G20 to pursue a new kind of social justice, all of whom wanted to share and air their views peacefully. The carnival-like atmosphere with brass bands and stereos blasting music as the slow-paced procession weaved through the streets was something that Petra had never experienced before. The message "We are here to try and make a better world and protest against the G20" from Italian trade unionist Nicoli Nicolosi ignited the spark from which the beginning of Petra's WorkLife dream was formed.

Her experience in London impacted her so deeply that on her return to Poland, she began to research global poverty. As she learnt about the inequality and injustice throughout the world, she knew she somehow had to find a way to play her part in eradicating it. This led her to discover the field of international development. Immediately she knew she had found the path she needed to take to do what she wanted to do in her WorkLife. Further research led her to finding a global development studies degree being taught at the Faculty of Political and International Studies (FIPS) of the Jagiellonian University in Krakow – the oldest and the best higher education institution in

"For the past five years, I've sat next to Sheryl and I've learned something from her almost every day. She has a remarkable intelligence that can cut through complex processes and find solutions to the hardest problems. *Lean In* combines Sheryl's ability to synthesize information with her understanding of how to get the best out of people. The book is smart and honest and funny. Her words will help all readers – especially men –to become better and more effective leaders." (Mark Zuckerberg, Founder & CEO, Facebook)

From the inside flap:
"Sheryl Sandberg's *Lean In* is a massive cultural phenomenon and its title has become an instant catchphrase for empowering women. The book soared to the top of bestseller lists internationally, igniting global conversations about women and ambition…

"Ask most women whether they have the right to equality at work and the answer will be a resounding yes, but ask the same women whether they'd feel confident asking for a raise, a promotion, or equal pay, and some reticence creeps in…

"In *Lean In*, Sheryl Sandberg… draws on her own experience of working in some of the world's most successful businesses and looks at what women can do to help themselves, and make the small changes in their life that can effect change on a more universal scale."

"Eleanor Roosevelt once said, 'No one can make you feel inferior without your permission.' With stories from her own life and carefully researched data, Sheryl Sandberg reminds women that they have to believe in themselves and reach for opportunities. More women than men may need that advice, but I'd bet that both genders can profit from this very well done book." (Marjorie Scardino, Former CEO, Pearson PLC)

Lean In, by Sheryl Sandberg, was originally published by W. H. Allen in 2015 (240pp., ISBN 978-0753541647)

Poland and one of the leading universities in the region. She applied and was accepted onto the course.

Three years later, when she had completed her degree, she went on to do an MA in Humanitarian Action at the University of Warsaw. On graduating, she joined an organisation that was a platform for Polish NGOs involved in international development cooperation, democracy support, humanitarian aid and global education. She was part of a small team, and during her three years there, she got exposure to all areas of their operation. She gained invaluable experience supporting organisations who supported the front-line people – the people on the ground who were giving the practical and emotional support to people who were suffering injustice.

Moving her WorkLife to London was the biggest part of her dream and a natural next step for Petra. Because of her experience as a teenager, she felt that being in London would open up a wider range of opportunities that would enable her to have an even greater impact in her work. She didn't have a grand WorkLife plan. She was simply following her dream and going where it took her. She was in effect taking a step-by-step approach and figuring things out along the way.

This was where Petra encountered her first obstacle. On her arrival in London, she began to apply for jobs, but unfortunately, her CV didn't get past first base with recruitment consultants, resulting in her not being invited for interviews. Try as she might, she couldn't get a job within the industry. She simply couldn't get her foot in the door.

After weeks of job searching, reality struck. Her savings were dwindling, and she needed to work to earn a living. So she took a step back and considered her skills and experience that could be transferable to another role. She recognised she had strong administrative and organisational abilities and began to apply for roles that demanded these skills. Her search led her to an administrative role in retail at the organisation she's with today.

A leading retail organisation, it's a great company to work for: she works with people she likes; her good work is recognised and rewarded; and during her two years there, her WorkLife has advanced. But although she's grateful for the opportunities she's received, her heart just isn't in it.

Thankfully that's OK because Petra's story doesn't stop there.

That's because her intention is not to stay in this role. Her step-by-step approach to her WorkLife led to the idea to continue to look for opportunities within international development alongside working her day job. Petra's determination was driven by her dream, and while she knew she needed to bide her time for the right opportunity, she also wanted to be proactive in making this happen.

Thinking it through, she recognised she wanted and needed to keep her hand in within her chosen field. This led to her next step, which was to become a volunteer with Amnesty International, which had a branch support network close to her home. Wanting to make a positive impact in her role, she offered her administrative and organisational skills, together with the fundraising skills she had gained in her work in Poland. This led her to become involved in fundraising events, where she applied all of these skills.

The experience this opportunity gave Petra was immensely satisfying and rewarding. It gave her a sense of fulfilment and allowed her to stay on the path of what she knew was her real purpose in her WorkLife. Actually, her experience gave her so much more beyond this. Her genuine interest in people helped her to build a strong network of contacts. Being non-British, this was important to Petra because she'd arrived in the country not knowing anyone, which made it difficult to learn about opportunities.

In particular, Petra made a strong connection with James, who led the volunteer group. James had a wealth of knowledge and experience within the industry. Very quickly, through Petra's dedication, hard work and initiative, he saw her potential and came to value her as a key member of the team. Petra shared her dream with James, along with the obstacles she was focused on overcoming. James shared these words of wisdom:

"Taking control of your own WorkLife development will allow you to stay true to your passion and purpose, and this is possible even in the most challenging times."

Recognising she had a love of learning through reading, he went on to suggest a book that she might find to be helpful in navigating her path.

Book Wisdom

The book was: *Lean In* by Sheryl Sandberg.

The book description spoke to Petra: "In *Lean In*, Sheryl Sandberg – Facebook COO and one of *Fortune* magazine's Most Powerful Women in Business – draws on her own experience of working in some of the world's most successful businesses and looks at what women can do to help themselves, and make the small changes in their life that can effect change on a more universal scale."

Picking up a copy, the words of praise for the book encouraged Petra:

"Sheryl provides practical suggestions for overcoming and managing the challenges that arise on the 'jungle gym' of career advancement." (Condoleezza Rice)

"The key to opening some of life's most difficult doors is already in our hands. Sheryl's book reminds us that we can reach within ourselves to achieve greatness." (Alicia Keys)

The message that resonated most strongly for Petra was Sandberg saying that as well as believing everyone should have a long-term plan, she also believed everyone should have an eighteen-month plan. Actually, this message caused Petra to stop dead in her tracks. She suddenly had the realisation she had never planned her WorkLife. Well, other than the sense of knowing that she wanted to work within international development, which informed her choice of study, which in turn informed her first job choice. Then, in turn, this informed her move to London, which took her back to where the exploration of what her WorkLife purpose was had begun, which in turn led her to understand how she could fulfil that purpose. She hadn't planned. She had simply followed her dream and her purpose in her WorkLife.

Petra decided it was time to work on her long-term and short-term WorkLife plans. She began by modifying Sandberg's thinking on these two fronts to her own situation. Immediately she struggled with her long-term plan. She just didn't have the clarity other than to continue to follow her dream and her purpose – to make a positive impact by making a difference, working within international development.

So, she moved on to her short-term plan. She also struggled with this, which caused her great frustration. She just couldn't see the wood for the trees. The process was painful. She felt she had been knocked to the ground. She put her planning to one side for now.

For a second time since she had arrived in London, she took a step back to consider what she could do next. Reflecting on her WorkLife since she arrived in London and evaluating her situation, she was reminded of how much she'd accomplished by looking for opportunities outside of her work. By offering her skills and time, she had also created opportunities to develop new skills, knowledge, experience and insights into the industry – while all the time expanding her network, making new connections and developing good relationships. She thought that continuing to focus on building relationships would be helpful for her to do until she was ready and able to come back to her plan.

Petra's passion for pursuing a career in her chosen field was very apparent. Because of this, the others in her network were happy to make introductions to people who they considered it would be good for her to connect with. She was grateful for this and always prepared well for each meeting by finding out more about the person and their organisation, compiling questions to ask that would help her understand both day-to-day activities and the demands of the role, and also their perception of the future of the industry. This was valuable information for Petra for when the time came for her to resume her job search. This is because her intention was to not only apply directly for jobs advertised, but also to approach organisations speculatively for jobs relating to future projects, with the purpose of bringing her name to front of mind when they were ready to begin the recruitment process.

Petra always enjoyed these meetings and found people were really helpful and generous in sharing their thinking. That was until she met Mary, who began the meeting by asking why she wanted to move from where she was, when she had a perfectly good job, and so many people were out of work, going on to say: "You should be thankful to have a job."

Petra was stopped dead in her tracks. She didn't respond, not knowing what to say. She somehow got through the rest of the meeting, which thankfully was short. But it left her feeling deflated and questioning her decision to want to make a career transition.

Later that evening, Petra was co-hosting a fundraising event with James on behalf of Amnesty International. She shared with him what had happened in her meeting with Mary. She told him what Mary had said had knocked her for six and that for the first time, she was really doubting that she could achieve her dream. She said she now realised how naive she was arriving in London, expecting everything to fall into place. She said she felt stupid because she didn't even think to have a plan. She said there was so much she could have thought through that would have allowed her to have made a plan, but that in her naivety, the thought didn't even cross her mind. What Mary had said had brought all of this home for her, and she was questioning if she should, in fact, give up on her dream and be thankful for the job she had. She went on to say that there were a lot of good things about it, and that maybe she could make it work in a way that was more fulfilling.

James asked her why she initially deemed the move back into international development to be important. She shared her story of the awakening she'd experienced as a teenager at the Put People First Campaign. How this had allowed her to know that she wanted to play her part in raising awareness of humanitarian assistance and global interconnectedness. She said the reason she wanted to move back into international development was because she believed she had a passion that would enable her to make all of this happen.

James asked if these reasons and the move were still relevant and important.

The answer from Petra was a resounding 'Yes'.

James also shared these:

Words of Wisdom

"It's important to remember, when you ask someone for their advice, opinion, feedback, they'll feel obliged to give it. You then need to figure out whether to take it on board or whether to think, well that may be good advice for someone else but in line with what's important to me and knowing what I know about what I want to achieve in my WorkLife life that's not for me right now."

He went on to say: "It's also important to surround yourself with people who believe in you, who believe that change can take place even in the toughest of circumstances, and who also believe change is good."

It was at this point that Petra was reminded of the old adage that other people's behaviour is about them, not you.

And finally, as they were leaving the venue, James thanked her for helping to plan, manage and run that evening's event. He went on to say what he appreciated most was the specific focus on the practical planning and implementation phases she brought to all the projects she'd worked on.

For a third time in a short space of time, Petra was stopped dead in her tracks. But this time, it was different. Answering James's questions led her to evaluate her reasons for wanting to follow her dream. This, followed by his parting words, gave Petra the clarity she had been lacking about her situation. All of a sudden, she was seeing herself and her situation in a brighter light.

All of this allowed Petra to pick herself back up, and it gave her the impetus to continue her pursuit of her chosen WorkLife. In doing so, she discovered a great opportunity within her own organisation. As part of their corporate social responsibility, they worked with a number of charities, one of which was a human rights organisation. Through her organisation's intranet, she discovered an opportunity that involved a two-day-a-week secondment for eighteen months.

She prepared her application, which first had to be approved by her manager, who didn't relish the prospect of losing her, but at the same time, wanted to support her. This then had to be presented to the board of directors, and it was approved.

Petra now felt able to go back to her short-term plan. She considered what she wanted to get out of the secondment over and above the hands-on experience, and she developed a plan to help her achieve her objectives. She did this by thinking of targets she could realistically accomplish with her new team, which she suggested and were accepted. These were mainly around fundraising – a key element to her role, and one she had experience of from both her work in Poland and her voluntary position at Amnesty International. Her new manager was happy for her to take a proactive role and was impressed with both her approach and the suggestions she put forward, which demonstrated her in-depth understanding of the organisation and the world they operated within.

She then set more personal goals for learning new skills within the eighteen months, drawing on Sandberg's advice to self-question, by asking herself: "How can I improve?"

Sandberg's words rang true in that she knew that if she was afraid to do something, it was either because she wasn't good at it or that she was too scared to even try. In fact, Petra felt everything Sandberg said was written for her, right down to wanting and needing to develop her negotiation skills. So she followed through with the approach Sandberg had taken, gathered courage and let her new boss know this was an area she would like to develop. He was happy to facilitate this when opportunities arose, proving the old adage that when the student is ready, the teacher will come.

Epilogue

Petra is now getting stuck in and enjoying her secondment, creating the next chapters of her unique WorkLife story, which is helping her to gain more clarity on her long-term WorkLife plan.

WORKLIFE BOOK CLUB

As the story came to a close, Florian reached out and refilled their glasses, which served to bring everyone's presence back to the table and to each other.

Benny was a little lost in thought.

Benny: Interesting.
Maggie: For sure, there's a lot to unpick and discuss.
Florian: Can I suggest we do that over the selection of tapas Chef Pérez has prepared for us.

At this point, food was on everyone's mind, and they all readily agreed.

Florian caught their waiter Gael's attention, communicating they were ready for their entrée.

Arriving with their tapas, Gael introduced each of the dishes: a Spanish omelette, cured ham served on a crunchy bread, a vegetable paella and a *paella mixta* (meat, chicken and seafood), steamed mussels served with lemon, a traditional *calamari* and *calamares del campo* (country-style fried vegetables), sizzling garlic prawns, croquettes, *chorizo, pimentos de padrón, patatas alioli,* sautéed spinach with pine nuts and raisins, sun-dried tomatoes, Manchego cheese, a mature vegan farmhouse cheddar, and a selection of olives. He said that the perfect wine pairing to tapas were the wines they were all enjoying.

Gael's pride in describing the food he was introducing led Saoirse to ask: "Where does your passion for these dishes come from?"

Gael smiled and said his passion for Spanish food is part of who he is and began as long ago as he could remember. Preparing food and eating together as a family holds great memories for him. His dad is British and has wonderful memories from his childhood of holidaying in Spain with his family. He wanted to explore the country further, and when he was in his 20s, he spent one year driving through Spain on his motorbike. One day he rode up on his motorbike to the village where Gael's mum lived. They met, fell in love, and his dad never returned to live in Britain. His dad says, to fall in love with Spain is special. To fall in love in Spain is the kind of special that seeps through every fibre of your being and remains in your heart forever.

His father's stories of journeying around Spain, the people he met, the places he explored and discovered, the food and traditions he experienced gave him a great sense of curiosity to learn more about his own country. And so, as a student, he set off on his own motorbike adventure to discover the different foods of Spain. He would set up camp, and at the end of the day he cooked a meal for himself with the ingredients that were available to him. Those ingredients were pretty extraordinary, even more so as a student, because he was operating on a shoestring budget. The memory of that time and the meals he created remain with him.

He followed his passion in his WorkLife, first to work in a restaurant in Barcelona, where he was born, then to work in a restaurant in Madrid. Everyone he worked with at both these restaurants lived and breathed a passion for the food they served. It was in Madrid that he had a chance encounter with Florian, which led him to move to his restaurant here in London. Coming to London was always his dream. Working with the team here makes it easy to keep his passion alive.

He finished by saying that he still takes culinary road trips through Spain on his motorbike. When he does, he's always looking to discover traditional Spanish cuisine that he hasn't experienced before and new dishes created by chefs who pride themselves on celebrating local seasonal ingredients and close relationships with farmers and food producers from the area. Sons and daughters of Spain looking to honour the traditions they grew up with but with a more modern sensibility. He always shares his discoveries on his return to London with Florian and the team. Together they seek to bring their extraordinary discoveries to their guests.

Saoirse voiced what the rest of the group were thinking, saying: "That's such an interesting and beautiful story."

"Thank you," Gael responded.

Checking they had everything they needed, he said: "*buen provecho*" (enjoy your meal), and left the group to do just that.

Saoirse reached for a selection of tapas

Saoirse: It's interesting that Gael said it was his dream to move to London. It was Petra's dream too. I can relate to that, not in the sense it was my dream, but that I wanted to experience London at some point in my WorkLife. It has taken me time to get here. It's many years since I left Ireland, and there are many places my WorkLife has taken me in-between.

Annie: I moved from Scotland to London, not because it was a dream either, but because it has a vibrant tech industry, and I wanted to be part of that. Shoreditch, of course, is known as the Silicon Valley of London.

Benny: Ah yes, Silicon Roundabout – where Shoreditch, Old Street and Hoxton meet. For me moving to London was to experience working in a different vibrant city. I love city life, and I loved New York, but I wanted to experience a city that was new and different to me, that was also vibrant. The city shapes us. The city has dreams and desires, and it is acting them out through us, yet we think it's the other way around. I don't know where I first heard that, but it's something that has remained with me.

Pascal: As a management consultant working in a city such as London is really important to be able to advance your WorkLife. Simply because there are more opportunities. My partner and I toyed between London and New York, then Philippe was offered a position as Art Curator at Sotheby's, which was too good an opportunity to turn down. Once we made that decision, shortly after that, I was offered my position at the global management consulting firm I'm with today, and everything just fell into place. We both loved our life in Paris, which is an amazing city to live in as well, but we wanted to experience another city. We love our life in London, but we will go back to France at some point. France is in our hearts.

Maggie: I was born and bred in London. Not far from here, actually – Bow, and now I live in Shoreditch. I'm an East End girl and a Londoner through and through. I love it. I've never thought of living anywhere else.

Florian: For me, it was always a dream. I think I always felt that to make it in the restaurant business. I needed to make it in London. I thought if I could make a success of my WorkLife here, that meant I was a success. It is a measure that many people in my industry use. But of course, there are many others who measure success in other ways, that are more important to them. I never really had a definite plan in the beginning. Over the years, I learnt to plan. But starting out, arriving in London, I can relate to Petra's story.

That's actually why I chose this case, because I think I still have a lot to learn when it comes to WorkLife planning – for myself, and also to be able to support the team that work with me here, and at my vineyard and winery in Spain, in helping them develop their WorkLives, whether they're following a dream or a plan.

Benny: I think WorkLife is important as a viewpoint when planning, as opposed to 'career plan' or 'life plan', because you can't plan one without the other.

Florian: I agree. Petra's case demonstrates this. So much outside of her work helped her stay on her WorkLife path, and in time helped her to plan. For example, the volunteering work she did, put her in a good position to apply and be accepted onto the secondment programme, which in turn led to her planning.

Saoirse: I've always struggled with planning, call it WorkLife plan, career plan, life plan, or whatever plan you want to call it. A question I really hate because I can never answer it is: where do you want to be in five years? I haven't the slightest idea. I'm still trying to figure that out. It was really heartening for me when Sandberg said she didn't plan her path and that careers do not need to be mapped out from the start. I agree with her that career ladders don't apply to most people; and that the ability to forge a unique path with occasional dips, detours and even dead ends presents a better chance for fulfilment. I'm living proof of that, as I think is Petra.

Maggie: On the other hand, Sandberg says while she doesn't believe in mapping out each step of a career, she does believe it helps to have a long-term dream or goal. I can relate to that. My dream has always been to become a police officer. Choosing to undertake a policing degree was such a straightforward and easy decision for me on leaving school. But that was as far as I had thought it through. Beyond that, my path was very hazy. That actually worked in my favour because had I been too specific, I may not have been open to discovering that I could train to become a dog handler, that wasn't even on my radar, but now that I've discovered it, it seems such an obvious choice for me. I wake up every morning and have to pinch myself when I remember I'm following a WorkLife path that embodies my purpose and my passion. Policing and dogs. I think that's what Petra had too – a dream to follow her passion. That's what helped her to navigate her path when she got blocked by external barriers – the difficulty of getting a job within her sector, having to change her WorkLife, trying to re-enter her chosen industry after being away from it.

Saoirse: That's true. Sandberg says a long-term dream doesn't have to be realistic or even specific. For Petra, it was specific in that she had a desire to work in a specific field – international development – to make a difference through human rights. I can relate to having a long-term dream, but for me, it wasn't specific. If anything, it was very vague. I wanted to travel the world and to have professional autonomy as a writer. I didn't know if that was realistic, and yet it was. I simply followed my dream, with no great plan, I simply discovered the next steps I needed to take along the way.

Florian: I actually like the idea of an eighteen-month plan. In the past, I've always had a tendency to overestimate what I could achieve in one year. As Sandberg says, one year seems too short, and two years seems too long.

Annie: I found it encouraging when Sandberg said that when the tech bubble burst and the industry was still reeling from the aftershocks, that on giving herself four months to find a job, it took her almost a year. Though I entered the industry much later, when it had recovered, it still took me time to find the right job when I transitioned into cybersecurity. I found it encouraging because it served as a reminder that industries do recover and also that it can take time to get the next job when you go through a change.

I think the same can be said for Petra. Her industry had suffered, and it took her time to get back into it, having changed direction for a time. I think it's fair to say we were all following our intention, which could be loosely defined as a plan, but in no way a definite plan. We were simply following our chosen path, on which each of us encountered obstacles. I don't think a detailed plan would have helped us – even an eighteen-month plan – because we were impacted by external influences and the actual reality of how long things can take. I think there are times when a 'loose' plan is good enough.

Florian: Taking time out to change direction. What's time when you're going to work for forty or more years, Annie. I think it's the same for Petra. She's got her foot back in the door. I think her WorkLife will pick up pace and take off again. I think time is an important concept when considering plans or planning, it can often be an unknown quantity, and in a sense, you've got to factor that into your plan. 'Loose' planning is something I think you, Petra and Sandberg have in common when each of your pursued your path. Perhaps unknowingly at the time, but over time the importance of that factor came through.

Annie: Yeah, but it took both their stories for me to have that realisation. Going back to what you said about pace: as much as I'm enjoying working at Whitehall, I do miss the fast growth I experienced as a software engineer at the start-up. It grew so fast. There was so much to do, and I learnt so much. Sandberg reminded me how exciting that was, and it's true what she says about bigger corporations – politics and stagnation sets in.

Benny: Well, you are in the land of politicians. What do you expect?

Annie (laughing): True.

Florian: Is keeping up with potential cyber threats not fast-paced, or do you mean something more than that?

Annie: Yes, it is, but in a different way… I think reading the book gave me a sense of nostalgia… and Petra talking about following Sandberg's advice and setting more personal goals for learning new skills within the eighteen months rang a chord with me. I feel I should challenge myself more and adopt the same approach… I need to think it through. It's got me thinking… at the startup, I was reactive, in the sense that the rapid growth allowed me to know what I needed to learn, what I needed to get better at. Back then, I could have easily answered the question: "How can I improve?" But not now. We have annual appraisals, and so I sit down with my line manager, and we agree on areas to work on, but to be honest, it doesn't really stretch me. I want to be stretched more, but there isn't scope within my role or department that I can see that will allow that. I think I need to figure out my longer-term plan as well as my shorter-term plan – my five-year plan… I've never thought or planned that far ahead before

Benny: While we can overestimate what we can achieve in one year, we can underestimate what we can achieve in five years.

Maggie (with a cheeky smile): Ah, Benny, our California Man, is back.

Benny didn't rise to the bait.

Benny: I'm a planner. My work demands it. We're continuously developing marketing plans through analysis of current market data and future trends. Eighteen months, five years, both really help to have clarity on what we as a team need to be doing, and what I as a manager need to be developing within the company, the team and myself. I need to be forward-thinking to anticipate future trends and success of a product or service. It's the same for the success of our people. The approach I take is to work backwards from the five-year plan, identify the gaps from where we are now to where we want to be in five years, then plan to make it happen.

Pascal: To help a company to develop any specialist skills that it may be lacking, I work with both eighteen-month and five-year plans. I need this to provide objective advice and expertise to companies.

Maggie: That reminds me. I have a joke for you, Pascal.

Pascal had shared with the group that for some reason, people like to tell management consultants, management-consultant jokes. That there are people who make up management-consultant jokes and then post them on the internet, that for some unknown reason people would search for, just so they could tell a management consultant a management-consultant joke.

Maggie couldn't believe people did that. She has a deep curiosity about human behaviours, and to satisfy that, she had a look at what was out there on the internet. She found there were a lot of people sharing a lot of jokes. They were all so cheesy. She just had to share one:

Maggie: There was a glass of water on the table. One man says, "It's half full". He is an optimist. Second man says, "It's half empty". He is a pessimist. Third man says, "It's twice too big". He is a management consultant.

Pascal raised his eyebrows over his coordinated business attire (a mustard yellow suit with a red tie, red pocket hankie and red classic Clark Kent designer spectacles) – a reaction that always managed to convey: "I've heard them all before".

Pascal: Sandberg talks about how people miss out on great opportunities by focusing too much on career levels. My industry needs to be more open to the possibility of even greater change. But most businesses are focussed on doing the thing they've always done, and people spend their time getting efficient at that thing to help them advance their career. The problem with that is in an environment that's ever more volatile and less predictable, people need to explore new and different ideas and ways of working. They fight it because they think it will push them back, and they'll lose their hard-earned ground. Petra's case disproved this because it offered her a chance to learn new skills, which meant she was actually moving forward.

Benny: As Sandberg says: "The cost of stability is often diminished opportunities for growth."

Pascal: It's not clear cut, though. While I advocate for short-term and long-term planning, it's always with the proviso that there needs to be scope for flexibility and adaptability.

Saoirse: My philosophy has always been that planning too far in advance can close doors rather than open them. And also, I believe too much planning can keep you from living in the moment and missing moments, and some moments are not to be missed. I believe in following the rhythms of our WorkLives. As in having no plan, because, well, sometimes we just have to let the moments happen.

Maggie: I think the key is to keep it simple. Sandberg's suggestion of having a spreadsheet with just one column to evaluate opportunities in advancing your WorkLife – potential for growth – is a simple yet effective strategy.

At this point, Gael arrived to clear their table, letting them know their main courses would be along shortly. He then brought the wines Florian had selected as the pairing to their main course.

Florian poured Benny's wine

Florian: Benny, I've chosen Torres Natureo Syrah to accompany your steak. I think you'll find it has an exceptional flavour, and an interesting fact is that it was the first de-alcoholised red wine in Spain.

He then poured the wine for the rest of the group.

Florian: As a teenager, I went to the San Vino wine festival in Haro, La Rioja, Spain. It remains one of my craziest, best, and most memorable experiences. People travel from miles away, carrying every kind of container you can think of, each one of them full of red wine – including boots! Though I never did get to find out if they had been worn! It takes place every year on the feast day of the patron saint San Pedro, beginning with people celebrating mass. After the mass, the wine battle starts. People throw red wine at each other, and soon everyone is soaked. If you want to join in the wine fight, you have to wear all white and tie a red handkerchief around your neck. That was where my love of Rioja wine began.

He laughed.

Saoirse (smiling): I love that story. I might even plan a trip to experience it.
Benny: This is fantastic stuff.

Everyone nodded in agreement as they swished the wine around the entirety of their mouth, allowing it to come in contact with all of their taste buds, relaxing and seeing how the aftertaste was before taking another sip, as directed by Florian.

Gael arrived at the table with their main courses. Having checked they had everything they needed, he wished them: "*Buen provecho.*"

Florian watched as they each took their first bite.

Florian: How is it?
Pascal: This is so moist, and there is just enough fat here to just blend in with the meat, and when you just put it in your mouth, it just melts, doesn't it?

The sound from the group conveyed their agreement and the immense pleasure they were experiencing in that moment.

Annie: This burger is a mouth-watering pleasure.

Silence prevailed for a few moments as everyone savoured their meal.

Benny: This reminds me of the experiences I have when I take my personal quarterly offsite to think about and plan for what I want in my WorkLife.

Saoirse: What's a 'personal quarterly offsite'?
Benny: Every quarter, I take one day that I spend alone, thinking through what I want to achieve – what I want to do in my WorkLife over the course of the coming three months. Then I create a plan to make it happen. I leave the hustle and bustle of London, which actually helps to quieten and focus my mind. I'm working my way around the coast of Britain, so I get to enjoy the sea air, and I always include an overnight, so I get to experience the great places to eat in the area too.
Saoirse: That sounds like an interesting and enjoyable way to approach planning. I think even I could manage that.
Benny: It's an initiative that I rolled out for everyone at my company. It's built into their WorkLife planning programme.
Annie: Wow, I wish we had something like that where I work.

Silence prevailed for another few moments as they each relished their meal.

Saoirse picked up the wine bottle to read the label.

Saoirse: There's also an element of labelling in Petra's story... just like there is in so many things today... a sense that we're supposed to put a label on everything. Petra said she had the realisation that she had never planned her WorkLife. She had a dream, and at every stage she took the next step to get her closer to that. That could be easily labelled as a plan, but Petra just doesn't think in this way, and as a result, she thought she'd never planned her WorkLife. But yet she had moved her WorkLife on at every stage, without having to give it a label. She had a dream. That was her long-term plan. She took the steps she needed, at each step of the way, in pursuit of her dream – that was in effect her short-term plan. She just hadn't labelled it. And when she did try to plan, she struggled with it. I think this is because it went against her natural way of being, of doing. I think of planning as being restrictive, and I think it could have restricted Petra had she over-thought it.
Maggie: And yet when she tried to plan and then stepped away from

it, and began reflecting on everything she had accomplished since her arrival in London. The thing is she had actually achieved this by actioning her 'non-plan'. I think you're right, Saoirse. She didn't think or label what she was doing as being part of any plan – short-term or long-term, but actually, her actions could be considered as a plan. They certainly played into progressing her WorkLife in the short term through everything she gained in her volunteering work, and I think this will continue to serve her well in the long term. Sandberg talks about how overriding our natural tendencies is very difficult. I think this is what Petra was encountering here. I also think at this point in Petra's story, she was experiencing a lack of clarity, and this is why she struggled with the plans.

Pascal: I agree, and I know it's easy to see, looking from the outside in. Petra had a natural ability to do what was needed at each step of the way. For example, in preparing for each meeting she had, she put in so much work to ensure she came fully prepared. This helped her in the moment to get the most out of each meeting, and it also served to help her in the long-term because of the knowledge and insights she was gathering to help understand the future of the industry. This was really effective planning, but she just didn't think of it in that way. That's why people were so helpful and generous towards her. Sandberg talks about a guy who caught her attention because he took the initiative to pull a group together and integrate all their ideas – before that, each team had submitted ideas, but no one was coordinating, which left the presentation disjointed and unwieldy. Because of what he did, she's been helping him ever since and often calls on his input to help solve problems. This helps the company and creates ongoing opportunities for him. People like to help when they see someone is putting in the effort and when they see someone with potential.

Maggie: Except for, "you should be thankful to have a job Mary." The villain of the story.

Benny: Yeah, but, it's as James says: when you ask people for their advice, opinion or feedback, they'll feel obliged to give it. Sandberg talks about effective communication starting with the understanding that there is my point of view (my truth) and someone else's point of view (their truth). Rarely is there one absolute truth, so people who believe that they speak the truth are very silencing of others.

Maggie: There's a quote in the book from Eleanor Roosevelt: "No one can make you feel inferior without your permission." Mary might not have made Petra feel inferior, but she did make her question whether it was right to follow her dream. That remark could have crushed Petra's dream. She was very vulnerable at this point, but thankfully James helped her navigate through this. If Mary was the villain of the story, James was the hero.

Benny: Here's the thing, things don't always turn out precisely the way we hoped. Actually, they rarely do. Sandberg shared this sentiment throughout the telling of the ups and downs of her own story. For me, the positive thing about Petra's story was that as painful as her experience was, it actually became the starting point for something greater. When she reflected on everything, she realised how much she had already accomplished and also how much she had to offer to a potential employer. In picking herself back up, I think she had an even greater sense of clarity in pursuing what she wanted. That opened up her eyes to the opportunity within her organisation.

Florian: I really like the role that James played in all of this. First by suggesting the book to Petra, then by asking: "If the reasons she initially deemed the transition to be still relevant and important?" This is a simple yet such an insightful question that brought Petra to her resounding "Yes," and brought her back to her path in pursuit of her WorkLife dream.

Benny: James also talked about the importance of taking control of your own WorkLife development. I think people can be and should be in charge of their own destinies.

Saoirse: Yes, but nothing in anything James said was about planning. I think had there been, it could have stifled Petra. I think James recognised Petra is more a big picture thinker than a detail person. It's not that she can't do detail, she can, but she just needs that big dream or vision to know what the details are – or the steps as she calls them. The great thing about what James said – the words of wisdom he shared – was that it was vague in the sense that it allowed Petra to take her own meaning from it. That, together with the book, got her thinking and opened her mind up to possibilities.

Annie: That's how Petra functions, I think. She learns through experiences, whether it's a real-life experience, as with the march she attended as a teenager, or the metaphorical experience she took from the book. I think her experiences guide her more than a plan.

Maggie: James's parting words of thanks made me smile. Thanking her for all her 'planning' help. If that hadn't switched her bright light on, I don't think anything would have done.

Saoirse: You say that, but quite often, the things we do naturally, we tend to take for granted, and we don't perhaps value them as other people do. Also, signposting is sometimes needed, especially at times when we can't see the wood for the trees.

Annie: All of this led to the turning point in Petra's story. Finding, applying and being accepted onto the secondment programme.

Florian: Yes, and she was able to work on her plan this time. I think the difference with the eighteen-month plan here was that Petra thought about it in relation to her secondment. Thinking about it in this way, she was focused on making the most of her secondment in a way that would allow her to get the most out of her time there.

Pascal: Working through her plan also gave her the impetus to speak up and ask her new manager for the opportunities she wanted. I think for sure her short-term plan allowed her to make the most of her time.

Maggie: It also allowed her to be brave, I think. To push herself to put herself forward for things that scared her – for example, the opportunity to develop her negotiation skills. I agree Petra has a natural ability to make things happen by simply going about her WorkLife, but I think her eighteen-month plan while she's going through her secondment will serve to give the things she's making happen even more depth and purpose.

Saoirse: That's true.

Annie: The more I think about my situation (not feeling stretched and not seeing scope for growth in my role or department) and then thinking about what Petra did (what she asked for in her secondment), and Sandberg's advice on setting more personal goals for learning new skills in the next eighteen months, makes me realise I've contributed to my own lack of growth. At first, I was settling into the role and the organisation, and I was focusing on managing my WorkLife as opposed to developing it. I think that's important, but somewhere along the way, I became complacent. I've been maintaining the status quo for too long now. I've got to figure out what I want and need to do to change that. I'm going to think about my short-term and long-term plan. I think that will help me.

Although the group was newly formed, they were already comfortable together. There was an energy from them as people that was really unique. This led Annie to be open about her in-the-moment thinking. Normally she was a very reflective person and thought through things before she shared them. While the others didn't know that, they sensed she was processing her own situation in the moment, and was having a breakthrough in her thinking, and needed their quiet, supportive presence.

Saoirse: I think Petra and Sandberg are both strong role models from whom you can glean much wisdom and a practical approach to help your plans.

Benny: Yes, I found Petra and Sandberg to be engaging characters through their positive traits, which helped them to overcome their own challenges, and to help other people along the way.

Pascal: I also liked that we got to see their vulnerabilities too. WorkLives are not easy. Everybody has ups and downs, it requires bravery to show your vulnerabilities, and yet that's what makes a character in a book or a real person a strong role model because their strength of character comes through in how they handle difficult situations.

Saoirse: I agree. However, I was initially put off by the book's description: "looks at what women can do to help themselves". My reaction was that discriminates against men. I was pleased that Petra's story quickly moved beyond that, and also that the book is helpful for both women and men.

Benny: I know what you're saying, but unfortunately, Sandberg was speaking to many women's experiences.

Saoirse: I believe that women and men need to help each other. I liked that the book got to that.

Maggie: I understand what you're saying. A few months ago, I was asked to be part of a steering group for inclusion and diversity in our organisation. I felt the reason I was asked was because I was perceived as an advocate for inclusion and diversity because I'm young, I'm black and I'm a woman. I felt I was being stereotyped as someone who would have an agenda. And I do have an agenda, and that's to do work that I enjoy. I strive to do good work. I want to learn, grow and develop. But I don't want to be part of someone else's agenda. I don't want to be chosen to be an advocate because I fit some perceived stereotype. You talk about labels Saoirse, I felt I was being labelled, and I cannot abide labels either, and I won't have anyone put a label on me. So, I said no.

Benny: I agree with your logic Maggie. When I was in New York, I was asked to take on a similar role. I felt I was being asked because I'm a white man, and because of that, it was believed that I had no skin in the game, and so the perception was that I would be unbiased in my advocacy. It didn't feel right to me, and so I said no. I believe there's a lesson in every situation. The important thing is to figure out the lesson and not waste it. If we find the lesson and learn from it, it's often even more valuable than if we'd simply gotten lucky. While I felt I made the right decision in saying no, I didn't feel I'd learnt the lesson, but what you've just shared has helped me to realise that perhaps I had after all.

Maggie: That's interesting you say that. Because as much as I, too, know that I made the right decision in saying no, I haven't really let it go. I feel there's more to what happened for me to make sense of, to find the lesson and learn from it, as you say. It helps to know that it can take time to have that breakthrough learning, and I feel I will get there. Thanks, what you've shared really helps.

Florian: One lesson we know Petra learnt was around her move to London. This was the first time she faced such a big obstacle. She recognised she hadn't thought it through, and simply following her dream let her down. Her learning experience through reflection was that this was a point along her path, where had she thought through more of a plan, it would have served her better.

Benny: Yes, and building on this, her story talks about how she arrived in the country not knowing anyone and how important it was for her to build a strong network. I don't think she directly set out with a plan to do this, but it was an underlying element, and I think it's something that she will continue to build on. I'm not sure if she'll consciously consider it to be part of her plan, but subconsciously she will know it is. Sandberg talks about this too, in a way that applies to Petra, in that meeting people and building a network can be an indirect or direct part of a plan depending on the person. I think this is another lesson Petra will take from her experience.

Saoirse: Sandberg says that her company works hard to create a culture where people are encouraged to take risks. I love her favourite question: "What would you do if you weren't afraid?" I love it as a question for me to ask myself, and it also brings me back to Petra. She took a brave leap of faith, moving from Poland to London, leaving a good job and comfortable position behind, to progress her WorkLife.

Reading between the lines and from my own experience, a move to a city like London can provide more opportunities, but it's not without its risks. I think she will have experienced fear, but she pushed beyond it. Along the way, she experienced obstacles, which I think would have reignited her fear, but again, she pushed beyond it. Her process and her journey was slow, at times almost to the point of standstill, and yet she remained steadfast in pursuit of her dream, her passion and purpose. That, to me, is what is amazing about Petra and her story.

Pascal: Indeed.

Florian: The story was presented as 'The Case of the Short-term and Long-term WorkLife Plan'. But actually, there was a lot more to it than that. There were a lot of underlying themes or threads to the story.

Maggie: I agree, it brought a lot of threads together, and I think we were able to work through the connections to planning.

Benny: I liked that aspect of it because I think it's representative of WorkLife. Nothing is ever about just one thing. It's about uncovering what lies beneath that and also identifying what's connected to it that might be impacting it.

Annie: I thought of it as having an element of a mystery to it, and we worked to put the pieces together.

Gael demonstrated his skill as an attentive yet in no way intrusive waiter by arriving again at the point where there was a natural lull in their conversation. Enquiring how their meal was, as he cleared their table, he asked if they were ready for dessert.

The response from everyone was that the meal was wonderful, but they didn't think they could eat another morsel.

Florian: You can't leave without experiencing our signature ice cream, which is made from wild flowers and the sweetest of the sherry family of wines – Pedro Ximénez, which our pastry chef, Chef Fernández has created. Its lightness is perfect to finish your meal. He's adapted it to create the same wonderful lightness using Torres Natureo Rosé, a sweet non-alcoholic wine. The wines are served to accompany the dish.

When Florian put it like that, it would have been rude of them to refuse.

Gael arrived with their ice cream, along with accompanying glasses of wine. Once again, on checking they had everything they needed, he wished them: "*Buen provecho.*"

Saoirse's "Sublime" summed up the experience of this combined pairing for the whole group.

EPILOGUE

As their meal came to an end, Florian asked what was the single most important learning they had each taken from the case – the story, the book, the discussion.

Maggie: The key to breaking habits is the same as for all natural learning – increase your awareness. The first step in breaking a habit is to bring it into the light of your awareness. That's what Sandberg alluded to in her book, and that was what allowed Petra over time to change her thinking and approach to planning. Both Sandberg and James played a part in enabling this for Petra – in showing her, her own light, she was able to do what she needed to do to create her plan.

Annie: Everything in life has some risk, and what you have to actually learn to do is how to navigate it. We can't control every event, but we can control our response to it. Having a loose plan, as both Petra and Sandberg did – even though they may not have realised it when they were trying to overcome the obstacle they each faced – was good enough to help them through. I now realise unknowingly, this approach helped me too when I was faced with an obstacle.

Pascal: An event isn't over until you've learnt from it. People – individuals and in organisations – should develop a fascination with what doesn't work. Focusing on mistakes means you eliminate a lot of second-guessing when faced with future challenges. This will allow you to plan to avoid the same mistakes happening again and to also apply this learning to other challenging situations.

Saoirse: Weaving a bigger purpose into your WorkLife from the start makes it easier to navigate obstacles or setbacks and to motivate yourself around your dream. I think the best way to plan your future is to create it. I think that's true of life, both in and out of work. Now, that sounds like an oxymoron because how can you plan if you're creating your WorkLife, especially when, at times, it will be from a place of the unknown. The answer is we never know what's going to happen, but we can consider the likely scenarios and plan for some of them. By definition, you can't plan for every eventuality, and that's where following your bigger purpose and dream will help in guiding you through your next steps.

Benny: I think plans help us realise our potential and to believe in our potential by holding up a mirror so we can see our blind spots, and they hold us accountable for working through our sore spots.

Florian: Having something that's a real opportunity within our grasp makes planning easier. Because we're following something important to us. We're following our dream. And if we've had obstacles that came close to destroying or taking that dream away from us, we'll do whatever we need to do to ensure we get back on our true path.

That brings me in a roundabout way to the quarterly offsite that you talked about, Benny. I get a sense it could help people to follow their true path. I think this is something that I would like to adopt to support everyone working here and at my winery in Spain. I mentioned earlier that I chose this case because I still have a lot to learn when it comes to WorkLife planning – for myself, and also to be able to support the team that work with me in helping them develop their WorkLives, whether they're following a dream or a plan.

I'm also involved in different initiatives with my fellow restaurateurs, many of whom you'll meet along our culinary journey together. Together we work to attract people into the profession across all ages and from all walks of life. We have days throughout the year where we celebrate the work of both front- and back-of -house staff. We've created cocktail competitions for bartenders (both alcoholic and non-alcoholic) and also for baristas and for chefs to create their signature dishes. We create opportunities for people across all backgrounds to work in our restaurants, bars and hotels. We have exchange programmes with restaurants throughout the world.

That's how Gael came to work here – and Nancy (who is from Bow, Maggie) went to work in Madrid. We also work together in supporting the people and the companies who are suppliers in some way to our industry.

I'd like to understand more about your process, Benny, if you could talk me through it over a coffee when you have time. I think it would really help me in helping the people in my own business, my industry and my community.

Annie: Can I join you both? I think it would be really helpful for me.

Pascal: What I see in my work is that more and more people are becoming more interested in working for themselves. It's the rise of the creator economy. In the coming years there are going to be more people setting up in business themselves, individually or with family or friends – small enterprises. It's something I'd like to be involved with in some way, by way of giving back or forward – my knowledge, my expertise, my skills. I'd like to come along too, Benny, and I'd also like to learn more about the initiatives you're involved with, Florian – perhaps over the coming weeks, if that's OK with you both.

Saoirse: Can I come too? This is all so fascinating to me, and there may also be some way that I can give back or give forward through my writing. I consider myself to be part of the creator economy. Through my writing, I connect with people through shared interests and values – food, drinks, music, supporting other creators – the people behind the food, drinks and music. There are platforms that enable other creators and me to do this in a way that we can support ourselves financially.

There's also a theme in Petra's story, in Gael's story and in our stories too, and that's Chance Encounters. For Petra, it was a chance encounter with the representative from BOND at the youth hostel. That really is the place from which her WorkLife story began.

For Gael, it was his chance encounter with you, Florian, that brought him to London. And it was in visiting your restaurant, bar and café that brought about our chance encounters, which brought us here tonight.

I'm always drawn to stories of chance encounters, and it may be that I can write about experiences based on this. I get a sense from what you've said about the initiatives you're involved in, Florian, and from the people we're going to meet as you take us on the culinary tour you have planned for us, that there will be many stories of chance encounters to tell. And also stories from what you say about the rise of the creator economy Pascal.

Maggie: I agree. This all sounds so fascinating. I'd like to come too, to learn about the offsite planning and also to learn more about what's going on in my neighbourhood and ways in which I can perhaps be involved.

Florian: Absolutely everyone. How about I organise a fish-and-chip supper for us to meet over. In keeping with the theme of our culinary adventures and my promise to take you on a culinary tour of our neighbourhood, and in recognition that Britain's first fish-and-chip shop was in Shoreditch. Annie, I can promise you the best plant-based fish fillets.

He laughed.

Florian: I hasten to add, the origins of Britain's first fish-and-chip shop is much disputed, and there have been many claims to fame as to who created the culinary fusion that became the emblematic British meal. There is, however, a Spanish and Shoreditch connection, both of which go back a long way. The tradition of fish battered and fried in oil is said to have been brought from Spain, or Portugal, which was under Spanish rule at the time, by Jewish immigrants who settled in England in the sixteenth century. This was prepared and eaten for Shabbat for dinner on Friday evenings. Charles Dickens mentions "fried fish warehouses" in Oliver Twist. Dickens is said to have visited Shoreditch to gain inspiration for his works, and Oliver Twist is said to have lived in South Shoreditch.

The group loved these little snippets that Florian had woven together to give a sense of their neighbourhood history, cultures and food, and they were all definitely up for a fish-and-chip supper.

Benny: And yes, I'd be more than happy to talk you through the offsite planning. As part of the process, I've designed an approach that supports people to carry out weekly reviews with themselves – or daily should they choose to. To help analyse what they accomplished in a week, problems they had, what still needs to be accomplished. They then develop a plan and strategy for the coming week. I'd be happy to talk you through all of that.

The group all expressed their thanks.

Florian: Thanks, that sounds like a plan.

LETS
ADORE And ENDURE
Each Other
Ethnicity should never be a barrier to opportunity.

Interlude 1

Personal Quarterly Offsite Assignment

Accompanied by a Fish-and-Chip Supper

The diner-style fish-and-chip restaurant made the group feel they were stepping back in time to the 1950s as they arrived for their onsite lesson in personal quarterly offsites over a Friday evening fish-and-chip supper. The old-fashioned booths and counter barstools in sea blue and white, white Formica tables and counter tops, black and white tiled flooring, whitewashed walls covered with black and white photos of diners from days gone by – both locals and celebrities – together with holiday memorabilia scattered around the room conveyed both a retro and seaside vibe.

The humble and much loved British traditional fish-and-chip supper of fresh fried fish in golden, crispy batter served with chips, mushy peas, tartare sauce, ketchup and slices of soft white crusty buttered bread had been the mainstay of this popular chippy for many years. According to the owner, Reggie, remaining true to his pledge to support British fisherfolk and farmers in serving up fresh fish delivered from third-generation fishmongers and the best of British-grown potatoes, while also continuously evolving to cater to a range of dietary and lifestyle preferences, was what made his restaurant worth its salt (and vinegar).

Born and bred in the East End, Reggie started his WorkLife in the fish-and-chip industry aged just ten, when he got a weekend job cutting up newspapers to wrap the takeaways in. Fast forward several decades, and Reggie is still on hand, lending a hand and regaling customers with stories from the Second World War, when he was in his early teens: how he played his part in keeping morale among Londoners high by serving up their favourite British staple food. Reggie was known to quote Churchill when he called fish and chips our "good companions". According to Reggie, Churchill, in recognising the importance of the meal to the national morale and fighting spirit of a nation at war, was the reason he made it the one food that was never rationed.

Their waitress Victoria, Reggie's granddaughter, brought menus, pots of tea with accompanying mugs, and a jug of water to their table. Having just turned sixteen, Victoria was following in her grandfather's footsteps in her first weekend job.

Victoria let the group know that the catch of the day was cod in a choice of batters – traditional or beer, both of which were secret family recipes. She said they used banana blossom as the vegan fish alternative catch of the day because its texture was much more similar to traditional battered cod than tofu.

Victoria's bright and bubbly personality was infectious, causing Saoirse to ask what she enjoyed most about working there.

Victoria said she loved her grandad's love of fish and chips and his passion for keeping their family brand, which was steeped in tradition, alive – while also wanting to remain progressive. She said his pledge to support the British fishing and farming industries in serving their customers the best produce had always come from a place of sourcing from sustainable suppliers. That her grandad's openness and love of learning made him both a great teacher and student. She loved learning from him, and he loved learning from her.

Over the years, she had watched as he gave lessons in preparing everything they served from scratch. The lessons she said came with a great sense of pride. She loved how now he sought learning from her and how he eagerly supported her when she researched and wrote about recyclable packaging for an essay on environmental awareness. He then sourced the packaging she had written about and had a fish-and-chip lunch delivered to her class in the packaging, which included takeaway cutlery made from biodegradable corn starch. She said they now use this packaging for all takeaways.

Florian asked if she knew what she wanted to go on to study.

Victoria said she didn't, but that she was interested in both environmental issues and marine life, and so perhaps something in those areas.

The group all went for the catch of the day in their preferred batters and were quite happy to accompany this with their mugs of tea. Victoria let them know she'd bring along fresh pots with their food.

Saoirse: I love hearing stories that connect younger and older people. It's just so heart-warming. And stories that serve to remind us that we can all learn from each other regardless of age is both lovely and true.

Sipping their mugs of tea, the others all smiled in agreement.

Maggie: Ah yes, that reminds me of something I learnt from my old dad.

She laughed.

Maggie: He's not that old, but I did learn something of interest. When I told him we were having a fish-and-chip supper and how you had told us, Florian, that there have been many claims to fame about the origins of the first fish-and-chip shop. He said to me that Malin's, which was on the Old Ford Road, in Bow, close to where I grew up, was the first fish-and-chip shop in the UK. I looked it up, and it was established in 1860 and served up fresh fish and chips for over a century until it closed its doors in the 1970s to make way for a housing project. In 1968, it was awarded a plaque in recognition that it was the oldest fish-and-chip shop in the UK. There was also a BBC documentary made there, about the history of the UK's fish-and-chip industry.

My dad said he has fond memories of growing up and running to the chippy for Friday evening family fish-and-chip suppers, which always came wrapped up in newspapers. I loved discovering that the neighbourhood I grew up in has this connection to the history of fish and chips, and by extension, my family are part of that history.

With a sense of earnestness, Benny addressed the group.

Benny: Before I talk you through the offsite planning, I think it's only fitting that we raise our mugs in recognition of the importance of the role that Maggie's family and neighbourhood played in the history of the fish and chip.

They all laughed and raised their mugs to Maggie's family and neighbourhood and the history of fish and chips.

Benny smiled.

Benny: And now to the offsite planning, but before I get into the detail, I'd like to share what prompted this practice for me because that plays into the approach I take.

As much as I love my work and always have, there was a point when I first moved to London that I felt I'd lost my sense of purpose in what I do and why I do it. I had a sense of complacency in that I was going through the motions every day, but my energy and motivation had waned. I didn't know why this was because I knew I was doing work I loved, but yet something wasn't quite right, and I couldn't figure out what that was.

Back home, whenever I was stuck in my thinking or knowing what to do, I would take a day or two, get out of New York City and hop on the train to Long Island. I love train journeys, and although I always have a book with me to read, I invariably end up staring out the window, which allows me to switch off and encourages my mind to wander and wonder. On arrival taking a walk along the beach intensifies my wandering and wondering thinking.

So I took a couple of days off and headed out of London to Brighton for what would become my first quarterly offsite.

I thought about my lost sense of what I was doing and why I was doing it and realised these are the questions we use when working with companies to define mission statements.

So, I posed those two questions to myself:

1. *What do I do?*
2. *Why do I do what I do?*

And I let my mind wander and wonder about them on my train journey and, after having checked into my accommodation, on my first walk along the beach. Then I stopped for a coffee, took out my journal and started writing everything that came to mind. There was a lot, and I went with the free flow of being in the moment, getting my thoughts out of my head and onto paper. It felt liberating. I continued this practice for the rest of the day, walking, allowing my mind to wander and wonder on the two questions I had posed to myself, then stopping for a drink or something to eat and journalling on what came up for me.

Having slept on it, I woke up with more thoughts that I immediately wrote in my journal. Then I took a walk along the beach before breakfast, and I felt a sense of clarity, in that I felt I could now start to answer the questions more concisely. And so, after breakfast, I sat with a coffee and started to do just that. I didn't re-read everything I had written. I didn't feel I needed to. I had allowed my mind to wander and wonder, and I'd gotten all my thinking that came from that onto paper. It was as though I had cleared the way to get to the specifics of what those questions meant to me.

I came back to question:

1: *What do I do?*

My answer: I work with companies to establish their brand identity. I do this by embracing the combined power of story and voice by figuring out what to say and the best way to say it.

2. *Why do I do what I do?*

My answer: Because I like original and effective work that captures people's imagination and inspires them to take action.

But here's the thing, my answers weren't new to me. I'd known that all along, but somehow I'd lost sight of it and was going through the motions day on day. While I was happy to have clarity on my What and Why, I questioned if I needed more to regain my lost energy and motivation. I felt I was missing something. And so I continued to walk and journal, walk and journal, walk and journal, for the rest of the day.

Then the following day, I woke up with the answer. I had

allowed my learning to stagnate. Learning has always been an energising motivator for me. There are different ways in which I learn. For example, I learn so much through my client work, but I'd handed off a lot of my client work. There were a couple of reasons for this:

1. I'm responsible for the day-to-day running of the business, and this was taking up much of my time;
2. Part of my work in developing people is to get them more involved in client work. Hence I had handed off on that. I knew I needed to regain some involvement in client work. I also knew this couldn't be done by taking back what I had handed off because this would cause a ripple effect of what I was feeling: lost energy and motivation within my team.

I felt frustrated when I first had this realisation; but I also had the awareness that before I could become more involved in client work again, I needed to let go of some of the day-to-day work involved in running the business. I knew this was an area of work that people in my team wanted to learn more about as part of their development plans. That was enough to give me my starting point to figure out how I could overcome the stagnation in my own learning, and at the same time strengthen the flow of learning within my team.

From here, I asked myself two questions that have become my guiding questions for the quarterly offsites I've taken ever since that first trip to Brighton, and they've served me well.

1. *In eighteen months from now, what do I want to have accomplished?*

My first answer was: I want to have tested my 'Flow of Learning' idea within my team, and if successful, have begun or be ready to roll it out as part of people's WorkLife learning, development and growth planning programmes.

2. *What do I need to build into my day, week, month to help me achieve this?*

My first answer was: I need to identify the areas of my day-to-day work that handing off on will help the team's development. I then need to action these.

As I follow through on my actions, my answers to those questions at my continuing offsites help evolve my next steps.

There were two more actions that came out of that first offsite that have remained with me ever since.

I mentioned there are different ways in which I like to learn. When I realised that it would take time for me to get back to the learning I took from my client work, I had another realisation. Another way I love to learn is through reading, but because I had been so busy with my day-to-day work, I had lost sight of that too. Once I had that awareness, that was much easier to get back to, and get back to it I did. I now read for at least two hours a day, and the beautiful thing about doing that was that it had an immediate positive impact on my energy and motivation. Learning through reading is powerful in so many ways.

The third action that came out of that first offsite that has remained with me ever since is also related to another way in which I love to learn. I've always loved exhibitions at art galleries and museums. They've always inspired my thinking and opened up my mind to new ways of thinking, seeing and doing things. But I had thrown myself so much into my work. I hadn't been making time to go to exhibitions.

Again, once I had this awareness of how I had been depriving myself of something I love that fuels my creativity, thinking and learning, I was immediately able to build it into my week. That's the great thing about London. There is so much going on in the world of arts. There is always a wonderful exhibition to go to. That also had an immediate impact on my energy and motivation. Learning through art is also powerful in so many ways.

Those two last actions also served to remind me how our life in and out of work are so intrinsically linked that they cannot and should not be separated. That's wonderful because it means there is so much scope for us to learn, both in and out of work, by taking a holistic approach to learning through what we love doing.

And that's it. That's how I approach my quarterly offsites. It began by having clarity on those first two questions:

1. *What do I do?*
2. *Why do I do what I do?*

Following on from that, the two questions that I've focused on for every offsite since then are:

1. *In eighteen months from now, what do I want to have accomplished?*
2. *What do I need to build into my day, week, month to help me achieve this?*

Taking time out each quarter – a day, or an overnight – is, I believe, an essential part of the practice. Because it allows me to create the space for my mind to wander and wonder. The train journeys I take, the walks I go on, the journalling I do, adds to this. I always come back to London with more energy, motivation and focus on following through on the action points I've identified to push my eighteen-month plan. I have weekly check-ins with myself to help stay on track.

I did go on to roll out the practice within my company, which I developed based on this.

I hope that was helpful and my way of telling it made sense.

Annie: Thanks Benny, it was helpful, and it made sense. It's definitely something I'm going to do.

The rest of the group echoed Annie's words.

And with that, Victoria arrived with their food and tea.

Picking up two slices of the soft white crusty buttered bread that accompanied their food, Maggie asked if they were familiar with the chip butty. Annie and Saoirse laughed and said they were. Benny, Florian and Pascal laughed and said they weren't.

Maggie: If you permit, I will give you a lesson in preparing the perfect chip butty.

They all laughed as Maggie proceeded to create a sandwich filled with chips, indicating they should follow suit, letting them know that in her humble opinion the only accompanying condiments needed were salt and vinegar, but Maggie said that was a personal choice, and if they really, really felt the need to add ketchup, mayonnaise or even brown sauce, that while she wouldn't understand that need, she would be respectful of it.

They all laughed again and were guided by Maggie's personal choice.

Benny bit into his butty.

Benny: This is surprisingly good. I have an odd sense this is giving me a rite of passage to something, though I'm not sure what that is.

Personal Quarterly Offsite Assignment

Now it's time for your personal quarterly offsite, with your accompaniment of choice.

Develop the practice of taking time out each quarter (a day or an overnight) to create the space for your mind to wander and wonder.

Then follow these three steps:

STEP ONE

Begin by gaining clarity on these two questions:

1. *What do I do?*
2. *Why do I do what I do?*

Develop the practice of journalling, and write down everything that comes to mind. Go with the free flow of being in the moment, getting your thoughts out of your head and onto paper.

Continue this practice until you feel a sense of clarity, in that you can now answer the questions more concisely. There's no need to re-read everything you have written. Having allowed your mind to wander and wonder, you've gotten all your thinking that came from that onto paper. That has enabled you to have cleared the way to get to the specifics of what those questions mean to you.

Note: It's always good to return to these questions by way of checking in with yourself to remain on track in doing what is important to you in your WorkLife, and to maintain your motivation, energy and drive in pursuing this.

STEP TWO

Following on from that, the two questions to focus on for every future offsite are:

1. *In eighteen months from now, what do I want to have accomplished?*
2. *What do I need to build into my day, week, month to help me achieve this?*

STEP THREE

1. Focus on following through on the action points you've identified to push your eighteen-month plan.
2. Have weekly check-ins with yourself to help you stay on track.

WORD OF WISDOM

As with Benny, you may discover you have been depriving yourself of things that have always inspired your thinking and opened up your mind to new ways of thinking, seeing and doing things because you've thrown yourself into your WorkLife and haven't made time for the activities that fuel your creativity, thinking and learning (for Benny, that was reading and attending exhibitions). If you have this discovery, you also have the ability to make the changes needed to bring whatever that is for you back into your WorkLife.

2

February

The Case of Creativity Being Imagination and Imagination Being for Everyone

Featuring *It's Not How Good You Are, It's How Good You Want To Be*, by Paul Arden, accompanied by British cuisine

The welcoming British pub with its wood- and coal-burning open fire was the perfect place for the group to briskly walk to from their respective streets of Shoreditch on a snowy February Monday evening. Florian knew that the local hub and community pub that the manager Tom and his team had created, which the locals were proud to welcome all into, was the ideal spot to hit the spot. With its traditional British cold-weather comfort food from small plates to stews, it provided a tasty respite from a cold winters evening.

As they sank into the comfort of their Chesterfield armchairs taking in the warmth of the roaring fire, the manager Tom came over and introduced himself. Leaving food and drinks menus, he let them know that they had created a special Dry January cocktail menu, that was so popular it had become a fixture throughout the year. He suggested they might like to try their house special hot buttered rum with cider winter cocktail, which was great with or without the booze.

"How do you achieve that – with or without?" Benny asked.

Tom said in composing cocktails they begin by thinking about the flavour of the base element. In making a drink that can go either way (dry or with alcohol) – the basic principle of what flavours naturally work well together or brings out new elements of each other remains the same. They build the cocktail based on this, which also takes into account the spirits that may be added, the flavour of which needs to enhance the non-alcoholic components.

"Thanks, that's really interesting," said Benny. "I'll have the non-alcoholic version of your winter cocktail please."

"Well, I've never drunk butter," said Maggie. "But my beat partner John, who drinks bulletproof coffee before we start every shift, swears by it and tells me I haven't lived until I've sipped on butter, so I'm definitely up for the alcoholic version please."

So was everyone else.

Pascal: I'm always intrigued by the charm of British pubs. At weekends Philippe and I love to explore London or take a drive into the countryside and experience the quintessential characteristics of the pubs we discover en route that contribute to that charm. We've met some interesting characters too, all of who have a good story to tell, many of who will claim their local is the oldest pub in Britain. While each pub is unique and different, they also have commonalities; the characteristics of interesting old buildings, many with wooden beam ceilings, nooks and crannies – are those the right words? I think it's a British expression?

Saoirse: I think those are the right words, it definitely helps to explain what you mean. And I agree. I also like to explore and discover great British pubs. I love the wonderful names they have. I read a book called: *The Old Dog and Duck: The Secret Meaning of Pub Names* by Albert Jack, an English writer and historian. He says his

mission in life is to track down the hidden meanings and secret stories behind everyday things we take for granted. He set out to find out about the history of pubs – where they've come from and what their names mean. The stories he shares are really quite fascinating.

Annie: The pub is also at the heart of community life in villages, towns and cities throughout the county. When I go back home, I'll always pop into my local, alone and chat to the bartenders, and to catch up with friends – Christmas is especially great for that when we're all back home for the holidays. My family love going for a Sunday roast, which back in the day used to mean a nut roast for me, but over the last few years it's gotten better. Last time I had a vegetarian wellington.

She laughed.

Annie: It was actually quite exciting. I seem to remember raising a glass in its honour.

With that, Tom arrived with their drinks, to which they raised their glasses in honour of their winter cocktails and their second WorkLife Book Club meeting.

As they took their first sip, Benny's words summed up the experience for everyone: "This is the kind of drink that warms you from the inside out."

Tom suggested a selection of small plates to start, explaining that in seeking to revive traditional British pub culture, they had devised a menu that went back in time to when a bar snack was an accompaniment to a drink. They had worked to a brief of quality British pub fare that one can eat with one hand, leaving the other hand free for a drink. They now serve these small plates as both bar snacks and starters to a sit-down meal.

Everyone liked the sound of that. The house-special stews were the order of the day for everyone for their main course, with a selection to choose from, which included a hearty winter vegetable stew with chestnuts and rosemary, a chicken stew, a classic beef red wine stew, a beef and stout stew with carrots, a Lancashire hotpot, a rabbit stew with mushrooms, and an oxtail stew with dumplings.

Florian suggested English pinot noir red wines to accompany their meal, saying: "The lightness in body and richness in texture means this wine is versatile and can be paired with a number of foods and is easy to drink."

With their food and drinks orders taken care of, Benny began to read the case he had chosen for this month's discussion: The Case of Creativity Being Imagination and Imagination Being for Everyone, to which the accompanying book was *It's Not How Good You Are, It's How Good You Want To Be*, by Paul Arden.

"I read this book regularly. It's like my little holy book that I skim through every now and then. It's about advertising and the workplace, but I find a lot of the content can be applied to just about anything." (Mozhdah Jamalzadah, Afghan singer, actor and talkshow host)

"...A wonderful book by one of the most brilliant men I have ever met... I met him when he worked as creative director at Saatchi & Saatchi and he was simply inspirational - as is this practical, unpretentious little book." (Amanda Platell, journalist)

IT'S NOT HOW GOOD YOU ARE, IT'S HOW GOOD YOU WANT TO BE.

The world's best selling book by **PAUL ARDEN.**

PHAIDON

From the inside flap:
"*It's Not How Good You Are, It's How Good You Want to Be* is a handbook of how to succeed in the world: a pocket bible for the talented and timid alike to help make the unthinkable thinkable and the impossible possible.

"The world's top advertising guru, Paul Arden, offers up his wisdom on issues as diverse as problem solving, responding to a brief, communicating, playing your cards right, making mistakes, and creativity – all endeavours that can be applied to aspects of modern life.

"This uplifting and humorous little book provides a unique insight into the world of advertising and is a quirky compilation of quotes, facts, pictures, wit and wisdom – all packed into easy-to-digest, bite-sized spreads. If you want to succeed in life or business, this book is a must."

Paul Arden (1940–2008) spent a stormy 18 years in advertising and then found his Alma Mater in Saatchi & Saatchi in 1977, where he worked for 15 years. During his tenure as Executive Creative Director he was responsible for some of Britain's most successful advertising campaigns – including British Airways, Silk Cut, Intercity and Fuji – and famous slogans, such as 'The car in front is a Toyota' and 'The Independent – It is. Are you?'. In 1993 Arden set up the film production company Arden Sutherland-Dodd and began a successful second career as a writer with a weekly column in *The Independent* and several publications including *Whatever You Think, Think The Opposite* (2006) and *God Explained In A Taxi Ride* (2007).

It's Not How Good You Are, It's How Good You Want to Be, by Paul Arden, was originally published by Phaidon Press in 2003 (128pp., ISBN 978-0714843377)

The Case of Creativity Being Imagination and Imagination Being for Everyone

"You're not creative." These words stunned Aisling into silence. She couldn't believe Max, the person she was having a meeting over coffee with, actually thought this of her. Although she didn't speak any words in response, the look on her face obviously spoke volumes, as Max tried to recover from what he had said.

But let's back up a bit to Aisling's story:

Aisling has worked for several years as a WorkLife coach and learning practitioner. As a WorkLife coach, she helps people gain insight and inspiration in their chosen area of work and then supports them in working towards achieving what is important to them in their WorkLife. She is known for her ability to help people recognise and take ownership of their strengths and potential, as well as helping them assess their challenges, to determine where they are stuck, and to then work with them to uncover solutions to move forward. As a WorkLife learning practitioner, her focus of work is on soft-skills development, which she describes as being a combination of people skills, social skills, communication skills, emotional intelligence, personable attributes and traits – skills that make it easy to get along and work well with other people.

She was in the early stages of developing her work further; and, with a team of performing, visual and literary artists, she had created workplace and community theatre – theatrical productions written following research into organisational challenges and desired outcomes. The plays formed the centrepiece of learning and development, stimulating discussion and debate.

Aisling often gets asked how the idea of combining learning and development with workplace and community theatre came about. Because she helps people to tell their WorkLife story, she wrote a short story to tell this part of her WorkLife story:

"My WorkLife began in the world of finance, which I really enjoyed while I was doing it. That was as much to do with being in a good environment and working with great people as well as the job itself. But it did become mundane towards the end because I'd been doing it for so long, and so the time came to move on. But move on to what? That was the million-dollar question!

"While I was figuring out what I wanted to do next, my friend Pauline asked me to deliver the job-search element of a programme she was teaching. She had been let down by the original trainer at the last minute and needed someone to stand in. I had no experience in this, but Pauline persuaded me that all I needed was a common-sense approach. This was in the early days of the internet, so I couldn't get the course material I needed online. Instead, I drove the two-hour round trip to my nearest bookshop and returned home armed with enough books to develop a one-year training course – a tad excessive for the two days I needed to prepare for!

"I had two days to develop the course and travel to Ireland to deliver it. The client wouldn't pay the last-minute high-priced airfare, so I had to travel from England to Wales by train, get the ferry across to Ireland, catch another train, and then a bus. I barely slept for days. Instead, I did what I always do when I am out of my comfort zone: I over-prepared, then I went with the flow.

"And it went amazingly. I really connected with the people attending. All of whom had been impacted by a recession and downturn in the job market. Because of this, their confidence, self-esteem and spirit were low. I knew we had to work through this before we could work on the practical sessions I had planned. So my plan went out the window, but that was OK because having over prepared allowed me to be in the moment of knowing what to do and to go where the flow took me.

"I got the group talking about their WorkLife achievements – things they had forgotten about, or had taken for granted, or had never considered to be anything special. We all sat in awe, listening to the amazing stories being shared, and through this, they each began to realise how much they had to offer to employers. Once they had that realisation, we were then able to move onto the practical elements of their job-search campaign, preparing their CVs in a way that represented their skills, attributes and their amazing achievements to date, along with their potential. We planned their job-search approach, practised interviews, and explored how they would negotiate the job offers coming their way by considering what they wanted over and above the package being offered – whatever flexibility in the offer was important for each of them at their particular WorkLife stage, including:

- Regular salary reviews – while understanding there may be factors that may make a lower salary acceptable initially; the current status of the job market; the fact that many of them were entering an industry that was new to them, it was important to ensure there would be regular salary reviews;
- Continuous support in their professional and personal learning and development;
- Flexible working hours;
- The ability to work from home;
- More holidays;
- Good networking opportunities;
- Industry and cross-industry conference attendance;
- Access to WorkLife coaches and mentors;
- Tuition reimbursement;
- Professional dues and memberships.

"The group really enjoyed the in-the-moment learning they took from the negotiation role-play scenarios that they themselves improvised and devised. They explored different ideas – lower and higher status, body language, dialogue – and worked to refine each of these elements.

"As I made my long return journey home, I was buzzing. It was a little surreal because I was both exhausted from lack of sleep and energised from the experience. I began to write down the amazing stories I'd just heard, the stories that had transported the rest of the group and me into the world of each of the storytellers. I knew I had experienced something that was both meaningful and magical, and I wanted to capture that.

"I somehow knew this was what I was meant to do: help people manage, develop and transition their WorkLife in line with what was important to them. I don't think I was able to define it exactly as that in that moment. I think that evolved over time. But I do remember having a strong sense of my WorkLife purpose, knowing I had found my passion. I also knew I wanted and needed to do this properly. To serve people, I needed formal training: a solid theoretical base to build my knowledge from. As one of my beliefs in life is that 'when the student is ready, the teacher will come', I found the perfect pathway. I undertook a degree in Career Coaching and Management and then secured a position with a career consultancy agency. This allowed me to gain practical experience and to develop my skills – to ultimately launch my new WorkLife.

"My learning and development have always been important to me, and now I was in a position where I was working with individuals and organisations on their learning and development programmes. The individual coaching work came easily to me, but I felt inhibited delivering the group work – I suddenly became quite wooden! To overcome this, I undertook a Foundation year in Drama, along with several shorter acting courses and a year-long directing course that led to me being Assistant Director on a production of Hamlet, which went on to be performed at the RSC Open Space in Stratford-upon-Avon – my claim to fame!

"It was then I had my eureka moment of how the techniques, structure and methods of theatre are significant in the world of WorkLife learning and development: the unique skills sets performing artists have had to develop in their craft brings learning alive. This is 'learning by doing' enabling the practice of new skills sets and behaviours in a safe, supportive, challenging and creative environment.

"I was now able to combine my knowledge and experience of WorkLife coaching and WorkLife learning resources with drama-based techniques, collaborating with performing, visual and literary artists, and our workplace and community theatre programmes were born. Our work enables individuals and teams to be more active, spontaneous and flexible, freeing their minds to use their imagination in being inventive and original. The intrinsic nature of our work helps foster creativity, team spirit and emotional intelligence.

"This is a win/win for me because, along with a love for learning and development, I am also passionate about the Arts, and now I've created a WorkLife that embodies what's important to me. I work with interesting people helping them to manage, develop and transition their WorkLife, supporting organisational learning and development programmes, and I work with a team of performing artists in delivering the work – a definite win/win, don't you think!"

Aisling's next steps were to develop an online platform bringing learning, the arts and technology together to support individuals in their WorkLife learning and development. She was meeting with Max to discuss how to do this. They had worked together before. He's an actor with a background in graphic design. She was talking about what she could bring to the project. She doesn't remember exactly what she said, but it was something about creativity, to which Max blurted out those fateful words: "You're not creative!"

While she was stunned into silence and didn't respond with words, her facial response obviously spoke volumes, as Max tried to recover, saying: "I think of you as being honest, trustworthy, caring, I just don't think of you as being creative." She was still dumbstruck.

Somehow the conversation moved forward, and as it did, Aisling came to realise that Max didn't actually know her very well. She also realised that she was partly responsible for that, because she doesn't tend to talk about her work because she thinks her work should talk for itself. But it was very apparent it hadn't talked to Max. Anyway, they got through the meeting, discussed what they needed to discuss, agreed what they needed to do next, and said their goodbyes.

As Aisling walked home, she was mulling things over in her mind. During the meeting it had become very apparent that Max hadn't taken the time to discover anything about her, over and above the work they'd done together, nor did he see beyond what was in front of his eyes.

There was a time when what Max had said would have crushed her. But because she practices self-awareness and self-feedback through self-questioning, it didn't. She asked herself:

Is what Max said true?

If yes, why?

If no, why not?

This is the answer that came to her:

"I believe what's most creative about me, and my approach to my work is that I see connections between the detail and the bigger picture, I see what's possible, I see people's potential, I enable people to see things in new and different ways. I know this because people tell me. It's what they say is creative about me."

Then as she continued her walk home, something that later became very surreal happened. It was late in the evening, and the streets were deserted, and on a well-trodden London footpath, there was a book on the ground. There was no one around who could have dropped it, so she picked it up and brought it home.

Book Wisdom

The book was *It's Not How Good You Are, It's How Good You Want To Be*, by Paul Arden. It's quite a quick read filled with quotes and short stories, and so Aisling read it immediately on getting home. This is where the surrealism happened, with these words of wisdom:

"The most popular conception of creativity is that it's something to do with the arts.

"Nonsense.

"Creativity is imagination, and imagination is for everyone."

Words of Wisdom

Aisling shared what had happened with Max with her dear and wise friend Christina, who knew Aisling and her work very well. Christina was a little outraged on her behalf, asking if Max actually knew anything about her work. Wanting to ensure she didn't dwell on this, Christina also pointed out other areas where she considered Aisling to be creative. For example, she enjoys cooking, and when she has friends around, she likes to make it an experience: the setting, the food, the drinks, and so on. Christina was, in effect, reinforcing Aisling's own belief that there are many ways in which people are creative.

Aisling believes that you can always learn more from every situation and that you should always try to. She strives to be attentive to real-life challenges that people experience in their WorkLives. This drives the learning programmes she develops. A quote from the book served to remind her of this: "Don't look for the next opportunity, the one you have in hand is the opportunity."

Through her work, Aisling was very aware of the misconception of creativity being something to do with the arts. She had worked with creative people across all industries and sectors, including professions that were considered by many to be non-creative. Accountancy is one such profession that seems to attract that label, yet Aisling had worked with accountants who blew her away with their creative prowess. She had also worked with accountants who took a more cautious and perhaps a little less creative approach in their work. But the same could be said for people she worked with from the arts. Some really impressed her with their creative approach to their work, others less so. Another quote from the book clarified for her why this is: "In their need to prove their worth, creative people often produce work which on the surface appears clever but has little substance."

Wanting to find a way to enable people to recognise that creativity was imagination and imagination was for everyone brought Aisling back to a recent experience she had when working with her team of actors. They had a table reading of a script Aisling had written for a short workplace theatre play. At the end of the reading, there was silence around the table, and when Aisling asked what everyone thought, one of the group said, "Well, it's different." The rest of the group murmured in agreement. Now, Aisling happens to believe that different is really good. In fact, that's what she strives for in her work, but it was obvious to her that the group thought of different in this instance as being anything but good. They're a good group of people, and wanting to help out, they began to share their experiences.

Aisling valued the skills and experience the team brought from their training and work as actors to the workplace and community drama work they did together, but this particular piece of work was different to anything they had done before, and their suggestions didn't work for Aisling. She held back from saying anything because she wanted to encourage open feedback and not discourage them or shut their ideas down. Although they were having a table read and discussion and weren't improvising ideas, in Aisling's mind she was thinking of one of the golden rules of improvisation: Don't Block. 'Blocking' in improvisation means that one player's game offer is not accepted by the other player, but instead is rejected or ignored. Blocking often causes the scene to stagnate, and so Aisling didn't want to block anyone's ideas; but the thing was they were blocking her ideas.

Thinking about what she could have done differently in that moment brought Aisling back to an experience she had when she'd begun work at the career consultancy agency she had joined on completing her studies. At the time, the employment market was buoyant, and people who were unhappy in their WorkLife were willing to leave jobs that weren't fulfilling to them to carve out a more meaningful WorkLife. Some had already identified the change they wanted to make and needed support in making the transition. Others needed to discover what WorkLife path would bring them the fulfilment they were seeking. Located in the City of London (the home of banks and law firms), the agency attracted a significant number of bankers and lawyers for whom their work was no longer meaningful. Because Aisling had worked as a banker, she was surprised that she never got to work with them as their coach, but instead she worked with clients from the world of law.

Her curiosity led her to ask William, the managing partner who assigned clients, why this was. He replied: "When I first began to partner career coaches and clients, I put coaches who had themselves been lawyers with lawyer clients. But then I began to realise that for some reason, this wasn't working as well as I believed it should have had. When I looked into why that might be, I saw that they were getting stuck on the technical aspects of the job. Because the coach knew the job and the industry so well, they couldn't see the bigger picture, which meant they weren't able to help their client see things differently to what they themselves were seeing. Then I began to partner lawyers with career coaches from backgrounds that had nothing to do with law, and the work was completely different. The lawyer didn't expect the coach to understand the technical aspects of their work, and because of that, they didn't get bogged down in detail but instead were able to look at things differently, which in effect opened up new ideas for them to explore."

That is exactly what had happened in Aisling's experience with the actors. Because they know their work so well, they were focusing on what they knew had worked in other situations, which although different, they believed could be applied to this new piece of work. Except for Aisling that didn't work. Another quote from the book summed this up for her: "Experience is built from solutions to old situations and problems. The old situations are probably different to the present ones, so that old solutions will have to be bent to fit new problems (and probably fit badly). Also, the likelihood is that if you have experience, you will probably use it. This is lazy. Experience is the opposite of being creative." The impact of what the actors were doing was the same as the impact of the career coach with a background in law working with a lawyer – because they were focused on their experience of what was, they were blocking themselves from looking at things differently. Because of that, they couldn't see the possibilities of what could be.

Aisling was further reminded of when she shared with the actors that she cringes when she thinks of the first performance they had put on. This was because she had packed too much into it. Although they hadn't replied, she knew by their faces that they felt really bad for her and didn't know what to say. But Aisling didn't feel bad about it because to her way of thinking, if you're not embarrassed by what you did last year, you're launching too late. And there were several times when Aisling had spent too much time perfecting an idea, only for someone else to launch ahead of her, and that she did feel bad about. Although she cringes about their first performance, she had also learnt so much from the experience that was really valuable. And that more than compensated for any embarrassment.

Aisling realised that she had to take ownership for her role in how the situation had played out, or rather how it hadn't played out. She was so focused on wanting to encourage the flow of ideas, but by not saying anything, she had, in effect, brought about what she was trying to avoid – she too had been a blocker. She had a responsibility to share her ideas, her thinking and her vision for this new piece of work. The team needed to know this to have a better understanding of who she was and what she was about. She now knew she could have shared the story of her experience from when she first began working at the career consultancy agency. This story would have given them the understanding they needed without shutting them down or blocking them.

Again, the book summed up perfectly for Aisling the ownership she needed to take in her role, both in her work with the team and in her work with Max: "The art is to inspire, it's up to you to have the vision that allows them to expand into something they haven't done before. It's for you to lead them along the path of enlightenment."

She thought back to the experience she had all those years ago when she delivered the job-search element of the programme her friend Pauline was delivering – the experience that was the cause and effect of where she was now in her WorkLife. She remembered how when she had gotten the group talking about their WorkLife achievements – things they had forgotten about, or had taken for granted, or had never considered to be anything special – they had all sat in awe listening to the amazing stories being shared; and through this, they each began to realise how much they had to offer to employers. She realised that although she had worked with Max and the team of actors to create stories, she had never facilitated a session where they could all share their stories with each other. This is such a powerful exercise to help people realise their own potential, to include their creative ability, and also to help others learn more about the people they spend time with and to see them in a new and different way. Aisling knew this is something she needed to do, and she knew this would help her in leading Max and the team along the path of enlightenment.

Epilogue

All of this excited Aisling. She had been struggling to manage these pieces of work, both with the team and with Max, and this gave her a way forward. Her own experiences also gave her great material to work with and to develop into workplace and community theatre. She knew other people would have experienced the challenges she and her team had faced in how they had blocked their own creativity and, in doing so, had closed down their individual and collective imaginations.

So Aisling made herself a coffee, and sitting with her laptop, began to write the first scene for her idea for a workplace and community theatre play: The Case of Creativity Being Imagination and Imagination Being for Everyone.

WORKLIFE BOOK CLUB

As Benny stopped reading, he reached for a drink of water and smiled at the group, who had all been listening thoughtfully. Tom, who had been attentive to the group's needs, recognised this was his cue to pour their wine and bring over their selection of small plates. This comprised of scotch eggs, vegetarian and non-vegetarian cocktail sausages, sausage rolls, toad in the hole, whitebait with mayo and lemon, a mushroom and a chicken liver pate on toast, beetroot and red onion tartlets, a melty mushroom wellington and pork scratchings.

Saoirse tasted the wine.

Saoirse: My first experience of British wine was last summer when my friend and I walked in the Surrey Hills. We started out on what was supposed to be a three-mile walk through the hills, our destination being a wine estate for a late morning vineyard tour and tasting, followed by lunch. But we got horribly lost. Not being familiar with tree types, instead of taking a turning at the big old oak tree as per our directions, we took a turning at some other kind of big old tree. Our three-mile walk turned into a three-hour trek. We missed the tour and the tasting, but they did fit us in for a late lunch and much-needed refreshments. I remember how quickly we forgot about our weary feet as we sipped upon their wonderful rosé, sitting at our table overlooking the vineyard. The view was spectacular. It was a really special experience, which seemed so far removed from the busyness of London we had left behind that morning, and yet the train journey to several destinations on the Surrey Hills winery walks is less than an hour.

Pascal: This is quite a decent wine. It's got its own character. I didn't know England had the climate to ripen red grapes.

Florian: Pinot noir is a grape that can thrive in cooler climates, and it really likes the climate and soil we have here. It's taken time, though, and lots of experiments and hard work to get it right. The de-alcoholised wines are a more recent development.

Benny: Ah, so maybe some creativity and imagination thrown in?

Florian laughed.

Florian: Ah yes, the case we're here to discuss, and not the case of the British red wine.

Benny: Before we get started, I must profess I chose the case, not just because the title piqued my interest but also because it features

Paul Arden's book. I was a great admirer of the man and his work, and I've always loved his thinking.

Saoirse: I really like his thinking too. Although it was a quick read, I found it quite profound in the way it got me thinking. I can understand why it had such an immediate and surreal impact for Aisling. It gave her more profound answers to the questions she had posed to herself and was mulling over.

Florian: I agree, and the description is true in that he gives original and logical answers to everyday questions.

Maggie: Not least the question: "What is meant by the word creative?" And all the misconceptions that go with it.

Benny: 'Creative' is a word that features heavily in all our briefs, and it's as Arden says: "It means something completely different to each client." I think this is what Aisling experienced with Max: the word 'creative' held different meanings for both of them.

Pascal: The misconception that creativity belongs to the arts is so true. I experience this so often in my work with clients – from people who don't perceive themselves to be creative because they don't work in the creative industry, and yet their creative prowess is remarkable. I love that moment when people realise how much creative ability they have, and also when that's recognised by other people.

Benny: It can often be the opposite in my industry. People think they're more creative than they really are, or they want to be seen to be. As Arden says: "The word 'creative' is the currency with which ad agencies operate. Without it, there are no agencies."

Saoirse: It's that whole labelling thing again. People just love putting labels on everything, and then people want to live up to that label or are expected to.

Maggie: It's that whole awards thing too. I so agree with Arden when he talks about not trying to win awards. Here's the thing. Today there's an award for everything, and when there's an award for everything, there's an award for nothing. They just have no meaning.

Benny: As Arden says: "Awards are judged in committee by consensus of what is known. In other words, what is fashionable; but originality can't be fashionable because it hasn't as yet had the approval of the committee. Do not try to follow fashion. Be true to your subject and you will be far more likely to create something that is timeless. That is where true art lies." These words, this thinking, is why I admire and respect this man and his work so much. It also relates to the challenge Aisling was experiencing in wanting to create something that was original. She was met with resistance and what seemed like non-approval because it was different – the table read for the piece she was working on with the actors and also her thinking: "If you're not embarrassed by what you did last year, you're launching too late."

Maggie: Talking about originality, Arden says: "Being right is based upon knowledge and experience and is often provable. Knowledge comes from the past, so it's safe. It's also out of date. It's the opposite of originality." Is safe so bad? And can you actually say it's out of date? In my work, knowledge and experience that is provable and safe is good, and it doesn't mean that it's out of date. And it's certainly not a lazy approach. When Aisling was talking about the team of actors she worked with sharing their experiences because they wanted to help, was that such a bad thing? Surely they could have built from that. They didn't have to reinvent the wheel, as it were. I believe creativity can come from knowledge and experience. It doesn't have to come from something new or different. Arden also says: "If you can't solve a problem, it's because you're playing by the rules." I get a sense that both he and Aisling think that rules are bad. I don't think they are, or I don't think they have to be, and I also don't think they stop problem-solving, or cause blocking, as Aisling puts it.

Saoirse: I took the 'being right' or the need to be right as being the important part of that message or the learning to be taken from it. Arden says: "It's wrong to be right." And "It's right to be wrong." I think when people are trying too hard to be right and are scared to be wrong, that that's what prevents originality, stops problem-solving, or causes blocking.

Florian: He also talks about anything being possible, if you start from a place of not being afraid of getting things wrong. That I think is the message or learning that Aisling was trying to get across when she talked about: "If you're not embarrassed by what you did last year, then you launched too late." I can relate to that. There have been times when I delayed moving with ideas because I was trying to perfect them when really I needed to have pushed forward with them much more quickly. I was playing safe, and because of that, I lost out on opportunities.

Then at some stage, I stopped trying too hard to get everything perfect. I always got things to a place that I believed was the best I could do at that moment in time. I knew if I took longer, I could get it to an even better place. I made a choice to trade perfection for the best at that moment, and when I did, I was no longer trying to be infallible. I was in the unknown, as Arden says. There was no way of knowing what could happen, but there was also more of a chance of it being more amazing than if I tried to be right – or perfect in my case. I took a leap of faith, and if I hadn't, I wouldn't have the businesses I have now.

It was scary, though, I ventured into the unknown in so many ways with my restaurant here in London and my vineyard and winery in Spain; but if I had played it safe and had wanted to be right at every stage of my journey, well, I wouldn't have what I have now. I only have that because I did get things wrong. Because like Aisling, I learnt so much from those things that did go wrong. Much more than had I gotten everything right.

Maggie: "If everything seems under control, you're not moving fast enough" – Mario Andretti.

Saoirse: I like that Arden says: "When it can't be done, do it. If you don't do it, it doesn't exist." I can relate to that so much in my WorkLife. Particularly around my blog, which originated from my love of live music, craft beer and gin. At first, it was simply a way of sharing the adventures my passions took me on and the experiences I encountered along the way.

Over time I began to share the stories of the people behind the music, the breweries and the distilleries, appreciating the impact they have on the community and neighbourhood that supports them. When I began, it didn't even cross my mind that this could factor into the WorkLife I've carved out for myself, in a way that would support me financially, as well as honouring other things that are important to me, such as an independent WorkLife – and yet it has. This is what Aisling did as well. She created something that didn't exist, and she achieved this by being different, by doing something that was different.

Benny: "What the mind can conceive, the mind can achieve" – Clement Stone.

Maggie: "We don't see things as they are, we see them as we are" – Anaïs Nin.

Benny caught Maggie's eye. He wasn't sure if she was playing with him by throwing in the quotes from the book, some of which he knew she found cheesy. She smiled sweetly at him – she was, in a tongue-in-cheek sort of way. But it was also a slight tactic: she had struggled this month getting into the case, the book, and now the discussion. There was something about it all that was irritating her. It had evoked a strong negative reaction within her. Although unflappable for the most part, Maggie had what her family and friends knew to be an explosive side when something got her goat, as they laughingly referred to her infrequent but entertaining outbursts. And so, she was tactically playing a little to avoid showing her hand – or rather as a way to hold her tongue... for now.

Annie: Going back to what you were saying, Saoirse, about what you said about you and Aisling carving out your WorkLives by creating something that didn't exist. Arden says: "You will become whoever you want to be." I think that's more about imagination than creativity, or it's about creativity being imagination.

Florian: He poses the question: "Where do you see yourself?" And then goes on to talk about Victoria Beckham, when she said she wanted to be as famous as Persil Automatic. He said it wasn't how good she was that mattered but how good she wanted to be. And what was interesting was that she didn't compare herself to another performer, but she saw the fame of Persil Automatic as her yardstick. That in itself makes her different from so many people, and Arden claims that it was this highly original imagination that got her to where she is today.

Pascal: You can achieve the unachievable – firstly, you need to aim beyond what you are capable of. Arden advocates for the need to develop a complete disregard for where your abilities end. I'm not sure if Aisling had a complete disregard, but she did aim beyond what she thought she was capable of. In sharing her backstory, we first saw this when her friend Pauline persuaded her that all she needed was a common-sense approach to be able to deliver the work she had no experience in. And then how she had gotten the group to talk about their WorkLife achievements when they were lacking confidence or feeling blocked. I think that helped them to aim beyond what they believed they were capable of. Arden talks about trying to do the things you are incapable of. That requires imagination because you don't necessarily know what that is.

Annie: He also champions firing up people's imagination. Aisling realised this when she reflected on the table read, and she recognised the responsibility for this lay with her. I'm quite reflective myself, so I can relate to Aisling not knowing this in the moment. This is something I'm striving to overcome, but I find it challenging.

Pascal: This is something that I continuously have to work at to get the right balance. Yes, perhaps Aisling needed to share her vision more clearly; but on the other hand, as Arden says, if you brief too tightly, it wouldn't have allowed the freedom for the actors that they needed to make their work work, and that was what she was employing or collaborating with them for.

Benny: I agree it really is about getting the right balance. And as Arden said: "If you get stuck, draw with a different pen... Change your tools, it may free your thinking." That's what Aisling discovered through reflection. She knew she could get her message across by sharing her story of when she began working as a WorkLife coach. And she knew doing this wouldn't shut them down, which is the thing she wanted to avoid. All of this comes with experience, and I think taking time to reflect is a very helpful practice.

Florian: It is so important not to shut people down. It can cause people not to suggest ideas because they might not be listened to, or they might be concerned what other people will think of their ideas, or even worse, they might worry that people will think their ideas are stupid.

I have to work really hard on getting this right, too, with the people I work with. I think Aisling not saying anything in the moment and taking time to reflect on it was the best way. I got a sense they were quite a newly formed team, or maybe it was just that this was a new piece of work. In time she will find a better way of managing this in the moment.

Annie: "You're not creative," those words were crushing. How do you react to that, to what was unsolicited feedback?

Saoirse: Words have consequences. They have power, a power that can be used to knock down or to build up. Wisdom, truth and self-awareness are the arch-rivals to words that have caused a person to be knocked down. They are the superpowers that will build them up again.

Oh! That sounded like a headline followed by a sub-heading. I'm sorry, I can't stop myself sometimes. I've been a writer for so long, that I slip in and out of thinking in headlines and sub-headings, then I forget and I speak them aloud.

I suppose that was a lead in to the learning I took from what Aisling did as she walked home. While she was taken aback in the moment, she knew herself well enough to know the importance to question if the truth was being spoken. This was her inner sage at work.

Florian: Effective self-questions will help to get to the important truth. And the questions Aisling asked herself were really simple. This allowed her to give herself feedback based on the truth – her truth. That approach will help to resolve reactions to unsolicited feedback – good, bad, ugly or indifferent. As Arden says: "If you ask the right questions, you get the right answers."

Maggie: Was Max the villain or hero of the story?

Pascal: I think he was both. I don't think he meant or intended to crush Aisling with what he said, but that did make him the unintentional villain of the story. But what he said did cause her to stop, think and question both what had happened and also the role she had played, in her interaction with Max and the team of actors. This, in turn, allowed her to know the changes she needed to make to do what she needed to do. This also makes Max the unintentional hero of the story, I think. He had no way of knowing the impact his words would have. It could have played out either way.

Annie: Christina was another hero of the story. I think it's good to have people to remind us of who we are, what we've achieved and what we're capable of. That's a theme that's running through this story for me. Aisling facilitated this with the group in Ireland. Even though she didn't know anything about them, she instinctively knew that by asking them to talk about their achievements would allow them to recognise who they are, what they've achieved and what they're capable of. And before that, her friend Pauline did it too, in a less obvious way, but she still managed to help Aisling realise what she was capable of.

Arriving with their main courses, as Tom began to serve the group, Saoirse asked how he had come to work within the food and drink industry, enquiring if it was a long-held passion that he had always wanted to follow.

Tom said no, that his long-held passion was theatre, and he had actually studied drama at university and worked within theatre at the beginning of his WorkLife. He had formed his own theatre company and had been involved as an actor, a writer and a director. With his team, he had created a community hub that brought people from all walks of life together.

In between jobs, he worked in pubs, pulling pints and serving bar food. He said he started becoming more involved with behind the scenes work around the time when 'small plates' started becoming a trend, which was the same time he had joined the team here. He became fascinated with how Chef Jones, when creating each dish, paid attention to acknowledging the past while welcoming the future.

He had become involved in writing the menus, and drawing from his background he wrote a script to tell the story of the pub and the stories of the people who made it what it is. He also wrote the backstory behind the food and the drinks. He approached it by writing a script that described the action, the characters, the setting. He built it around hardcore ideas that could be shared with other people so they could explain the pub's vision. He told stories about the produce they used and how they strived to source from local suppliers as much as they could. He talked about local markets and small businesses and the integral role they each played in supporting the community they served. He then told their stories, and this helped people envision where their food comes from and to talk about it with a sense of pride.

He said his love of theatre brought him to where he is now, but that it took time to seep into his pores, into his DNA, that not only was he in the right place but that he was in the place he was meant to be. He said it had become a love to be here every day and that he thinks of it as a theatre of craftspeople practising their different crafts daily. Cooking, often costuming for the themed events they run, lighting, sound. So many performers, so many front-of-house people, so many behind-the-scenes people, all of whom are needed to keep all the operations running.

Everyone was fascinated by Tom's story and his storytelling abilities. He had drawn them into his world. A secret world that existed on their doorstep.

Saoirse: I just love Tom's story, and I love how he instinctively knew he needed to tell the stories behind the pub. I think it's very similar for Aisling, who spoke about knowing in the moment what to do with the group in Ireland – in getting them to talk about their achievements. She got them to tell their stories in the same way Tom worked with people to tell their stories.

Annie: Aisling also said she went with the flow. In the situation with Max and the actors, while she didn't know what to do in the moment, she also went with the flow as such, in that she let it play out, and that was good enough. Tom went with the flow as well. He said it took time to seep into his pores, into his DNA, but by letting it play out and going where it took him, he eventually found himself at the place he knows he's meant to be. The lesson I'm taking from this is that you don't have to have the answer in the moment. Sometimes you will, which is great, but when you don't, the important thing is to go with wherever it takes you and trust that you will figure it out, and that your inner sage will help you.

Pascal: Something that Arden says sums this up for me: "Do not put your cleverness in front of the communication." In Ireland, Aisling was in the moment and knew what to do; with Max and the actors, while she was also in the moment she didn't know what to do. She didn't try to be clever. She allowed it to play out. In both instances, she used her imagination, either in the moment or later, by allowing her mind to wonder. Imagination is not about being clever. It's about being curious, and that's where creativity comes in.

In my work, sometimes I'll have the answer I need in the

moment, other times I won't. When I started out, that really bothered me, and it bothered my clients who were paying a lot of money for my input, and there were times when I did bow to the pressure I was feeling and tried to come up with something clever. Then one day, a senior partner in the company who was also my mentor took me aside and said almost the exact same words to me as Arden said: "Instead of trying to find a quick fix, spend time finding out what the problem is, and you will discover the solution." Because I was putting too much pressure on myself in the moment, my vision was blurred. I needed to step away to figure out what I needed to do and to do that. I needed to let it play out. That was a scary place for me, the not knowing, and while I wasn't explicit in saying that, it was very obvious to everyone, and that caused a sense of nervousness within myself and also within my client. But yet, when I did step away as such and let it play out, I stopped trying to be clever and always having the right answer immediately. When I did that, I was able to see the problem more clearly, and from that, a solution always presented itself. But to say that was a scary place to be at that point in my WorkLife is a big understatement.

Benny: I can relate to that, and something Arden says sums up how I overcame my biggest challenge. Or one of them – there have been a few. And that's: "That if you are willing to not take yourself too seriously, it indicates to others that you have confidence and competence." I was so intent on having to get things right and having the answer in the moment that I was really intense and not a good person to be around or to have in a meeting. To say I blocked people was an understatement. I'm embarrassed to say it, but I crushed people too, like Max, not intentionally, but in effect, I shut them down and, looking back now, most likely caused them to doubt themselves. It was actually Paul Arden who saved me from myself. I discovered his wisdom a long time ago, and through this, I learnt to take my work, but not myself, too seriously, and when I did that, things began to change. I was more open to seeing solutions around me; and when people began to realise that, they were more open in sharing their ideas, in the knowledge and confidence that they wouldn't be crushed. While Aisling's story wasn't explicit in saying she was experiencing something similar, I think there was some of this at play within her mind. I say that because I think it's something that most people experience when starting out or starting something new. These situations bring about a sense of intensity that can crush or block. Time brings confidence and competence, which in turn will allow people to lighten up, and that's when creativity flows because it's following the journeys people's imagination are taking it on.

The quietness of the group spoke volumes to their respect to Pascal and Benny for sharing their personal stories and their openness in being vulnerable and sharing what they could clearly see were painful recounts of difficult moments in their WorkLife. They were, in essence, picking up on the thread that was running through Aisling's story, and although the unfolding or telling of their stories was a natural occurrence in following the flow of the conversation, as opposed to an exercise Aisling had initiated in her story. Regardless of how it had occurred, it served to demonstrate the power of sharing stories. Whether that was about achievements or challenges didn't matter. What did matter was that they were getting to know themselves and each other better and at a more deeper level in the context of their discussion.

Florian continued this sharing of stories.

Florian: Arden talked about how easy it is to take something that is great, and through the power of consensus turn it into something good. I did that in my first job as manager. I was promoted to the role, and I wasn't ready for it. I couldn't lead or make decisions, and so I made it that everything we did, had to be agreed on by the group. We had a team of great chefs who were so creative and imaginative in the dishes they prepared, but I took that away from them. One by one, they began to leave. Most of them didn't give a reason other than it was time to move on. The food and drinks industry is a small world, and I now realise they were afraid to speak up because they believed whatever they said would follow them and would be the thing they would be remembered for, for their time at the restaurant.

There was, however, one exception, and that was Pedro. He told it to me straight. He told me that we had a great team, all of whom were confident in their work, and that I took that confidence away because I was so hell-bent on getting consensus at every step. Not only was I micromanaging the running of everything, but I had the whole team involved in micromanaging each other. I didn't just block their creativity and imagination. I totally crushed it.

The restaurant started going downhill, we were losing customers, and eventually, I was sacked. I was asked to leave before I ran it completely into the ground. It was the hardest and most painful lesson of my WorkLife and one that took me time to recover from. I actually took time out because I believed I didn't have what was needed to run a successful restaurant. Running a restaurant, as Tom says, is like putting on a theatrical show. It needs creativity, it needs imagination, and I didn't believe I had that.

In a crazy turn of events, it was Pedro who brought me back into the fold and back to the restaurant. He took over the job from me, and he was much better equipped to do so. He set out to rebuild the restaurant by bringing it back to its original greatness, and he persuaded me to come back and work with him in doing that. I swallowed my pride and went back. Pedro is a good man, and I knew instinctively he had my best interests at heart. I'm eternally grateful to him. Not only did he rebuild the restaurant, but he also helped me to rebuild myself from that crushing experience.

Once again, there was a quiet lull in the conversation, which expressed the respect of the group to Florian for sharing his story and, in so doing, his vulnerability.

Benny: The person who doesn't make mistakes is unlikely to make anything. When Arden talks about Benjamin Franklin saying he hasn't failed, he's had ten thousand ideas that didn't work, and Thomas Edison saying of the two hundred light bulbs that didn't work, that every failure told him something that he was able to incorporate into the next attempt. And theatre director Joan Littlewood saying, if we don't get lost, we'll never find a new route. As Arden says, all of them understood that failures and false starts are a precondition of success. I think that Aisling instinctively knew that too. She had an acorn of an idea, which she needed to grow, and before it could take root, she needed to feed it more.

Florian: Something Arden said brought me back to my experience and summed it up for me too. He talked about composing your ad from the weakest point, and to start knowing that it's a problem to be solved as an integral part of the idea. To treat it as an advantage and not a problem, and to involve the client. I was the weakest point or part of my story. I had caused the problem that needed to be solved. When Pedro brought me back, it could be said that I was the client as well, and by involving me, I became an advantage and not a problem. Sorry, I'm not sure if my analogy makes sense to the rest of you, but it helps me. Please excuse my self-indulgence.

Benny: It makes sense to me. I use the approach Arden talks about in my work.

Pascal: I understand what you're saying. I use this approach in my work too, and it really does help to open up people's imagination to solve the problem.

Maggie: I understand, I think, but I can't think of a situation I can relate it to. I need to mull it over.

Annie: I need to mull it over too. But can I take us back to the stories you've all shared, which were really interesting. I'm not a manager, and I have no desire to be. I'm an independent contributor, and I enjoy that. So I don't have a story to share of a failure in the same way you've talked about your experiences of things that went wrong and how what you learnt from that helped you. But in Aisling's story, she talked about Max not seeing what was in front of his eyes in terms of who she was and what she was about, and how she was partly responsible for that because she didn't 'talk up' her work if you like. Arden talks about: if you have the reluctance to push yourself forward, you will go unnoticed. You'll be a nobody as such. I prefer being behind the scenes, and I got a sense that Aisling does too. I don't know that I consider it as a failure, but it's certainly a challenge.

Saoirse: Arden says that it takes real courage to do something different and that wanting to seem different is not the same as wanting to be different. I can relate to what you're saying, Annie, about enjoying working independently. That's my preferred way of working too. And I get a sense it is for Aisling too, but because she's working with a team who she brought in, in a sense, she has responsibility not necessarily to manage them but definitely to lead them. It's a collaboration as such, where everyone has the responsibility to self-manage, but they also have to work as part of a team.

The challenge for me over the years as someone who enjoys working independently is at times having my voice heard, and I'm partly responsible for that because I've chosen to be a freelance writer. I don't want to be part of a corporation. Now that's not so unusual or different for writers. What I believe is different about me and my work are the stories I tell and how that's enabled me to carve out a WorkLife that's financially sustainable. It took courage because I had to create a new pathway. I wanted to do my own thing and do it my way, and I didn't want to compromise.

All the time, it was about having my voice heard. I'm talking about my blog. I was talking about something that was interesting to me, but so what? It wasn't breaking news stories which had an immediate interested audience. These were more 'nice' stories. And here's the thing, the word 'nice' has gotten a lot of bad press over the years. It was considered dull, boring, uninteresting, but I happen to think that 'nice' is understated and underestimated, and I think the world is waking up to that now. And people want nice, heartfelt, warming stories, simple acts of being nice to someone, and the frequent domino effect of that.

But that wasn't always the case. For a long time, people were only interested in the exciting, breaking news stories – and I've covered those, and I enjoyed it. But I also wanted to write 'nice' stories. But for a long time no-one was interested in those; and so, in the beginning, writing these stories was more of a hobby, they came from hobbies, or things I like – music, beers, gin – and I've started writing about coffee too. I always knew I wanted there to be more to it, but I struggled having my voice heard in making it more.

I'm rambling, and I'm repeating myself. I'm sorry, I'm probably not making any sense. I don't know what it is about this story, but I can relate to what you just said Florian. It's helping me make sense of my own experience, but I'm not sure if it makes sense to anyone else.

Annie: It does, actually. I think it is for me about having my voice heard, too, to be seen for who I am, in the way Aisling wanted Max to see her for who she was. For me, it's about finding a way to do that in a non-shouty way. Arden said: "To be original, seek your inspiration from unexpected sources."

Listening to Aisling's story, her WorkLife journey has followed this thinking. When she spoke about her eureka moment that led her to combine her learning and development experience with drama-based techniques. And how their work frees people's minds to use their imagination. And also listening to Tom's story and how his natural skills and attributes led him to the place he was meant to be. He's both front-of-house and behind-the-scenes. He has a gentle, yet really engaging way of drawing people into the stories he shares. I feel there's a lesson in here for me, but I haven't figured out what that is. I'm so reflective, I would love to have the in-the-moment learning you're having, but for now, I think it's enough to know that it will come to me. If I try too hard, it will have the opposite effect of freeing my imagination.

Maggie: What you've said makes perfect sense to me, Annie. I had a really bad reaction to the story, the book and where it was taking us at the beginning of our discussion. I think the problem I have is with the word 'creativity'. I got hung up on that word. Arden said: "All creative people need something to rebel against, it's what gives their life excitement, and it's creative people who make their clients' lives exciting." I was rebelling against the word 'creative' and the context of how it's so often used. If a word can be put on a pedestal, it would be that word. And it seems to be put there by so many people and represents something that should be revered. Something that is only for the chosen or the select few. Like a private, exclusive members club, which is all so pretentious.

The word 'imagination', on the other hand, I really like because it doesn't discriminate against anyone. It doesn't infer you have to be part of a special club. It's inclusive, and it's also individual. Simply put, imagination is for everyone.

The group nodded in agreement. They agreed with Maggie's synopsis of the word 'creativity' being put on a pedestal. They had all noticed she had been quiet this evening and hadn't said very much. But that was the great thing about the group. There was no pressure on anyone. They each said what they needed to say. Some said more. Some said less than others. Although this was only their second Book Club meeting, they all sensed that this was how it needed to be and that it would vary from week to week. There was also no expectation that they had to make really clear arguments. There was a lot of clarity in what they said, but there was also a little haziness around some of what they were saying. And that was OK because everyone recognised they were working through it in the moment, and it was bringing enlightenment, but there were places where that light was dim. There were no hard and fast rules. They had been brought together by a shared love of reading and were simply sharing an experience each month and going where that took them.

Benny: You know, Maggie, in my company we prefer to be thought of as 'productive' rather than 'creative'. We believe productivity fuels imagination. I fully get where you're coming from.

The contemplative lull in the conversation gave Tom his cue to attend to their needs. He recommended for dessert that they might perhaps like mugs of hot chocolate made from the award-winning chocolate from local chocolate makers at their workshop in the backstreets of Shoreditch. The hot chocolate was served with marshmallows, which Tom suggested they may like to toast on the open fire.

The group loved this idea, and they also loved how much they were learning about their neighbourhood businesses and how they supported each other.

Benny: I don't know if it's going to happen every month, but I love the underlying themes that we've uncovered or discovered last month and this month. Florian, you told us this pub is the local hub and community pub, where people come together, and no doubt share their stories. Pascal, you spoke about the stories the locals shared with you. Saoirse, you mentioned your interest in the stories behind the pubs. Annie, you talked about pubs being at the heart of community life. Tom has regaled us with stories that have a community theme to them as well. And, Maggie, if I'm right, I think our sharing of stories was helpful to you too. I think we're surrounded by stories here and in your restaurant too, Florian, at the tables, at the bar. Maybe especially at the bar, because many people will tell their story to bartenders, whether they know them or not. Even the walls can tell a story or many stories. For me, the underlying themes tonight have been communities and stories.

The group nodded in agreement.

Florian: There's also an interesting theme to Tom's story. Or maybe a better way of saying it is that there is a corresponding background or connection to his story and the story of this neighbourhood. Tom told us about his background in theatre. This neighbourhood also has a historical background in theatre. The Curtain Theatre, which was built in 1577, was London's second playhouse and

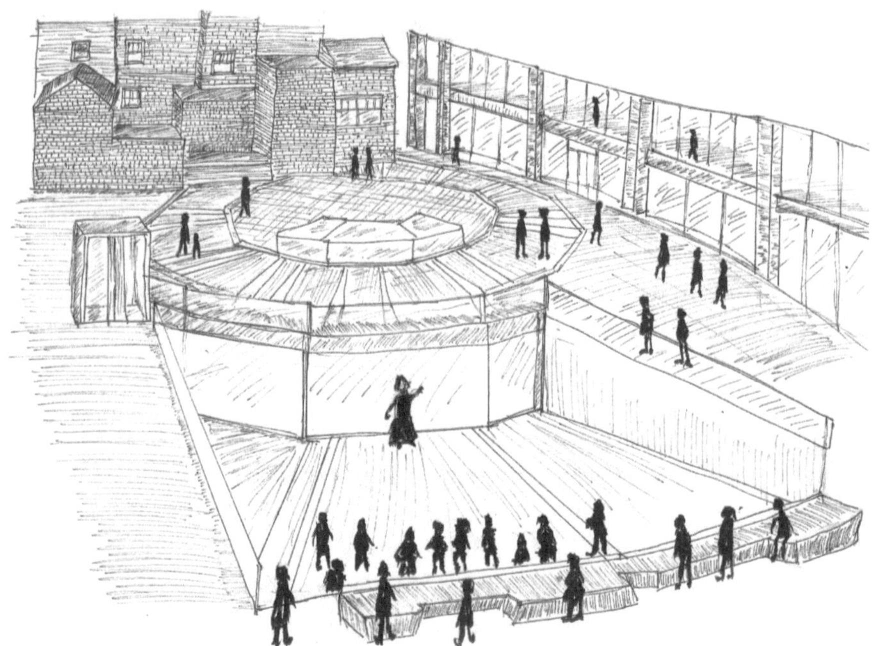

staged several of Shakespeare's earlier works, including Romeo and Juliet. In recent years archaeologists from the Museum of London announced that they had discovered the remains of the theatre during trial excavations. There are plans to develop the site, which include a Shakespeare museum, an outdoor auditorium and park, as well as apartments. The site already features street art paying homage to Romeo and Juliet.

Maggie: Oh, I've seen that. It's amazing, but I didn't know the story behind it. That's so interesting, Florian. I love these little snippets you share about our neighbourhood. I also loved Tom's stories and his storytelling abilities, which for sure came from his theatrical background, but also, bartenders are great at getting stories out of people. And relating his story back to the people on the course that Aisling ran in Ireland, who were retraining to enter an industry that was new to them. When you start to rethink your job as a set of skills, you can, in effect, work anywhere. I love that too.

And, yes, Benny, you're right, the stories being shared this evening really helped me to make sense of things – the case study, the book, our earlier discussion. I didn't understand my initial negative reaction to everything. The stories you all shared really did help. And I think that was because you were all so open in everything you shared. It felt quite raw, and perhaps that you were putting yourselves in a place where you were sharing and showing your vulnerabilities. Because of that, they were meaningful and magical – exactly what Aisling said she had experienced. So, thank you.

The group smiled in response.

EPILOGUE

Savouring the delicious hot chocolate and the cosy warmth of the atmosphere for a little longer before bracing the cold night air, Benny asked what was the single most important learning they had each taken from the case – the story, the book, the discussion.

Maggie: The important question is not what is creativity but what is imagination. Because there are a lot of misconceptions around what creativity is. And what it is means something different to different people.

Benny: Creativity exists in people in every walk of life, at every Work-Life stage, not just in the creative industries.

Saoirse: Creativity is fuelled by imagination, and stories play an important role in this. Because stories allow us to see what is possible. We also need the curiosity that can be provoked by a great question. Both stories and questions take our minds to a new place.

Pascal: We all get blocked. Sometimes it's our own mental blocks. Sometimes we're blocked by other people or situations. The way to get unblocked is to stop trying too hard, stop thinking we have to be right. We need to stop our critical thoughts and instead take a playful approach to ideas.

Florian: Anything is possible. You need to be willing to fail. You need to be willing to get things wrong in order to get them right.

Annie: Sharing stories, whether it's achievements, successes or failures, is a great way or a great tool to help people understand and appreciate who they are themselves, and also help other people understand them at a deeper level too. I learnt a lot about how to do that tonight through our discussion, in a way that was really natural, and I'm pleased about that.

I'm also pleased that the WorkLife Achievements assignment that Aisling used to help the people on the course in Ireland tell their stories is part of this case and that I can tap into it.

Because now that I understand how it works in practice, I think it will be really helpful to me, for myself and also I may be able to roll it out within my department.

Maggie: That's a good idea. That's something that I could possibly do at my work, and for myself too.

Could we meet for a coffee to each share one of our stories? A way of replicating what Aisling did with the group in Ireland. I'm curious to understand what that experience was like. Aisling said it was both meaningful and magical and that the stories shared had transported them into the world of each of the storytellers. I would just love to experience what the Achievement assignment brings about in reality in the sharing of our stories, if that's OK with everyone.

The rest of the group said that was something they would like to experience too, as they drained the very last drops of their hot chocolates.

My bounty is as
boundless as the sea
My love as deep
he more I give to thee
he more I have
both are infinite
Romeo and Juliet

Interlude 2

WorkLife Achievements Assignment

Accompanied by a cup of coffee or tea.

The only sound that broke through the early Saturday morning crisp February air as the group made their way through the sleepy streets of Shoreditch to Florian's café was the soft murmurs from the market street traders as they set their stalls up for the day.

Spitalfields Market is at the heart of Shoreditch life, and the community prides itself in having something for everyone. There's always something new happening, from modern to vintage fashion and art, to retro and rare vinyl record collections, from live music to tango dancing to street theatre. A foodie hotspot, it's said you can eat here every day for months and always have something new and different to try. The vibrancy from the hustle and bustle of the market attracts people from near and far who come to shop, eat, drink and soak up the lively atmosphere and the unique artistic vibe from the exciting happenings taking place.

On welcoming everyone, Florian and his baristas, Sam and Pilar, who the group all knew, prepared their much needed first coffees and teas of the day.

Taking his first sip, Benny said, "The first cup of coffee of the day is always the best, and this is really good. Thanks, Sam."

"So is my tea. Thanks, Pilar," said Annie. The others nodded in agreement.

Sam told them they get their coffee from a nearby roastery that takes pride in sourcing the finest coffee from farmers they've partnered with in different countries throughout the world. The company was built on the ethos of paying a fair price, allowing the farmers to invest in their farms, families and workers, to make better coffee for everyone. Pilar said they get their tea locally, too, from a tea shop that has longstanding relationships with individual tea estates, with whom they've established trustful collaborations. The estates source directly from different countries to bring distinctive teas to the world of tea connoisseurs.

Leaving them to enjoy their drinks, Sam and Pilar went to prepare coffees and teas for the market stallholders – a weekend practice that they, together with the other nearby coffee and tea shops, engaged in.

Saoirse: That's such a lovely thing to do. It really helps to create a great sense of community, which is quite unique, because as much as I know locals support the market, in numbers it attracts more visitors, and yet it emits such a strong feeling of community.

Florian: We come together as a community to keep both our neighbourhood and the market strong. It's a one-of-a-kind iconic landmark that serves locals and visitors alike. It's an essential establishment for our community. We work together to both preserve and enrich it.

There has been a market on the site for over 350 years. Since King Charles I gave a licence for flesh, fowl and roots to be sold at what was then known as Spittle Fields – a rural area of east London. During the time of the Commonwealth, the rights lapsed. It is said the market was refounded by King Charles II to feed the growing population of a new suburb of London. In the late twentieth century, there was a dispute between the owners, the City of London Corporation, and local residents about redevelopment, which resulted in office blocks being built on the site. Then what was remaining was rebuilt to include restaurants, shops and an indoor market. That's why it's so important to the community to keep the market alive. In so doing, we're protecting not only the market complex but also the community of people who live and work here – including individual and small independent businesses. The market is home to a community of both life-long traders and exciting new brands.

Saoirse: That really is interesting, and so important to know how we

all can and need to play our part in supporting our community. Thank you, Florian.

The others echoed their agreement to Saoirse's words.

Sam and Pilar's arrival with fresh cups of coffee and tea was perfectly timed, as the group was ready to share their achievement and story from completing the WorkLife Achievements Assignment.

Annie: Shall I begin by sharing my achievement and story? I can talk you through it in the format it was set out in the assignment.

Benny: That sounds good. I don't think we need to discuss or give feedback on the stories as we go. I think the idea is to continue the flow of storytelling by each taking turns to share our achievement and story. Does that sound OK?

The rest of the group said it was.

Annie: My Achievement & Story

THE SITUATION

My best friend, Isla, had found herself single again. Through her sobs of heartbreak, she said she just wished she knew from the start that it wasn't going to work out because of her dog, Duisa. She had been dating a guy who just wasn't a dog person. He tried at first, letting the dog hang out with them; but that soon changed, and he issued her an ultimatum, you've got to choose the dog or me. Isla chose the dog.

This wasn't the first time Isla was forced to choose her dog over a boyfriend, but she vowed it would be her last. She needed a way to find love with someone who would love her dog as much as he would love her.

Knowing that Isla liked to use dating apps, I jokingly said she needed a dating app that would connect dog lovers. Isla took my idea to heart and said knowing how skilled I was technically, that I was the best person to develop the app.

Wanting to help Isla through the heartbreak of her breakup, I somehow found myself agreeing to Isla's request.

THE ACTION TAKEN

So I went about developing a dating app, specifically targeting dog lovers in Edinburgh, where Isla was living. Within a couple of months, the prototype was ready, and Isla, having suitably recovered from her heartbreak, was ready to test it out. We had lined up friends from our uni days who were willing and able to help with the testing too.

THE OUTCOME OR RESULT

Not only did Isla find love with Angus, but Duisa also found love with his dog, Bailey.

As for the app, it had been a fun project that ended Isla's search for her perfect dog-loving partner. Dog done, we sent it to a home for retired apps.

THE SKILLS AND ATTRIBUTES I USED

I used my research and technical abilities to design the app, together with a sense of fun in creating it.

THE WAY I FELT AFTERWARDS

I enjoyed the experience of learning how to do something new. As well as it being a fun project, I also loved that I was able to help Isla with something that meant a lot to her. I just hopes it brings about long-lasting love.

Benny: Thank you, Annie.

Benny: My Achievement & Story

THE SITUATION

The nature of my industry made it possible for my company to be an early adaptor of the hybrid workplace, supporting a distributed workforce of both in-office and remote workers. The initiative brought about immediate employee happiness because of the flexible way of working that catered to their needs. But it also brought about concern for me. My concerns were related to how my company could support the mental health and wellbeing of our people in an industry where competitive deadlines are known to contribute to stress and burnout. I prided myself on creating a workplace where people looked out for each other and were adept at recognising warning signals that their colleagues were under pressure. My concern was, without seeing people in person every day, how they could maintain this practice of taking care of each other.

THE ACTION TAKEN

I created an initiative which I called: Caring For Each Other With High-Touch Communication.

High-touch communication in my world means real communication. Honest communication is championed. Banal communication is opposed.

I rolled it out within the entire workforce by making it that everyone was required to have a ten-minute conversation with two members of their team once a week. The fact that everyone had to do it alleviated any stigma that might arise when discussing mental health and wellbeing.

Working with my team, we came up with questions that would help to support honest communication. These included asking:

- *Do you feel you have enough time to get your work done?*
- *Are you experiencing any challenges?*
- *Are you finding ways to stay connected to the team?*
- *How can I be of better support to you right now?*
- *What do you need from me?*

THE OUTCOME OR RESULT

The act of dedicating time and resources in support of these check-ins sent a clear message to people that their mental health and wellbeing mattered. The questions instilled a sense of confidence in helping to recognise early signs of concern – from tiredness to restlessness to anxiety. The practice instilled trust in being able to speak up and ask for help, in the knowledge this would be supported.

THE SKILLS AND ATTRIBUTES I USED

I took a proactive approach in leading on this initiative. This came from a place of empathy, understanding and foresight. I created a process that enabled clear communication by helping people learn the practice of insightful questions and effective listening.

THE WAY I FELT AFTERWARDS

I felt both a sense of relief and pride in knowing I had found a way to remain true to my commitment to build and maintain a workplace where people looked out for each other and were adept at recognising warning signals that their colleagues were under pressure.

Florian: Thanks, Benny.

Florian: My Achievement & Story

THE SITUATION

I learnt that two members of my team were bad-mouthing one of their colleagues. I had worked hard to build a culture of transparency, where people could give constructive feedback to each other in saying what needed to be said. I believed this helped to avoid sustained misunderstandings and the need for rules.

I was reluctant to fire them because of their comments without giving them a second chance. This is because I knew that the openness of our culture could be difficult for new people who hadn't experienced the practice of direct feedback before.

THE ACTION TAKEN

I talked to them about what had happened, but I was met with hostility and defensiveness. They weren't open to hearing what I had to say. They accused me of monitoring their private conversations. This wasn't true. Their comments had been posted on a social media channel that they thought was private, but it was, in fact, open for everyone within the company to see.

THE OUTCOME OR RESULT

I felt I had no option but to fire them.

THE SKILLS AND ATTRIBUTES I USED

I felt I had remained true to my values to always treat people fairly, and my belief in giving a second chance whenever possible.

THE WAY I FELT AFTERWARDS

While this was not the outcome I had wanted, I considered it an achievement because I had managed a difficult situation with dignity. I had been open to finding a solution, but it hadn't worked out this time.

I applied the learning from the experience by ensuring new and existing members of my team have coaching support to help to learn how to give and take effective feedback.

I work to ensure that our key driving principle to maintain a work environment built on showing respect and kindness to each other is at the forefront of everyone's mind. To achieve this, people are regularly reminded of the adage that the company lives by: "That you only say things about your fellow workers that you would say to their face."

Maggie: Thank you, Florian.

Maggie: My Achievement & Story

THE SITUATION

I was aged twelve when I got into a fight. I had come to the defence of my friend Jim when he was attacked by two boys from the class above us. I had figured two against one wasn't fair, and so I had jumped in to even things up. The boys had been bullying Jim, and both he and I knew it wouldn't stop until he stood up to them. We both also knew that Jim being much smaller than the two boys, needed help in some shape or form to do this.

THE ACTION TAKEN

Jim and I signed up for a boxing class at school. The trainer focused on teaching proper form, which prevents injuries and demonstrates the importance of health and fitness routines such as stretching and conditioning. We practised our punches on heavy bags. Then when Jim felt ready, he challenged his bullies to a fight. This was actually sparring that was supervised by the trainer.

THE OUTCOME OR RESULT

Jim held his own with both of his bullies. He was both lighter and quicker on his feet. The boys saw he was able to defend himself with ease and left him alone after that.

THE SKILLS AND ATTRIBUTES I USED

Problem-solving – figuring out with Jim a way out of his difficult situation. A determined focus on developing my health and fitness to be Jim's sparring partner.

THE WAY I FELT AFTERWARDS

I felt a sense of pride that I had been able to support Jim in solving his problem through a practice of maintaining good fitness, health and wellbeing of body and mind.

Pascal: Thank you, Maggie.

Pascal: My Achievement & Story

THE SITUATION

I had connected Florian's and his fellow restaurateur's initiative of creating opportunities for people across all backgrounds and walks of life to work in their industry to the non-profit social enterprise arm of my company. We provide pro bono management consultancy support to help businesses in their community thrive and grow.

The restaurant I worked with had experienced significant growth over recent months. But with that growth had come a disgruntled workforce. It had gone from a happy to an unhappy workplace.

Conversations with the team allowed me to know that they were not aligned with what they wanted from the culture change this growth had brought about. Older people said they were experiencing ageism and that they had lost their sense of belonging. They didn't believe there would be opportunities for them to grow and develop in their roles. They had joined a company that they believed stood for diversity, equal opportunities and inclusion. They no longer believed that.

THE ACTION TAKEN

Recognising they had lost their direction, I suggested working as a team to develop a Guiding Statement: language of a future state of where the company wants to go. Something that all of the workforce can point to, strive for and move towards.

THE OUTCOME OR RESULT

Their Guiding Statement: To move forward by creating a diverse equitable work environment with a strong focus on belonging.

The statement is there for everyone internally to use when there are moments of difference.

This change has brought about a dedicated workforce, who are happy in their work.

THE SKILLS AND ATTRIBUTES I USED

I used my problem-analysis skills and my understanding of organisational transformation and individual change. I made recommendations to help the company achieve their desired outcome to build strong, trust-based relationships within their workforce. I led in helping the team recognise the priorities in implementing the changes.

THE WAY I FELT AFTERWARDS

My motivation and drive, passion and purpose in my WorkLife is to support motivated and talented workforces to be the best they can be. Achieving this always instils me with a sense of worthiness.

Saoirse: Thank you, Pascal.

Saoirse: My Achievement & Story

THE SITUATION

I was awoken by an early morning phone call and a cry for help from my niece, Niamh, who had gotten herself into financial difficulty and had the bailiffs banging on her door, threatening to take all her possessions. I managed to calm the situation by speaking to the bailiff, asking what I could do to help in that moment to stop what was happening. The bailiff said he needed an immediate payment of £3,000 to delay the proceedings and a commitment to a regular payment plan to clear the remaining debt of £30,000 within twelve months. I made the immediate payment, and although I had no idea how I could help Niamh pay the remaining debt, I committed to the regular payment plan because I needed to buy time for us to figure this out together.

Niamh's debt had accumulated from her student loans and living expenses that she was putting on her credit cards. She had studied art. Her main subject was horses, which came from her childhood passion. She had created equestrian-themed digital fine art prints, but up till now she had only taken small passive approaches to selling her work by hanging her art up in coffee shops, creating a website to show her work, and hoping for sales.

Niamh believed in her work, and so did I. Niamh knew it had real potential if she could only generate interest in it. This is where I came in.

THE ACTION TAKEN

I wrote about Niamh's story. I focused on her personal story: a young girl, following her passion, trying to get out of debt. I shared her journey in an honest and open manner. I shared the stories behind the prints Niamh had created – quirky and fun facts about the horses, their owners and life at the stables.

Together Niamh and I shared the story and the sketches across our writing and social media platforms, encouraging friends and followers to help share her story wide and far.

THE OUTCOME OR RESULT

Sales for Niamh's existing prints started to trickle in and quickly built momentum. Within two weeks, she had made enough money to make the first monthly payment to the bailiff. Then she started to receive orders from horse owners for hand-drawn sketches of their much-loved animal. She was able to charge more for these personalised prints. Within nine months, Niamh had repaid all her debt and, through the process, had established a profitable business.

THE SKILLS AND ATTRIBUTES I USED

Starting from a place of caring about Niamh, recognising and believing in her talent and potential and wanting to help her find a solution to her problem, I used my writing skills to help people connect to Niamh's story and to her art.

THE WAY I FELT AFTERWARDS

I was empowered to know that I had been able to work with Niamh to find a way to resolve what both she and I had initially believed to be an insurmountable problem.

Annie: Thank you, Saoirse.

That was an interesting exercise. I think sharing our stories was more structured than the storytelling Aisling initiated with the group in Ireland because we followed the format of the assignment. I believe theirs would have been more off-the-cuff. We know how well that worked. I think this worked really well too.

Maggie: I agree, and I think the assignment sets people up to be free-flowing in sharing their achievements and stories in a way that's interesting and also succinct.

Florian: It also helps to get an insight into who people are. For example, things we might never learn about our friends or colleagues in everyday communication.

Benny: It also opens communication up to interesting conversations.

Pascal: It's an assignment that elicits achievements or stories that can be helpful to share in different WorkLife situations – interviews, presentations, networking, relationship building.

Saoirse: I liked that we chose achievements from different times in our WorkLives, and were able to turn them into stories that gave a sense of who we are and what has been important to us at different stages.

Annie: I feel I want to know more about each of your achievements and stories. I've never been part of an achievements or storytelling group before. I think it's something I'd like to do again, in a social setting, and I also believe it would be a good exercise to use in our Workplace.

Maggie: I agree. Thank you, everyone. I really appreciate that we were all able to come together to experience what the Achievement Assignment brings about in reality in the sharing of our stories.

Benny: I think it was an experience we all enjoyed and appreciated.

Everyone smiled and nodded in agreement.

* * *

Your WorkLife Achievements Assignment

Now it's time for your WorkLife Achievements, with your accompaniment of choice.

Identifying your natural abilities (skills, attributes and unique capabilities) begins from a practice of increasing your self-awareness. That's because when you do things that come easily to you, you can take them for granted. You may not give much thought to the skills, attributes and unique capabilities you have used and how they fit with your values, purpose, passion, interests and motivated abilities.

To help you become more self-aware of who you are and what you do well, spend time thinking about the times when you felt a real sense of achievement. This might include anything you felt particularly satisfying, and felt proud of, or it might be a challenge you successfully overcame.

Outline something that you regard as a particular achievement in your WorkLife so far. It can be from your work or your life outside of work and from any stage of your life.

YOUR ACHIEVEMENT/STORY ASSIGNMENT

The Situation

The Action Taken

The Outcome or Result

The Skills and Attributes You Used

The Way You Felt Afterwards

DEVELOP A PRACTICE OF INSIGHTFUL SELF-QUESTIONING ASSIGNMENT

As your self-awareness in recognising and taking ownership of your achievements grows, ask yourself the following questions:

Now I have this self-awareness what does it mean to me?
What does it make me think?
How does it make me feel?
Will it make a difference in how I approach any aspects of my WorkLife?

DEVELOP A PRACTICE OF CONTINUOUS SELF-FEEDBACK ASSIGNMENT

Repeat Your Achievements Exercise for more of your achievements. Once you begin to become self-aware of who you really are when you are at your best, what it is you are doing that contributes to you being the best you can be, you will become more and more self-aware of your unique skills, attributes and capabilities. You will become unstoppable in owning your greatness.

WORDS OF WISDOM

As Pascal said, the stories you are writing about your achievements are stories you can tell in different WorkLife situations, from interviews to presentations, from networking to socialising, to building personal and professional relationships. They help you communicate who you are, what you're about, and what's important to you in line with your values and beliefs. Your stories are your way to show what's unique about you.

POW
ZAP
P
Mon - Sat
8.30 am - Midnight
Permit holders
or
Pay by phone
quoting location
or
Pay here
at machine
Display ticket
Max stay 4 hours

3

March

The Case of the Unconditional Apology

Featuring *The One Minute Apology* by Ken Blanchard and Margret McBride, accompanied by Indian cuisine

This month the group were meeting for a 'Ruby Murray' – Cockney rhyming slang for curry – in the land of curry houses, otherwise known as Brick Lane. Florian had suggested a long-established family-owned restaurant for their first Indian food shared experience.

Zoya, the restaurant co-founder and proprietor, welcomed them, and on showing them to their table, brought them warming cups of Masala chai (spiced tea). Florian enquired how her most recent trip to India (from which she had just returned) had been, telling the group that Zoya, and her husband, Vidur, love to travel across India and learn first-hand about the country's diverse regional cuisine.

Zoya smiled and explained to the group that she had been born in

India, and that was where her passion for cooking had been born, too, inspired by her mother and grandmother. She said moving to the UK in 1983, she brought that passion with her together with a vision for sharing her native cuisine with those who also enjoyed good food, which led her to opening the restaurant with her husband, Vidur. And now that their children were owners in the business too, that she and Vidur take time to explore India and the different regional cuisines, where they spend time with local people in the food-chain industry, from chefs to farmers to fisherfolk to street food vendors to families in their kitchens, absorbing the unique culinary techniques and traditions of people in each region. She said this helps her remain true to her original vision of bringing authentic, family and regional Indian cuisine to their diners.

She went on to say that they had just returned from Kerala and that when Florian had shared with her that he wanted to introduce them to great Indian food, in preparation for their visit, to accompany the traditional dishes already on the menu, she had prepared a few dishes which she had experienced in Kerala, and which she was planning to add to the menu, for them to experience also. These included *appam ishtu* – a thin pancake served with stew (originally a vegetarian dish, it is also served with chicken or lamb), fish *molee*, which is a famous fish stew with a significant flavour of coconut, and Kerala prawn curry (*cheemeen* curry), which is sprinkled with chilli and pepper. She said because of its long coastline Kerala is known for its variety of seafood. She had also prepared *thalassery biryani*, both the traditional version with marinated beef and a vegetarian option. She said the name comes from the seaport Thalassery, which was the centre of export for spices, and where European, Malabar and Arab cultures came together and influenced the cuisine.

She suggested a selection of appetisers to start, saying that appetisers served in Indian restaurants are typically popular Indian street food, which came about because Indian people love to eat at all times of the day, which prompted street food stalls to be set up at every corner to satisfy that need.

"*Dhaba*," Annie interjected.

"Yes," Zoya responded. "You know the word '*dhaba*'."

"Yes, I spent a summer in India, and I remember being introduced to *dhaba*," Annie said. "The word and the food and being told it means 'side of the road food stall', and there were countless to choose from. I also remember a saying: the best food isn't only cooked in people's homes, you also find it on the street. India was actually where my love of vegetarian food began. I got used to eating a lot of vegetarian food. India, I think, is one of the few places in the world where that's not a burden. I love eating Indian food wherever I am."

"That is so true and so lovely to hear," said Zoya. "Indian's are known for spreading throughout the world, bringing great food with them."

Arriving with their starters, Vidur introduced himself and their starters which included: onion bhajis, paneer and chicken tikka kebabs, fried cauliflower gobi, samosas, vegetable pan rolls, freshly baked paratha rotis, chapati and naan bread, red coconut chutney, minty yoghurt dip, pappadams and pickles.

* * *

As well as serving their own alcohol, the restaurant also had a Bring Your Own Bottle (BYOB) policy. On learning this, Saoirse had asked if she could bring the beer, which she believed, and they all agreed, was the best accompaniment for a curry.

She suggested she could do this for them to drink over the reading of the case study and as a pairing to the starters. She said that for the main courses, without knowing how spicy the curry they would each choose would be, it would make the pairing trickier, and having checked the pairings suggested on the menu, she herself was quite excited to try those. The same applied to deserts.

Saoirse had noticed that local breweries were among those who supplied beers to the restaurant. This included the Truman Brewery, which, together with a street full of curry houses, was another notable establishment for which Brick Lane was renowned.

In introducing the group to her favourite craft beers, Saoirse was mindful that she wanted to be supportive of local breweries, and she let them know that she would visit three east London breweries in selecting their beers. Asking if anyone would like to join her, she was met with a rapid round of affirmative responses.

And so, the previous day, the group, led by Saoirse and joined by

Florian's wife, Elena and Pascal's partner, Philippe, had set off on a tour of three breweries.

Their first stop was Truman's Social Club – a beer hall and cultural centre that brings people together to enjoy shared experiences of live music, street food and a beer or two, who also like to support and celebrate the people and community behind the artistic and craft scene.

As they enjoyed their first cold one, in their quest to discover their BYOB of preference for their first Indian food shared experience, Saoirse shared Truman's story, which they themselves describe as a tale of rise, fall and renewal.

Saoirse: The brewery was founded in the seventeenth century. Its rise was built on a foundation of great beer, great pubs and respect for the local community, and lasted over two hundred and fifty years. The fall and the closing of their doors were brought about by the dark period of the merger mania of the 1980s. Thankfully, the name remained because that enabled the renewal, as two local beer enthusiasts, James Morgan and Michael-George Hemus set out on a quest to bring Truman's back to its former glory. This was realised when they opened the Eyrie, the new Truman brewery in Hackney Wick. Fast forward a few years, the renewal was so successful, they found themselves in search of a bigger new home in which to grow their expanding brewery. This brings us to where we are today, Walthamstow, where Truman's continue to fly the flag for east London brewing.

Drinks downed, beers purchased, the group were on the move.

The second stop on their tour was Crate Brewery. A small and growing independent business. Once again, they put their tastebuds to work with the help of their barman, who told them there was a Crate for everyone and every occasion. And once again, Saoirse shared their story.

Saoirse: As a company, they're proudly independent. They have partnered with Silo, which is a zero-waste restaurant. Together they've created a space within their building that brings together food and drinks, homeware and gifts, a grocery and bottles shop. All with a focus on low waste and sustainability. They have strong ties to the community and being next to the river, they also have a riverboat that's moored right outside.

Drinks downed, beers purchased, the group were on the move again. The third and final stop on their tour was Hackney Church Brew Company – a brewpub named after the parish church over the road. As they sipped on their third cold one, Saoirse shared their story.

Saoirse: Their purpose is about more than great beer and great food. They say it's as important to them to create a great space that connects and supports the community. They source as much of their ingredients for their drink and food as they can within walking distance of the brewery. They brew their own beer, and they also support other local breweries. They want to help their local community to grow because, for them, without the community, there is no brewery.

This time having downed their drinks and purchased their beers, they headed to the on-site restaurant for a late much needed and well-earned, Sunday afternoon roast.

And so they had all arrived at the restaurant with their BYOB of choice. Florian had let Zoya know they would be bringing their own beers for the beginning of the meal, and she and Vidur brought along glasses for them, together with a jug of water for the table.

* * *

Saoirse poured her beer.

Saoirse: A fun fact about IPA beers served in Indian restaurants. IPA beers came about because brewers needed to keep beer fresher longer on their voyages from England to India. To do this, they added hops to preserve the beer better. This hoppy-style beer has a higher alcohol content than other craft beers and a more distinctive bitter taste too. The bitterness also helps to cool things, making the beers an ideal match for spicier dishes. An IPA also acts as a palate cleanser and is often drunk in-between courses to wash away lingering flavours of other dishes.

The group raised and clinked their glasses to a chorus of cheers to the beers.

Maggie: That's fascinating. I love all these snippets of history and current-day stories, insights into our neighbourhood – the businesses and the people.

Florian: I love it too. And having learnt the story of Truman's Brewery from you, Saoirse, the same century that saw the start of the original brewery also saw the start of Brick Lane market. The area continues to evolve, as you say, Maggie. Today we have Sunday Upmarket and Backyard Market, both of which operate out of the old Truman Brewery, with vendor-chefs serving up the best of street food representing cuisines from all over the world. I love their co-existence on the street that is **the** place to go for a curry in London, where you can try traditional and authentic cooking that celebrates the cultural diversity of our city. Brick Lane and

East London are special places. I love that our Shoreditch Chapter of the WorkLife Book Club allows us to explore, discover and uncover so much about our neighbourhood – as you say Maggie, the history and current-day stories, the businesses and the people.

The group raised their beers in a toast to Brick Lane, East London and the Shoreditch Chapter of the WorkLife Book Club.

This was Saoirse's cue to begin to read the case study she had chosen for this month's discussion: The Case of the Unconditional Apology, to which the accompanying book was *The One Minute Apology*, by Ken Blanchard and Margret McBride.

The Case of the Unconditional Apology

"A monkey could do it better"

Ray couldn't believe the words that had come out of his mouth. Neither could his team, who at first laughed because they thought it was a joke, but seeing the look on Jake's face, who was on the receiving end of this feedback, quickly realised it wasn't a joking matter.

Afraid of what else he might say, Ray decided he needed to remove himself from the situation, and so he took a walk.

But let's back up a little to Ray's story:

Ray was the manager of a team of twenty people within operations in a leading investment bank in the City of London. He'd been with the bank for over thirty years. In his earlier days and younger years, he'd been a trader at the front end of things. It was a demanding role that was high powered and fast-paced, which Ray enjoyed for the first few years, but after that the stresses of the job became too much for him, and he reached burnout. The burnout was quite severe, and he needed to take a one-year sabbatical.

Ahead of returning from his sabbatical Ray met with his manager to discuss his future with the bank. His manager was very supportive. Ray was a good guy, intelligent, hard-working and brought a lot to the organisation. Ray knew he wanted to get away from trading and from client-facing roles and wanted to move into what was then known as the back office, and so he took on a role in compliance. Although it

"A fabulous book by two warm, wonderful people whose caring and compassion shines through on every page. A classic, and a worthy companion to *The One Minute Manager.* Simple and effective, yet challenging and stimulating, *The One Minute Apology* is a book that can change your life. It can even change the world. Buy it. Read it. Make it part of your life. You won't be sorry!" (Sheldon Bowles, co-author of *Raving Fans!*, *Gung Ho!*, *Big Bucks!* and *High Five!*)

From the inside flap:
"The latest addition to the phenomenally successful *One Minute Manager* series of business classics by Ken Blanchard: this new parable teaches readers how to accept responsibility for their errors.

"The phenomenal business classic *The One Minute Manager* introduced three secrets of management: One Minute Goal-Setting, One Minute Praisings, and One Minute Reprimands. Now told in Ken Blanchard's signature breezy style, this enlightening business parable – the fourth secret of the One Minute Manager – presents a concept that, implemented properly, is one of the most powerful actions for improving company and employee morale. Step-by-step, Blanchard teaches readers how to accept responsibility for their errors and to deal with the cause of the damage while maintaining their integrity."

From the back cover:
"*The One Minute Apology* goes straight to the heart of all our business and personal relations, and is especially timely in the 21st-century business world. Through an engaging parable, in the style of the previous groundbreaking *One Minute Manager* classics, it teaches us step-by-step how to accept responsibility for our errors, making life better for friends and colleagues. We learn how, by improving morale, companies and employees can expect to reap the benefits of a genuine sense of integrity."

The One Minute Manager, by Ken Blanchard & Margret McBride, was originally published by Harper in 2011 (128pp., ISBN 978-0007160068) was very static and process-driven, it suited Ray. He was good with analysis and enjoyed it. More importantly, it helped to restore Ray's confidence in himself.

But Ray's career didn't remain static. With the support of his manager, over time and over the years, Ray worked in a number of different functions within the bank. This allowed him to continue to develop and to learn new skills, which kept him motivated.

In all of these roles, Ray was an individual contributor, and this suited him very well. He had no interest in managing people. Then the financial crisis hit, causing downsizing and restructuring with the bank going through a merger. A number of people Ray had worked with for many years who weren't on board with the merger jumped ship, and as a result, along with losing good people, the bank also lost years of important knowledge. Because of his in-depth knowledge, having worked across several functions, Ray found himself being promoted from individual contributor to manager.

Some of the positions that had become vacant were filled from the merging company, and some were filled by people working in other areas of Ray's existing bank. This was how Ray inherited Jake. Jake had been working with the bank for over fifteen years. He was a good guy, and everybody liked him.

Although known for having a good work ethic, his work from the day he joined Ray's team was not good. He was continuously missing targets, which impacted the team, and this is what caused Ray's outburst. He was at the end of his tether with Jake. Another late report ahead of an important meeting was the final straw and led to those fateful words coming out of Ray's mouth:

"A monkey could do it better".

Seeing the look on Jake's and the rest of the team's faces following on from his outburst, together with the anger Ray was feeling towards Jake in that moment, Ray knew he needed to take a walk to distance himself from the immediate situation, to calm down and to gather his thoughts.

'Walking meditation' is how Ray thought of this practice. It was a strategy his manager Nora introduced him to all those years ago when he was returning from his sabbatical and one that had served him well at times when he had felt overwhelmed and when he needed to turn off his self-talk and his thinking. Ray thought of Nora not only as his manager but also as his mentor and friend. Although she had long since retired, her wisdom remained with Ray throughout his WorkLife. It was something that he could tap into when he needed to.

The process was easy. He'd begin his walk by posing a question to himself, something as simple as "What do I need to know about x (situation/person)"? or "What one action can I take today that will help with x." He would then switch off his mind and self-talk by focussing on the beauty along his walk. When thoughts/self-talk began to filter through, he'd mentally acknowledge them, say thank you, then switch off again by refocusing on the beauty of his surroundings. Ray found this simple strategy quite powerful. It helped to alleviate the sense of feeling overwhelmed. By not thinking or listening to his self-talk, the answer he needed always came to him – sometimes in the moment or soon after, most often when he was getting on with his daily life, and other times he'd wake up with the solution of knowing what to do. This practice of self-questioning gave Ray the self-feedback he needed to evaluate what he needed to do next.

Ray's focus on quieting his mind to what had just happened took his walk on autopilot on a route he took each lunchtime, through a nearby park, then to his favourite bookshop where he often spent his breaks browsing the shelves, picking up a book, sitting and reading a chapter or two over a coffee. Ray had received the answer to the question he had posed to himself: "What the hell did I just do? How can I put this right?"

Book Wisdom

On becoming a manager, this bookshop was where he had discovered the *One Minute Manager* series of books, which he'd found really helpful. Ray immediately knew which of the *One Minute Manager* books he needed in this moment: *The One Minute Apology* by Ken Blanchard and Margaret McBride.

He entered the shop, picked a copy off the shelf, got a coffee and settled down in his favourite armchair, open to the learning that he knew he was about to receive through the book wisdom of *The One Minute Manager.*

From the key points of book wisdom that came to him from reading *The One Minute Apology,* Ray knew:

- He had to take full responsibility for his actions, regardless of the outcome;
- He had to apologise to Jake, and he had to do this with a sense of urgency;
- He had to demonstrate his commitment to making amends beyond this apology.

By the time Ray had finished reading, it was too late to go back to the office. He knew everybody would have left for the day, and knowing what he had to do the next morning, he also knew he needed the evening to prepare mentally, and this was best done away from the office.

He just needed to do a couple of things before leaving the bookshop. He messaged Jake asking him to meet early the next morning before the workday began. He suggested a nearby coffee shop because this meeting needed to be away from the bank. He let his assistant know he would be late into the office and asked that she rearrange his morning meeting.

And so, at 7.30 am the next morning, Ray and Jake met for coffee and a discussion, which Ray knew would not be happening if he'd addressed the issues with Jake earlier on. He knew he'd failed Jake and began the meeting, having thanked Jake for agreeing to meet early, by saying: "Jake, I owe you an apology".

Jake was taken aback, because of Ray's angry outburst the previous day, and knowing he'd screwed up with the report, he was expecting a further balling out.

Ray continued: "I've let you down in so many ways. You've always done great work in the past. That changed in the last year. Your work has been under par for some time, and I failed to address it, I failed to talk to you, I failed to ask you why this was happening, I failed to take time to understand what's been going on for you that was contributing to this. You've been loyal to the bank for so many years, you've been a great contributor, you've done great work, and I've let you down by not taking the time to talk to you when clearly something was not right. I am sincerely sorry I've let you down so badly."

Although taken aback for the second time within minutes, Ray's apology immediately struck Jake as being both sincere and humble. It caused Jake to blurt out everything that he'd been carrying around since he'd taken on his new role. Although Jake was visibly upset, Ray's apology gave him the courage to speak up, together with a sense of knowing that he needed to do this for his self-esteem and that this was his time to do so. He responded to Ray's apology by saying:

"I wish you had talked to me; I wish somebody had talked to me instead of making assumptions. I wanted to leave when the others left. I wanted to leave, but then I was offered a role on your team and told how much I was valued for my loyalty, and everybody assumed that's what I wanted. It wasn't, but I didn't have the courage to leave or to speak up. I've hated every moment of this merger. The people on our team are all good people, but I miss everyone who has left. I was expected to be able to pick up my new role straight away because of my knowledge of the business, but the work is so different to my old role, and I've been out of my depth since day one, but nobody said anything, and I wasn't offered any help. I assumed you were OK with me getting up to speed. But I could see by the look on everyone's face yesterday that they weren't surprised by what you said. They all looked sorry for me. Why didn't you say something? Why didn't anybody say something? I thought you all liked me. You must have all seen that I was out of my depth. If only someone had offered to help. Instead, I've become a laughingstock, someone to pity."

Ray knew this was the conversation he should have had with Jake a long time ago, in the same way, his manager had taken the time to talk to him all those years ago when he was struggling, when he was in a role that wasn't right for him.

Ray spent the next two hours listening and talking to Jake – really listening to understand what was going on for him. By the end of the conversation, Ray had learnt so much about Jake that he hadn't known before. Things he could have should have and would have known had he taken the time to have a WorkLife conversation with him, which would have allowed him to understand his motivations, his longer-term dreams and aspirations, how these fitted with his current role and how he could have helped Jake work towards achieving this. The more they talked, the more he realised how much he'd failed Jake on so many levels.

While he couldn't turn back time, Ray knew he needed to do what he could in this moment to help Jake, and that was to help him to move on from the bank, which is what Jake had wanted all along. You see, Jake's real passion is art. He's an artist. He studied Art at university, but due to pressure from his father, who was a banker and who didn't believe being an artist was a career, he buckled and entered the world of finance. Then he married, had kids, and his work afforded his family a good lifestyle. He had actually enjoyed his work to a degree because of the people he'd worked with, and before the merger, the work was actually OK. More importantly, it had allowed him to put his children through university.

His art had become a hobby, but the burning desire to be an artist had never left him, and of late it was all he could think about. It was risky, but financially he was in an OK place. He'd discussed it with his wife, and she was supportive, but Jake felt he needed a little more financial security for peace of mind. He had wanted to ask for redundancy settlement before he was offered the role on Ray's team. This had been offered to other people, but as nobody had asked Jake what he wanted at the time of the merger and instead offered him a secure position, he hadn't wanted to seem ungrateful, and so he didn't speak up.

Ray was in a position to secure a good redundancy settlement for Jake for his years of service to the bank. This is how the meeting ended, which was very different from how either Ray or Jake had anticipated it would have gone.

Ray knew if he'd taken the time to talk to Jake a year earlier to understand his WorkLife aspirations, or if he'd taken time to give him feedback on his work at the given opportunities over the year when Jake messed up, it would never have gotten to this. He could have helped Jake avoid the anguish and stress he'd experienced.

He knew he could have been a better manager if he'd taken the time to create a culture of feedback, not just for him but also for Jake's peers to give feedback to each other. A culture where Jake would have had the confidence to speak up and ask for what he wanted. A culture where it would have been OK for people to say "No" to something they didn't want to do.

Ray knew he needed to evaluate if he should, in fact, be a manager. Maybe he wasn't cut out for management. Maybe he was best suited to an individual contributor role. While Ray knew he had gotten a number of things right, he also knew he'd gotten some fundamental things wrong. He knew he needed to step back to evaluate his own role.

Epilogue

There's a happy ending for both Ray and Jake's stories.

The time Ray had spent analysing how he should have managed the situation with Jake allowed him to recognise that he did like his job and that he was good at it. He acknowledged he had gotten it horribly wrong with Jake, and he knew in his heart of hearts he would never allow that to happen again. To ensure it didn't, he did exactly what he should have done with Jake, with the rest of the team. He set up a time to have a WorkLife conversation with everyone. He now understood their motivations, their longer dreams and aspirations, and how these fitted with their current roles. He understood how he could support them in their development in achieving this and how this fitted into the team, department and organisation growth plans. He's working on developing a team where everyone is responsible for giving feedback to each other and where people feel safe in speaking up. He's writing his continuing WorkLife Story chapters.

Six months later, Ray received an invitation to the opening of Jake's first art exhibition at a renowned gallery in the City of London. On Ray's arrival, Jake greeted him warmly. Ray was struck by how good he looked, and he was blown away by Jake's art and his talent.

Later that evening, Jake took Ray to one side, and he thanked him for everything he'd done to help him achieve this. He thanked him for forcing the issue. He laughed and jokingly thanked him for almost 'firing' him. He thanked him for giving him the courage to speak up and say what he really wanted and for really listening. He thanked him for the financial support he'd arranged, which had made it possible to move onto the new challenge that he had for so long yearned and which gave him the success he was now experiencing. He told Ray he knew he had been spinning the wheels at work and that he had been too scared to take action, and that the space Ray had given him that morning to talk had allowed him to know what it was he needed to do.

Words of Wisdom

We can all do or say things that we later come to regret, an in the moment reaction that can leave us and other people feeling anywhere from slightly uncomfortable to totally destroyed. What we do next to be able to move forward will determine how the story ends.

WORKLIFE BOOK CLUB

Being observant that Saoirse had finished reading, Zoya and Vidur arrived to take their orders for their main courses and accompanying dishes. Vidur recommended the best beer pairings to accompany their personal curry choices, and the shared dishes they had prepared for them. He said a brown ale complements a hotter curry and also goes well with a vegetable curry. Indian pale ale, he said, helps heighten the spice of a flavourful biryani and offers a dominant flavour to a creamy tikka masala. A porter cuts through the richness of coconut-based dishes to balance out the flavours and give a savoury finish. And a light lager, blonde or amber ale works perfectly with milder food. Vidur's simple explanation helped the group in being confident in selecting their beer of choice.

Benny picked up his glass.

Benny: This beer is really quite good, Saoirse, and I'm really pleased to learn that Cobra Zero is the perfect pairing for my korma. I've always liked the story behind the Cobra brand – how it came about because its founder, Karan Bilimoria (later Lord Bilimoria of Chelsea), found other lagers too fizzy, harsh and bloating, meaning that he couldn't eat or drink as much as he would have liked; and how he found real ale to be great in a pub, but too bitter and heavy with food. And so, he had an idea to create a beer with the refreshment of a lager but with the smoothness of an ale.

I also like that his company went on to develop the non-alcoholic version. I remember when I first stopped drinking alcohol and on asking for non-alcoholic beers back home, I would get blank stares, but nowadays there's such a variety of non-alcoholic drink options, all offered without confused looks from wait staff and without judgement. In fact, the dry drinking scene has become quite interesting and exciting. I used to feel I was missing out. I don't anymore.

Annie: I can relate to what you're saying from a vegetarian point of view. I remember being at restaurants and the vegetarian option was a plate of tomatoes, which brought with it a sense that I had created a lot of extra work for them. I used to feel I was an awkward and unwelcome guest. But now it's so different, over recent years the dishes I've experienced have also become quite interesting and exciting. And perhaps none more so than Indian food, which has always been the perfect cuisine for vegetarians, but these dishes... and hearing Zoya talk about remaining true to her original vision of bringing authentic, family and regional Indian cuisine to their diners. It's bringing both the old and the new together, and that's what makes it so interesting and exciting.

Saoirse: Food and drink connects people, and in some way, it also connects with virtually every challenge the world faces. That's why I love writing my blog. There's so much to it, over and beyond the food and drinks, which is great in itself, but there is just so much more.

Annie: You're so right. Before we get into the discussion about the case, I have some exciting news to share. It's something that has come about from our first two meetings, which brought up a lot for me with how I was feeling about my work.

I was questioning how I could continue to develop when I didn't see any opportunities at work. Anyway, long story short, I approached a secondary school close to me, let them know my area of work is cybersecurity and asked if they might be interested in me giving a talk to their older students, students who are considering their university choices, and they said yes.

It was all a little surreal really because it happened so fast, and then because it's school hours, I needed to speak to my manager about time off, and he agreed immediately too. He said he wanted to work with me to help with my WorkLife planning, and is happy for me to manage my own development and wanted to facilitate me being able to learn new skills which I've identified, one of which is to teach something to others.

All of us eating together, and connecting over food and drink, and discussing the challenges people are facing in their WorkLives, through books and people's stories, helped me in figuring out how to overcome a challenge I was facing.

Florian: Wow, Annie, that's amazing, well done.

The rest of the group joined in with Florian's congratulations and clinked glasses with Annie.

Annie: The thing is, it came out of our discussions, and from you sharing your offsite planning, Benny. I took a day to work through that, and I also worked through the WorkLife Conversations Assignment that accompanies this month's case, which helped too. Then I shared it with my manager, and he really liked it too, and it may well be that I will get to share that with the rest of my team. He expressed an interest in that.

Another round of wows, well done, and clinking of glasses.

Florian: What made you think of offering to talk about cybersecurity? Was it because it's your area of expertise, or was it something else?

Annie: Well, yes, it was because it's my area of expertise, and because I've never taught anything to anyone before, I thought it would be best to start with something I know. And also, when I say I work in cybersecurity, people are always interested, so I sensed it could be something good to pitch. And Saoirse, it was also because I was intrigued with how you developed your hobby/side-hustle of blogging about something you're interested in into work. I was thinking maybe if there aren't opportunities to learn, grow and develop at work, I can create them outside of work.

Actually, I think I could have and should have done this some time ago, and that I might have been holding myself back or blocking myself. But I've had a shift in my thinking, which came about because of our discussions, so thank you, everyone, you helped me push through a barrier I had put up myself.

Maggie: Well, you're very welcome, but what was it that the book said about not using phrases such as 'could have' and 'should have' because they keep you stuck in the past and prevent you from taking your best course of action.

Annie laughed.

Annie: True, those words actually stood out on the page for me, as did the ones that followed: "That they also keep you from being honest with yourself," and that was true for me.

Maggie: Being honest with yourself was a theme that ran through Ray and Jake's story and also the Young Man's story in the book and the President of the company. It was only when each of them faced up to their truth that they were able to move on. It's what brought about their apologies – Ray to Jake, Jake to Ray, the Young Man to the President of the company, the President to the Board. I do wish the Young Man and President had been given names, though. I understand it was to set up the status of their relationships, but I think once this was established, it would have helped to personalise it more in the context of their relationship.

Benny: I thought that too, and I also had to get beyond some of the words used: for example 'reprimand', when the book talked about the principles of the One-Minute Manager, from which the One-Minute Apology evolved from. But I think this was more to do with the language that was used and was considered acceptable when the books were first written, and 'reprimand' has now been replaced by 'redirect'. I'm familiar with the series of *One Minute Manager* books, and while some language is outdated, other principles have stood the test of time. For example, that it only takes one minute to apologise, but of course, a lot of preparation needs to go into that one-minute apology.

Florian: Yes, I'm familiar with the One-Minute Manager and the three secrets, which are one-minute goal setting, one-minute praisings, and one-minute reprimands, which is now one-minute redirects, and the one-minute apology being the fourth secret. I agree too about the language, and I also agree about the principles standing the test of time – namely that all of these can be delivered in one minute, with preparation time, of course. As much as I am familiar with the first book, I liked that this book wasn't dependent on that and stood very well as a stand-alone book.

Maggie: I didn't read the first book, and I didn't get a sense I needed to in order to understand this book. I also thought this book stood very well on its own, but I did like that there was a connection to understanding the philosophy and wisdom of the One-Minute Manager, and how that unfolded over the course of the story when the One-Minute Manager invited the Young Man to spend the weekend with him and his family. But I'm curious now, what are one-minute praisings and reprimands or redirects?

Florian: We know them better today as in-the-moment feedback, given at the time or soon after something happens so that it's given in context. Praisings are positive feedback, and reprimands or redirects are constructive feedback. The *One Minute Manager* book advocates that praisings should be done in public and reprimands or redirects should be done in private, and that they need only take one minute.

Maggie: Thanks.

Annie: I liked that the book was written as a parable and was a quick read, and the key points it got across for Ray: he had to take full responsibility for his actions, regardless of the outcome; he had to apologise to Jake, and he had to do this with a sense of urgency; he had to demonstrate his commitment to making amends beyond this apology.

Ray's outburst, though – and those words in particular, "a monkey could do it better" – was hard to recover from. And blurted out in front of everyone!

Florian: He really was at the end of his tether with Jake. I can understand why it happened, but you're right. Those particular words were hard to recover from, and especially as you say, having blurted them out in front of the whole team. His manager Nora's wisdom – walking meditation, that served him well in this instance, and at other times throughout his WorkLife. I think it's good practice to distance yourself in a situation like this.

Pascal: Just taking five is good too. Or even just counting to ten if you can't leave the situation. That's enough to re-ground yourself if you like – to give yourself a little distance, calm yourself if needed, regain composure and to gain perspective.

Florian: I liked that Ray's manager Nora's wisdom stayed with him throughout his WorkLife. And I liked her idea of walking meditation, too: walking and posing questions, then reflecting on those through self-feedback. They help to focus the mind and turn off idle chatter and thoughts. That's such a simple yet effective strategy. It's one I'm going to borrow.

Saoirse: It's in-the-moment self-feedback that can be done quickly and effectively through posing a question to yourself, then quickly reflecting and giving yourself feedback. For example, the suggested questions to ask oneself: "What do I need to know about x?" "What one action can I take today that will help with x?" Those self-questions can be asked in the moment, and they can be asked of the other person too if the answer doesn't come.

Maggie: The same can be done for the question: "What the hell did I just do? How can I put this right?" That can be asked of oneself, and if the answer is not forthcoming, it can be put to the room – the other side.

Saoirse: Ray did let the situation fester. In-the-moment opportunities ,if taken, would have avoided an apology being needed – we often ignore something, hoping it will change, or go away, or resolve itself.

Maggie: So did Jake. Both parties needed to have spoken up earlier. But I understand how difficult this is to do. Both were hoping things would get better.

Pascal: I've managed many mergers and takeovers, and inheriting someone is very commonplace, and it can be difficult to manage because there is so much else going on. Similar to Jake and to Ray, too, people are having to get up to speed with new and different responsibilities. With the best will in the world, it can be really difficult to take the time needed to manage everything or stay on top of everything that's going on. Many people will be of the belief that things will settle down and take care of themselves, and so they don't actively do anything about it as such. That goes for managers and individual contributors believing that of themselves and of each other – in that they'll get up to speed and the other person will settle into the role. Yes, Ray needed to have said something earlier, but so did Jake. They each had a responsibility to themselves and to each other. Of course, they had that realisation at the end. It's finding a way to get to it at an earlier stage, but that isn't easy with so much else going on.

Maggie: The book talks about how people can get so far off track and lose sight of what's really important. I think Jake knew what was important for him, but as he said, he had been too scared to take action, even though he knew he was just spinning the wheels at work. What happened, the words spoken, were unfortunate for sure, but as Jake said, they forced the issue for him.

Florian: "If we watch the real-life drama unfold, the situation uncorrected, usually gets worst." Jake was really hurt when he had the realisation that Ray and the rest of his team had all seen what was happening, and yet no one spoke up. This is where one-minute feedback was needed: in the moment when people saw what was happening. It would then have been meaningful because it would have been in context and would help improve people's self-awareness (Jake in this case) and people's power of observation (that is, the team). This is what Ray identified he wanted to work towards to make it OK for everyone to speak up, and when it's in the moment, it's meaningful, whereas when people ignore what is going on, or, as with many organisations, feedback is given at appraisal time, by which point it's meaningless because the context has long since gone.

Benny: Teaching moments. And NO feedback sandwich – where the important thing you want to say is in the middle and dressed up by something 'nice' on either side, often causing the important thing to lose its meaning or (to keep with the sandwich metaphor), its rich flavour is diluted by the dressing.

Maggie smiled at Benny.

Maggie: Straight-talking the New York way is the best way, eh Benny.

Benny (laughing): Yes!

Zoya and Vidur arrived with the first of their main courses, accompanying dishes and beers. They let the group know that they would bring their remaining dishes a little later on, telling them that this is the traditional way in Kerala to allow time to savour the many courses that had been prepared. The group were immediately struck by the wonderful aroma from the beautiful mixture of spices that Zoya and Vidur described and how individually each spice influenced each dish in providing its unique taste. They were also struck by not only how delicious each dish looked, but as they began to taste each one, how the distinctively different and delicate flavours were just bursting with freshness.

Maggie: The tasty breathtaking flavour is definitely the order of the day and such attention to detail. As a family, we use lots of herbs and spices in our cooking too. Jamaican food has many influences from the different cultures that inhabited our island, including British and Indian, and Irish Saoirse, and Spanish Florian, and French Pascal, and American Benny. And Annie, I haven't experienced it... yet... but I have it on good authority that Reggae Burns is the island's way to celebrate your national poet: a night of reggae and poetry reading, haggis and plantain fritters, rum and whisky.

We have our own influences as well, of course the crops we grow and the wonderful array of seafood available. My grandparent's story is similar to Zoya's in that they love to share their native cuisine with people who love good food. They arrived in Britain from Jamaica in the 60s, and an important part of keeping their culture and heritage alive is through sharing their food. And when they're invited to eat in other people's homes, at my grandfather's insistence, my grandmother always brings a bottle of hot sauce. She presents it as a gift, but we all know there's another reason, too: it's in case they didn't flavour the food enough. As you said, Saoirse, food and drink connect people, and allows us to tell and retell stories to help us understand each other. Stories that make us laugh and cry and remember. Stories that help to keep so many memories alive.

When it comes to curries, I love mine hot, but I never knew what beer to choose that would stand up to strong, intense flavours. This beer most definitely brings drinkable harmony to fan the flames of my spicy vindaloo.

The rest of the group murmured in agreement as their tastebuds were awoken by the distinctive flavours of each dish, and accompanying beer, as they relished each mouthful.

Saoirse: Traditions are the stories that families, friends and communities write together. The sharing of food and stories is a shared experience across all cultures and one that, as you say, help to keep so many memories alive. Stories that make us laugh and cry because they can evoke both happiness and sadness. My parents loved to welcome people into our home, their friends, my friends, my sibling's friends. Both my parents have passed now, but while they were still alive, even after us kids had all moved out, our friends would pop in to visit. When they did, my mum would always have their favourite cake baked. We all loved my mum's cakes, and we all had our favourite, which my mum was quick to deduce, and would always present it proudly, saying: "I knew you were coming, so I baked your favourite cake". My family and our friends love to tell that story, and when we do, we're right back there in the moment of tea and cake, and everything is all right. It was an idyllic place then, and it's an idyllic place to travel back to through our shared memories and stories.

It was the little details that made the stories so memorable. To bring it back to the case, on the subject of detail. One thing I would have liked from the book was some detail about what the President had done that was so bad.

Maggie: In the beginning, I felt that too, but then as the story evolved, I got beyond needing to know. I think because it's presented as a short parable, there wasn't space.

Saoirse: I don't think it needed a lot of space, there were other stories in the book that were told concisely, and they really helped to understand different situations. I felt I needed the story of what had happened that was so bad. I don't know if it was something the President did or if it was caused by some other influences. The reason I felt this was because when the President first began to share the problem, at the emergency meeting with the Board of Directors, he was confident, then he was asked a few questions: "How long has this been going on? When was the first time you learnt of this? Why didn't you take action before now? Couldn't you have seen what the consequences of such actions might be?"

The book said he then refused to take responsibility, he became defensive and combative, and this made things worse. The Board members had never heard the President talk like this. When he stopped, silence filled the room. Everyone was stunned by what had just happened.

It was as though all the blame was being laid at his door (criticism, judgment, even though they had never heard him talk like this before), they were quick to point fingers of blame (why didn't they apologise too), they were so quick to turn (surely they have responsibility too). He was acting out of character (maybe in the same way Ray was in shouting or Jake was in not being up to the job). People need to stop and question and ask why, not attack. There would be less need for an apology if people call what is going on in the moment.

I think it would be difficult for anyone not to become defensive with questions like that. I think when people we know act out of character, we need to understand what's going on for them, and also how we might have contributed to that – all the Board members against one person – but yet he was the only one feeling bad, his behaviour was the only behaviour under the spotlight. Yes, there's a need to hold people accountable, but not by attacking.

Benny: "Most misunderstandings in the world could be avoided if people would simply take the time to ask, 'What else could this mean?'" – Shannon L. Alder.

Saoirse: Exactly. I really like that quote. And all of this was followed by the Chairman of the Board saying to him, "Well, we've heard all of your excuses and rationalisations. Frankly, I am unimpressed. If we don't resolve this quickly, our company's reputation in the marketplace will be ruined along with its stock value." Then his closing remarks, which to me might have started off OK but soon became an ultimatum: "After the weekend, we'll meet again. You deserve an opportunity to set the record straight. Between now and then, think carefully about what you plan to say and do. If you haven't come up with an effective way to restore our confidence, we may have to look for new leadership." Threatening, or what! It gave me a sense that there was something rotten to the core within the company – "Something is rotten in the state of Denmark", as Shakespeare wrote.

Annie: What was different about the Young Man was that he wanted to help. He saw that the man he admired was acting out of character, and he came to learn that the company was in trouble. But, unlike the Board members, he wanted to find a way to help. That was what was behind the One-Minute Manager wanting to help the Young Man help the President. He recognised what a rare young man he was. That was the Young Man's truth of character and it was Ray's truth of character too, albeit not as in the moment as with the Young Man. But he got there, when he finally saw that Jake was in trouble, and he found a way to help.

Pascal: It's also true what the book says about: "Many people say 'that's not my worry', they divorce themselves from the problem and steer clear from being involved. Psychologically they jump ship. Then, once things blow over, they join back in." Jake experienced people actually jumping ship, in that they left the company, which brought about the position he found himself in. Then I think he experienced people psychologically jumping ship: Ray, his team, they saw there was a problem, but they too distanced themselves from it, waiting for it to blow over. I've witnessed that so often in mergers or takeovers I've managed.

Annie: It was the Young Man's truth of character that allowed him to see the President's behaviour and actions weren't aligned with his truth of character. The President, the Young Man knew and respected, had given him a wonderful opportunity in joining the company and had continued to mentor him. As he said, "I wouldn't feel good about myself if I bailed out on him and the company now that they're both in trouble and may need help." That's what the One Minute Manager saw and valued. Ray's manager, Nora,

I think had the same reaction, and I think this served to remind Ray of this.

I personally didn't need detail of what the President had done that was so bad. As you say, Saoirse, other examples in the book provided detail, and that was great; but for me, not knowing what the President had done helped me relate to it in a way that was more generic, that could be any situation, and I liked that the book provided both specific situations with more detail and a generic situation with less detail, that I could make sense of it in my own way – from my own experiences.

And also the protagonist of the book, 'The Young Man', and the antagonist – 'The Company President'. Another important element in understanding the status of the relationship was that it gave an insight into how the President had helped the younger man realise his potential and championed his development. So we know it was a good relationship with mutual respect.

So I was OK too, with the book not giving the details of their names, but rather keeping with 'The Young Man' and 'The Company President' in the context of their relationship. Because it helped to remind us of the difference in status, which also served to remind us how difficult it can be to speak up when there is that difference in status. And yet, when the Young Man did speak up and said what he believed needed to be said, it brought the relationship to more of a level pegging. There wasn't a shift in status as such. It wasn't that there wasn't mutual respect to begin, there was, but the Young Man saying the 'hard stuff', the stuff that needed to be said, deepened a respect that was always there. It served to bring the relationship to another level.

Of course, when the Young Man was with the One-Minute Manager and his family, he was referred to by his name, which made sense in the context of those relationships – their families were friends and had holidayed together in the past.

Maggie: It's also how the Young Man did it. He approached what he needed to say – the hard stuff, in the same way, Ray had with Jake. He began with the words, "I owe you an apology'. He took ownership for not living up to who he should have been, for not being who the President admired him for being, or living up to the traits that the President admired in him – his forthrightness. He admitted to seeing that things were wrong but that he didn't have the guts to tell him the truth. He admitted that he was part of the problem, and not the solution. He admitted that he felt ashamed that he hadn't told him the truth earlier but that he was afraid of losing his trust, or his job. His apology felt genuine, and in asking for forgiveness in failing him and assuring him it wouldn't happen again, that too felt genuine because it had come from a place of truth in an apology that was heartfelt. It was the same for Ray. His apology felt genuine.

Benny: And before that, the Young Man had sent him the 'Lincoln apology.' That had gotten the President thinking, for sure. Lincoln remains revered as a president in the US, as a man of great integrity and great leadership. And that story, that apology, served to demonstrate how even the greatest of men can get it wrong. Sometimes they too can fall below their own standards of behaviour. And of course, there was a lot going on for Lincoln in that moment, that his behaviour could easily be understood and excused, but for him, himself, it couldn't be. He would have had to live with it had he not done what he did to put things right. Beginning with an apology, then taking the steps needed to follow through. In the same way, the President did following his apology to the Board. He followed through with first suggesting the business plan he believed would turn the negative situation around and get the company back on track. Then once he had their approval, he set about making it happen. Ray also did this when following his apology. He listened to Jake, really listened. From this, he understood the action he needed to take to help Jake and to demonstrate his apology was genuine, and that was to secure the financial settlement that would help Jake pursue his dream.

Florian: These actions by these people – Lincoln, the Young Man, Ray – these are actions of good people, some might say leaders. Lincoln would have recognised the need for him to be a leader in his role. I think the Young Man did too. And I think Ray did as well, but I also think he was getting hung up on being a manager and everything that comes with that in terms of responsibilities. As opposed to when he was an individual contributor, and he was only responsible for himself and his own work, now he had a responsibility to his team. But he didn't have responsibility for managing others, and that was his hang up I think, and because of that, he didn't perhaps recognise his leadership qualities and ability. One doesn't have to manage others to be a leader, I think.

Annie: "A one-minute apology can be an effective way to correct a mistake you have made and restore the trust needed for a good relationship", I like these little summaries, at the end of each lesson, as it were.

Zoya and Vidur arrived with the remaining main courses and accompanying side dishes and beers, once again describing them by way of introduction to their origins. On introducing the prawn dishes they had prepared, Vidur told the story of how ahead of a seafood cooking class, their chef, Zian, took them out in a canoe to buy freshwater prawns, and how the fisherman displayed a fistful of prawns, each double the length of his palm. Zian encouraged them to haggle – no easy feat according to Vidur when accompanied by a fear of slipping overboard the bobbing boat. Zoya laughed and went on to share how then they observed in awe as Zian set to work on his two-ring camping stove, creating the most mouth-watering prawn dishes they had ever experienced. Vidur finished by saying, Zian had brought together beach flavours of coconut and citrus fruits to seafood fresh from the Indian Ocean.

Vidur and Zoya's story, the once again unique flavours as they began to taste the new array of dishes, brought about a lull in the conversation and their attention back to the restaurant. As the group looked around, they observed the quietness in which all of the staff moved around amidst the bustle of the busy restaurant. The manner in which they interacted with guests, at times respectfully quiet so as not to interrupt the flow of conversations taking place, and at times stopping to chat and to engage more when that seemed the more appropriate way to interact.

Florian: Over the years, as well as dining at the restaurant with family and friends, I also often stop by alone. I've met so many people who return time and time again – some of whom were just students when the restaurant first opened, who also return alone, or with friends, or to introduce their partners and children to Zoya and Vidur. Others who discovered it over the years, who also wanted to share the experience with their friends and family, or alone catching up with Zoya and Vidur and their family. The ambience is always so warm and welcoming. It provides a home-from-home experience for so many people from so many different walks of life.

Annie: What makes a place like that? I mean, how do some places achieve that while others don't?

Florian: That's something I'm always curious about. It's a little bit strange. What I mean is, people don't talk about the decor of this restaurant. I actually don't think it's changed much over the years. But despite not talking about it, people love it. And that's the strange thing, because I think it may actually be a subconscious thing that people aren't fully aware of. Because it represents a sense of homeliness, of coming home or coming back to a familiar place, that holds lots of good memories. And in a way, the food is the same but in a different way. It's unpretentious too, but it's also exceptional because of its full-flavoured, uniquely different tastes. People return time and time again for good reason. It's the kind of place you can come with your mother or your lover, and both are guaranteed to be impressed. The atmosphere is just lovely and warm in a relaxed, welcoming way, which complements the warmth of the food. The kind of place you want to stop and stay awhile and definitely come back to.

Saoirse: Many of us can see ourselves in those stories, those experiences – the story you just shared, Florian. The story Zoya and Vidur shared. The story of your family, Maggie. The stories that are unfolding in front of our eyes as we observe the people in the restaurant, and indeed the restaurant itself is made up of stories. Not only stories of food and drink, but people's stories, stories of their life experiences.

And also the side stories, whether it's the stories of the accompanying small dishes – the side dishes and their origins, or the accompanying short stories, asides or side stories if you like, in which so many more insightful experiences are shared by characters other than the main characters in the book. I really love how short meaningful stories are woven through the book. In the same way, I get a sense that short meaningful stories are being shared all around us here in the restaurant.

Maggie: Talking about side stories and to take us on a slight aside: I liked that story about Alfred Nobel, about how he read his own obituary when the paper misreported his brother's death as being his. Knowing that he would be remembered for destruction because he had been involved in the invention of dynamite, he set out to completely redesign his life so that he would especially be remembered for honouring the pursuit of world peace.

Have any of you written your own obituary? I find the idea very creepy, but I also like the idea of writing down what I want to be remembered for.

The group shook their heads, indicating they hadn't.

Florian: "The legacy you leave is the one you live." Those words are so true. In answer to your question Saoirse, no, I haven't written my obituary, but like you, I liked the story about Alfred Nobel – a wake-up call, as it were – and I also liked all of the other side stories or shorter stories, and the quotes. They really helped to get a lot of lessons across in a small book.

Saoirse: The bigger stories in the book too, and especially I think stories of first-hand experiences, good experiences but also stories of experiences that were bad. Even though we may not have similar situations or have made similar mistakes. We have all invariably made mistakes of our own that we can relate to.

Benny: That's true. I can certainly relate to how you coined up those words from the book, Saoirse.

Annie, you mentioned how you liked the chapter summaries. I really related to those too, in particular: "Without a change in your behaviour, just saying 'I'm sorry' is not enough." I can also relate to Ray's story of how he reached burnout and needed to take time out, a sabbatical. I related to that summary of Ray's experience because of something that happened in my life.

Benny paused briefly before continuing. That brief pause, the silent intake of breath Benny took, signified to the group that this was a poignant moment for Benny, and they respectfully gave him their full attention.

Benny: Before I moved to London, I, too, had taken a sabbatical. I, too, had reached burnout because of the demands of my job. I wasn't coping well, and like the President, my behaviours became quite erratic. I was pushing people away, although I couldn't see that at the time. I actually thought I was coping, or rather that I was doing what I needed to do to cope. The company was in a bad place. I knew this. I knew stuff that other people didn't know. I knew if we couldn't find a way out of that, it would bring about a lot of job losses. I was trying to fix it because I felt responsibility to these people, but I didn't share what was going on. My position in the company meant I had all this inside knowledge that I couldn't share because it would put the company in a weak position if our clients or our competitors knew this. I was hiding information from our shareholders because I was afraid they would withdraw their investments. So I can relate to what might have been going on for the Company President. I was keeping everything to myself because I didn't know who I could trust.

I wasn't eating. I wasn't sleeping. I started drinking. I began to find solace at the bottom of a glass. It went on like this for weeks, and eventually it spiralled out of control. I drove everyone away with my destructive behaviour – my colleagues, my family, my friends. My behaviour became so erratic that it couldn't be ignored any longer. At this point, I was spending my days and nights at the office, and any sleep I was getting was alcohol-induced. Then one morning I woke up to find my assistant standing over me on the couch in my office, with a mug of coffee and fresh clothes, letting me know the board members were in the board room waiting to speak to me.

I was told in no uncertain terms that I was going to a facility that could give me the help and support I needed. I tried to resist it, but it soon became apparent that if I didn't go of my own accord, they were willing to have me sanctioned. Talk about a wake-up call, although I didn't see it like that at the time. I thought everyone was out to get me, but I had no choice. I had to do what was being suggested. I now know that intervention saved my life. It was a long road to recovery, but I got there, and along the way, I had to make several apologies. That was part of my recovery, part of the twelve-step process. So, I know a thing or two about apologies.

My move to London gave me the new start I needed. I didn't immediately begin to socialise. Actually I didn't for a long time. Mainly because of being an alcoholic. I didn't want to put myself in situations where the drinks were flowing, and because as I mentioned earlier, when I first stopped drinking alcohol and on asking for non-alcoholic beers back home, I would get blank stares, which I felt came with a sense of judgement. So I just stopped putting myself in situations where there would be alcohol, where I needed to explain why I wasn't drinking.

He laughed.

Benny: But I felt being part of a book club would be a safe way to venture back out into social settings.

The respectful silence the group gave Benny demonstrated both their understanding that he was sharing something that had brought much pain – to himself and to others – and also their appreciation that he trusted them with his story, which was his truth, a painful truth from his past. Florian gave voice to this.

Florian: Thank you for sharing your story with us, Benny.

Benny smiled in response, and the group left a continued silence to give him the space to continue if he wanted to – he didn't. He had said what he had needed to say about his personal and professional situation. Instead, he brought the discussion back to the case and the book.

Benny: The book raises the question: "With serious mistakes, is apologising enough?" And goes on to say: "Not if the apology is merely words," and that "The power of the one-minute apology is deeper than words." That was true for me. One of the twelve steps is to make a list of all persons harmed and become willing to make amends to them all. The book brought me back to that, in saying: "It can be said in one minute, even though it requires a good deal more preparation time – there are no excuses, no self-victimisation, no drama. It's simple and to the point and very effective. The time-consuming part comes in being completely honest with yourself and taking responsibility for your mistakes before you apologise." I share my experience because it's my way of relating to it, but to bring it back to the case study, Ray did this too. From the key points of book wisdom that came to him from reading *The One Minute Apology*, Ray knew he had to:

- Take full responsibility for his actions, regardless of the outcome;
- Apologise to Jake, and he had to do this with a sense of urgency;
- Demonstrate his commitment to making amends beyond this apology.

And he continued beyond this when afterwards he took time to consider if he was right for the job. Unless you do that, your continued actions will not be effective.

Annie, you mentioned how hard it was for Ray to come back from those words, that outburst. It was hard, but it was also possible. It does require demonstrating a commitment to changing behaviours and following through on that. It's all about relationships. Sometimes we have to repair broken relationships. Other times, we have to build and maintain good relationships.

Again, the group left a silence for Benny to continue if he wanted to. Seeing that he didn't, at this point Pascal spoke.

Pascal: I agree, Benny, it is possible. In my experience, this line rings true: "Mistakes fester and poison relationships, no matter what else is going right, if your president doesn't admit his mistakes right away and deal with them by changing his behaviour, he will lose the confidence of the board, and careers and relationships will be damaged." This was also true for Ray. He too would have lost the confidence of his team, and careers and relationships would also have been damaged if he hadn't taken time to consider if he was right for the job, if he hadn't taken time to consider what he needed to have done differently, if he hadn't taken time to consider what changes he wanted and needed to bring about from the learning he took from the mistakes he'd made.

In mergers and takeovers, there's a lot at stake with relationships. The people left behind who survived the culling of jobs. 'Workplace survivor syndrome' is a phrase coined by organisational psychologists to describe the emotional, psychological and physical effects of employees who remain in the midst of company downsizing. I think this played into Jake not wanting to ask for what he wanted, as he said he didn't want to seem ungrateful. But he was unhappy. In my experience, while companies will offer support to people whose roles have been made redundant, by way of outplacement programmes, they don't offer support to the survivors; and yet, many will be going through issues impacting their wellbeing.

Florian: I think this phrase is very poignant: "The Young Man's journey brings us to our own discoveries about what we can do to make things better, at work or at home, with our own one-minute apologies." I can relate to that, and Ray came to relate to it too. Times of loss, or threatened loss, makes us appreciate and value what we do have that's good in our lives, both in and out of work.

Benny: It's true that the hardest part of apologising is realising and admitting that you were at fault. You mentioned the importance of self-awareness and observation, Florian. These are important soft skills and need to be part of people's learning and development. I actually think they're superpowers, but I don't think their importance is always valued or even recognised.

Maggie: I agree. Mistakes are compounded when we don't acknowledge that we got things wrong, and so we don't apologise. We ourselves are blinded to our behaviours. What we can't see, we can't change. Self-awareness and observation would really help with this.

Saoirse: It's also true that it takes common sense, inner wisdom and inner strength to admit you got it wrong and work to set things right. Self-awareness and observation would really help with this too.

Florian: "Any problem you have spins out of control the minute you avoid dealing with the truth." While I agree those words are true, I think of them being less so with Ray, in that he was trying his best to manage the situation he had found himself saddled with – going from individual contributor to manager. I don't think he was necessarily avoiding dealing with the truth about Jake's performance. I think it's as you said, Pascal. He was managing the fallout of survivor syndrome, needing to cope with the increased responsibilities that came with his new position. But I do agree that at the core of most problems is a truth you don't want to face.

Benny: "The truth will set them free. The truth is intolerant of deception. The truth doesn't give a lot of wiggle room, and for some that can feel very uncomfortable especially if they are living a lie."

Though Benny didn't bring the conversation back to himself, the way in which he spoke those words allowed the group to know that this was bringing up a lot on both a personal and professional level, and it was painful for him. Again their respectful silence demonstrated their understanding and appreciation of this. Allowing space to allow these words, this moment to linger long enough to allow the meaning to be acknowledged while also recognising that Benny didn't want to overtly make this about him, Florian gently brought the conversation back to the book and the case.

Florian: I like the ways in which, throughout the story, that the One-Minute Manager helped to ground the Young Man. For example when he said: "Being able to do something you enjoy while you're solving problems is a sign that you are mastering your life." I really like this. It's a reminder of how problem-solving techniques can be simple yet effective. For example, the One-Minute Manager saying to the Young Man that he would have time to play golf and solve his problem when he was so overwhelmed with finding a solution that he was on the verge of locking himself away with his problem. It's similar to Ray's technique of walking and thinking, posing questions, or reading over a cup of coffee. The solution always came to him when he took himself away from the immediate problem – combining it with something else or distancing himself from it.

Maggie: I also liked how the One-Minute Manager simplified processes. For example: "Surrendering and admitting you're wrong." When I first read that, I felt uncomfortable, it felt like something that would be very hard to do, but when I read the process, it softened it for me and helped me realise it's not hard:

"The surrendering process of the apology has two important parts – the first is about you and coming to grips with what you did wrong. The second is making sure the person or persons you have harmed feel that you know you made a mistake." I'm OK with that. It's a simple process yet extremely effective. Ray's story demonstrated that extremely well.

Saoirse: It was actually the next part that made me feel uncomfortable: "To surrender, you first let go of being right, and then confront the truth about your own failings by being one hundred percent honest with yourself. A fundamental concept to remember is: One minute of being honest with yourself is worth more than days, weeks, months or years of self-deception."

It made me feel uncomfortable because I can identify with it. There have been times in my life when I haven't been completely honest with myself, not in a way that impacted others, but in a way that impacted me or held me back.

The case is called 'The Unconditional Apology', and that is so true. So is the fact that to get to that, it requires unconditional truth to oneself – that can be hard, maybe even harder to get to.

Benny raised his glass.

Benny: Both unconditional apology and unconditional truth take courage and humility.

To which they all clinked glasses.

At this point Zoya and Vidur arrived at the table and began to clear the dishes. "Are you ready for desert?" Zoya enquired. Maggie laughingly replied: "I suspect if we were to say we couldn't eat another morsel, it might fall on deaf ears."

Smiling, Vidur said: "Your trip to Kerala would be incomplete if you don't get to taste the desserts we've prepared for you."

"And besides, no matter how much you eat here, you will always have room for dessert," Zoya said. And with that, they left the table, soon to return with a selection of desserts and accompanying beers that they were very quickly drooling over.

Saoirse: One of the favourite things I've learnt about beer is the discovery that there are beers you can have with dessert that enhance the end-of-dinner experience. For example, Belgian beers go really well with apple pie or strudel. And a nice stout is the perfect pairing for a chocolate-based dessert because of the chocolate undertones in a stout. I actually recently found a recipe for Guinness chocolate puddings, one of the most indulgent boozy desserts I've tried to date. And fruit-based beers make a delightful pairing with fruit-based desserts, as I think we're about to enjoy and appreciate.

Mouths full, the group nodded in agreement.

EPILOGUE

Maggie: I think circumstances were the villain of this story – not Ray, not the Company President. And I think the apology and the truth were the heroes of the story – a story about abstract heroes and villains, external influences and people's behaviours. That's the learning I'm taking from this month's case, book and discussion.

Saoirse: The underlying message/learning for me went deeper than the apology. For me, it was about what needs to be done to avoid getting to that place – to the President's behaviour becoming erratic, to Ray losing it. Behaviours that were out of character for both of them. I think for me, it's about creating that safe environment where people are willing and able to speak up, to say what is needed to be said, to speak the truth before things spiral out of control.

Annie: We can't go back and change the beginning, but we can start from where we are and change the ending. For me, that quote from the book is both profound and reassuring, and the learning I will take from the case study, the book, our discussion.

I also have an ask. The WorkLife Conversations Assignment that's part of the case can also be used within the workplace to have coaching conversations with your colleagues in helping them to develop and refine their WorkLife learning, development and growth action plans. Having gone through the process for myself, I'd like to experience what it would be like going through it with someone else. Would anyone like to do that?

Maggie: I would. I found it really interesting and inspiring how along with everything else you mentioned – the offsite planning, our Book Club – it helped your WorkLife development plan. I was actually going to ask you about your experience. It would be great to talk or work through it.

Annie: Great. Thanks, Maggie.

Annie then addressed the whole group.

Annie: If it's OK, I'd like to do this one-on-one with Maggie – to get a sense of how it works in practice, and also to build confidence by having a coaching conversation. It's not something I've ever done before.

The rest of the group smiled at Annie and Maggie, and said that was fine.

Annie: Thanks, and sorry I've interrupted the flow of us saying what we're taking from this month's meeting.

Once again, the group smiled and said that was fine.

Florian: "The one-minute apology is more than a technique, and it's certainly more than just words. It is a useful way to think and live more successfully." That line summarises everything for me.

Pascal: We all fall short of perfection. As a result, we all sometimes do things that are inconsistent with who we are. Our integrity is measured by how quickly we correct our mistakes and get back on course. That's the learning I took from everything we've read and discussed.

Benny: "Done properly, the one-minute apology is one of the most powerful things anyone can do to repair a situation."

Benny's words brought about a pensive silence within the group.

Annie was wondering if she had blocked Benny in saying what he had wanted to say earlier when he had begun to talk about drinking non-alcoholic beers. She had come in with her experience as a vegetarian. She didn't want to bring it up now and make a big deal about it. The moment had passed, so she decided to make a mental note to be more self-aware and observant of what was going on around her.

Maggie was also wondering if she goes too far with her jibes with Benny – if they are, in fact, annoying and silly and disrespectful. She too was making a mental note to herself, to be kinder – having fun at someone's else's expense wasn't kind. Even though she hadn't meant to be unkind, she was questioning if she had been.

Benny was used to these reactions within people. In fact, he felt it was a superpower within people who were highly self-aware and observant, but they didn't always recognise it or see it as this. He, too, didn't want to make a big deal of it, but he recognised from past experience that sometimes people can beat themselves up about what they did, or feel they did, and he always strived to find a way of addressing it, to ensure this didn't happen.

He had noticed that both Annie and Maggie had become pensive, and knowing that Annie was quite reflective and stopped short sometimes of speaking up in the moment, he didn't want this to happen, nor did he want it to take her voice away. He also didn't want to stop Maggie and her little jokes, which he actually quite enjoyed and found amusing.

The truth was, Annie hadn't blocked him. He hadn't been ready to say anything further earlier into the meal. In fact, he hadn't planned to say what he had said. The discussion and the ease of the group had taken him there naturally, and so he felt he needed to get this across for Annie and for everyone else too. And he also needed to let Maggie know that he was fine with her little jokes.

Benny: I want to thank you all for giving me the space to say what I said. It's not something I planned. It just came out because of the ease of the group, our conversation, the case study, the book, and actually at the beginning of our meal when I mentioned how exciting the 'dry' alcohol scene had become, that's all I felt the need to say at that moment.

And I was so pleased that you could relate to my experience from a food perspective, Annie, because I have in times past felt as a non-drinker that people considered me to be boring, which I think can be said of the concept people used to have about vegetarians.

He laughed.

Benny: But thankfully that is changing, and people are great about it now. Indeed it quite often opens up interesting conversations about the great non-alcoholic drinks that are available now, many of which are really interesting and exciting.

I'm not sure what your best experiences with vegetarian food have been, Annie, but there's one that I would like to suggest that perhaps as a group we could try together, and that's afternoon tea that's served at a hotel close by, that offers both a traditional afternoon tea and a vegan afternoon tea, together with both alcoholic and non-alcoholic cocktail pairings. Would you all be up for that, for one of our meetings?

Oh, and Maggie, I believe they serve potato chips as an accompaniment... oh no, they're not called that in good ole Blighty, are they? Let me get this right – it's crisps, right?

He gave Maggie the same cheeky smile that always accompanied her jokes.

Benny: Saoirse, do you have any beers up your sleeve to go with cake? Or stories of cocktails you've experienced with afternoon tea, Florian? Or stories about French cakes, Pascal?

Saoirse: Well, I do, as it happens. If carrot cake happens to be on the menu, an IPA beer is the perfect accompaniment to carrot cake.

Florian: I've experienced many wonderful tea-infused cocktails and many wonderful stories to go with them.

Pascal: And yes, I do, as it happens too. French chef Marie-Antoine Carême, who is widely considered the father of French cuisine, is said to have invented the cake.

Annie smiled at Benny and said that would be a definite yes for her. The change in her demeanour was immediately visible.

Maggie (laughing): Oooooh, I hope they have crisp sandwiches on the menu – it's the ultimate good ole Blighty sandwich.

Everyone laughed, and the rest of the group also expressed their agreement with Benny's idea.

Benny: Thank you. If I may suggest, we do it for our June meeting. I know that's a little while away, but June being my birthday month – I say month because I like to drag the celebrations out for as long as possible. Or rather I prefer a number of small gatherings as opposed to one big party. I really think afternoon tea is the perfect way to celebrate one's birthday while in good ole Blighty.

Once again Benny was met with laughter and agreement from everyone.

As a group, they had already begun to meet to celebrate each other's birthdays. It had started in January when Maggie had said in passing that she was a New Years baby. On hearing this, Florian had swiftly swung into action, picking up cupcakes from a popular nearby cupcake shop. He asked the others to drop in for a coffee at a time he knew Maggie would be popping in to sit and read awhile. When she did, the group, led by Florian carrying a giant, candlelit cupcake, surrounded by baby cupcakes, walked out from his café kitchen, steps in stride as they belted out Happy Birthday Dear Maggie. Maggie was thrilled, and it was the start of a new tradition.

Next up was to be a birthday brunch at a Breakfast Club to celebrate Florian's March birthday. They already knew they would visit Saoirse's favourite cake shop for cake and fizz for her May birthday. They hadn't yet decided what they would do for Pascal's September or Annie's November birthdays. Those decisions were still in the melting pot of ideas.

And now, Benny had presented them with the perfect idea to celebrate his June birthday.

That was, indeed, a fitting end to another great chapter of the Shoreditch branch of the WorkLife Book Club.

Interlude 3

WorkLife Conversations Assignment

Accompanied by breakfast

Annie and Maggie arrived for Florian's birthday celebration ahead of the rest of the group to talk/work through the WorkLife Conversations Assignment. They were greeted by Jason, who took them to their table in the glass-domed conservatory. It was the perfect pocket of leafy calm amid the hustle and bustle of Shoreditch life. Taking their orders, Jason soon returned with a pot of Earl Grey for Annie and an espresso pot of coffee for Maggie.

Florian had told the group about the idea behind the new Breakfast Club at the boutique hotel they were all familiar with. The hotel managers, and life partners, Sarah and Jane, both from Yorkshire, immediately fell in love with London life on their move to the city. They loved the anonymity of their new life. But over time, they began to miss the connection of everyone knowing everyone and each other's business – which made them laugh because that had driven them crazy back home and was behind their reason for moving to London.

Wanting to create some balance between anonymity (which sometimes fostered the sense of loneliness) and familiarity (in a way that didn't foster a sense of intrusiveness) brought them back to the breakfast clubs that were part of their lives growing up. Weekdays at school and weekends and holidays at the different clubs they'd attended, where they enjoyed a hearty breakfast and had time to connect with their friends and time to play before their day got underway.

And so the conservatory became the dedicated relaxed space for the Breakfast Club, where people could come with friends or colleagues or alone and get to know people over a hearty breakfast.

Maggie: I began working on the WorkLife Conversations Assignment, but I couldn't answer all of the questions.

Annie: That's OK because the assignment says you may not have all the clarity you need immediately. I didn't, and I'm still not clear on my bigger picture. So, I took the approach of working through what I could by mulling over the suggested questions, which led to conversations in my head, which I then journalled on. That, in turn, led me to identify action steps to help me develop my learning, development and growth action plans.

Maggie: I started as suggested by thinking about my dreams and aspirations. By asking myself what I will be doing at the pinnacle of my WorkLife – when I'm feeling challenged, engaged and not wanting anything else. But immediately I was stumped, I couldn't answer that.

Annie: I couldn't answer that either. So, I moved on to the questions that help to understand your bigger picture.

What size of company do I imagine working for?

I'm not sure about that because I've worked and enjoyed working for both small and big, so I parked that one for now.

Maggie: I've only experienced working for a large company, and I enjoy it – for now anyway. Whether that will always be the case, I don't know. I think I want to park that for now too.

Annie: What industry do I want to be in?

That was easy for me. The tech industry is definitely right for me, now in this moment and into the future, too, I think.

Maggie: Policing is definitely the right sector for me. For now, and for the foreseeable future, working as a dog handler is the right area for me. I'm not sure if that will change in the long term, but for now, I feel I'm in the right place.

Annie: Do I want to be in a very individual contributor-type role or a management-type role?

Again, that was easy for me. There's no question. I want to be in a very individual contributor-type role.

Maggie: I collaborate in my role with my beat partner John. We work well together, and I like that, but I feel in time I may want to be part of a bigger team, and maybe even a management-type role. I don't know what that means yet, but I'm open to discovering what it could be.

Annie: I didn't feel I had enough information to begin to articulate my envisioned future from answering those questions. And so, as suggested in the assignment, I'm continuing to reflect on what all of this means as I go about my daily WorkLife.

Maggie: I think that will be the same for me.

Annie: I moved on to the next step: Getting into the Detail:

That required me to actively think about what my WorkLife looks like by looking at what I'm doing today and what I want to be doing in eighteen months, then identify what the gaps are in where I want to be. I was able to work with that, and I did it by answering the proposed questions:

How can I improve?

My answer was that I needed to push beyond the place of complacency I'd been at for far too long.

Maggie: I think I need to improve by engaging or connecting with more people at work.

Annie: Then I asked myself:

What am I not good at?

I'm not good at presentations. I've always held back on putting myself up for sharing ideas in a group situation.

Maggie: I'm not good at networking. I hate small talk that's contrived and banal, and so I avoid any kind of formal networking.

Annie: Then I asked myself:

What am I afraid of?

I'm afraid if I were to present something, I wouldn't communicate it in an interesting way, and people would find what I say boring and uninspiring.

Maggie: I'm afraid of how I'll come across in a networking situation.

When I'm out of my comfort zone, I can come across as being quite intense, and then if I try to lighten the situation, I can come across as being quite flippant.

Annie: Then I moved on to: Creating My Self-Coaching Plan. I rated myself on the area I identified – presentations, which provided a baseline for improvement. As I never give presentations, I was starting from zero, really.

Maggie: Although I'm not good in formal networking situations, being part of our Book Cclub has definitely helped me in social networking situations. So, I'm going to give myself a rating of five.

Annie: The next step: look for opportunities where I can work on improving the area I identified I want to improve upon; look for opportunities to become good at what I have identified I'm not good at; and look for opportunities to overcome my fear in areas I have identified I'm fearful of. This led me to approach the school to give a talk on cybersecurity. That's my area of expertise. If I'm going to be good at giving a presentation on anything, instilling knowledge in others, to teach them what I know, it had to be that.

Maggie: I'm going to have to figure out which networking event at work is the least formal, a step up from our Book Club as such, and start from there. I think something that might be set in a sociable, fun setting but has some element of formal networking structure to it too.

Annie: The next step is to set time aside to assess how I'm doing. Rate myself and compare it to where I began. Then from my re-evaluation, give myself feedback on how I'm doing to help me identify what I want and need to do to continue my improvement plan. I actually feel my first presentation went really well. I prepared well, and they responded well, listened attentively, and interacted with me by asking good questions, demonstrating their understanding. I felt I'd answered their questions well, and I felt I had communicated clearly and in an interesting way. So, I rated myself a five. From zero, that's a significant jump, and I was pleased with that. Their questions let me know what else I could say to make my talk more informative upfront, which is part of my improvement plan. I asked my manager if I could approach more schools in our borough to give my talk, and in so doing, teach them about our profession. He said yes, and so I'm following through on that.

That's pretty much where I've gotten to with the assignment. However, I am following the step: Developing a Practice of Continuous Self-Feedback

Looking beyond my workplace to detect shifts and changes that might impact my WorkLife learning, development and growth planning. I'm trying to be aware of my company's growth areas and limitations, as well as changes in the skills that my industry will require. I'm also trying to look to good practices across other industries.

I hadn't been doing this up until now, and I think it contributed to my stagnation. I believe this is really important to me in becoming clearer on my bigger picture.

I'm also following the step: Develop a Practice of Insightful Self-Questioning Assignment. At the moment, I'm doing this by considering the answers to the suggested questions in the assignment and building that into my presentation:

Are you optimistic about the industry's future?
Are there specific reasons you feel this way?
Do you see new opportunities?
What do we need to get better at? Faster at? Smarter at?

For now, this is enough for me. From this, in time, I think I'll be able to craft my longer-term WorkLife vision.

Maggie: That's really helpful, Annie, thank you. Once I've attended my first networking event, I can follow the process to assess how I did and identify what I want and need to do to continue my improvement plan.

I can see the benefit of Developing a Practice of Continuous Self-Feedback, and I think that will help me in understanding my longer-term vision, too. I think that's something I can begin to do as well.

The assignment says a simple way to Develop a Practice of Insightful Questions is to do this by having conversations to stimulate good dialogue. That's exactly what I need for networking to overcome my fear that I'll come across as too intense or too flippant. I think the questions in the assignment will open up interesting conversations, and they'll also help my longer-term vision.

Thank you, Annie, that has really helped to understand how the assignment works. I'd been feeling blocked because I got stuck at the initial Bigger Picture step. Now I know I can park that for now, move on to the other steps, which I feel I can do. Gaining perspective as I go will enable me to come back, in time, to fleshing out what the Bigger Picture means for me.

Annie: You're welcome, Maggie, and thanks, it's really helped me too. I'm not sure if it was a coaching conversation per se, but it gave me a sense of how I could go about having a coaching conversation. I mentioned my manager liked the idea of the offsite planning Benny shared with us. If we roll it out within our team and department, I can put myself forward to demonstrate how the WorkLife conversations work and have coaching conversations with my colleagues.

Maggie: That interests me as well. That was a mutually beneficial WorkLife coaching conversation, I think it's fair to say.

Annie: Absolutely. Now, where are the others? I've worked up an appetite working through the assignment. I'm ready for breakfast.

Right on cue, the others arrived, laughing and chatting, arms filled with fresh flowers. Benny presented Annie and Maggie with fragrant bunches.

Benny: We couldn't go to Columbia Road Flower Market and not bring you beautiful blooms.

Maggie: Why, thank you, kind sir. Happy birthday, Florian.

Annie: Happy birthday, Florian, and thank you so much for the flowers. They're beautiful.

Florian: Thank you. How did your WorkLife Conversations Assignment go?

Annie: Excellent, we enjoyed it. Were you all at the flower market?

Benny: Yes, it turns out great minds think alike on Sunday Mornings

in Shoreditch. It also turns out you never know who you will bump into when you stop for a coffee.

Saoirse (laughing): And such timing. We were all in the coffee queue at the same time.

Benny: Like I said, great minds!

The rest of the group laughed as they laid down their flowers, took off their coats and took their seats. Florian introduced his children to Annie and Maggie: Emilia and Mateo, who had come to London to celebrate his birthday.

Together with Elena and Philippe, the group were a birthday party of ten, which seemed very fitting to celebrate the birthday of a man who loved bringing people together, and the ethos of the Breakfast Club: a place you want to take your friends and meet new friends.

Jason arrived with their menus and took their drinks orders – they were sticking with coffees and teas… for now, anyway.

"Gosh, I hadn't noticed how the place had filled up," said Annie. "We were the only ones here when we arrived. Now it's buzzing."

"It's a popular spot for locals and market-goers at weekends, especially Sundays with the flower market and Backyard and Sunday Upmarket in the Truman Brewery happening as well as Spitalfields Market," Florian observed. "Weekdays it's a hive of activity for workers. People working nearby drop in for breakfast, a coffee or a meeting, people coming with their laptops to work for a few hours, and locals dropping in as well."

"It's got a great artistic vibe to it," Pascal remarked.

"Ah, funny you should say that," said Florian. "We've got the artist in residence at our very table."

Florian smiled at Elena, who laughingly said, "Oh, Florian!"

Turning to the rest of the group, Elena said: "The hotel partners with the Other Art Fair, which showcases a different artist at each participating location."

"Oh yes," said Philippe. "That's a wonderful initiative in giving art lovers access to some of today's most exciting artists, all under our Shoreditch roofs."

"The paintings in the corridor, right?" Maggie asked. "I saw them earlier, they're wonderful."

"Thank you," said Elena.

"I'm going for a proper look," continued Maggie. "Or should I say a 'private viewing', seeing as I'm in the company of the artist in residence."

With that, Maggie stood up and was joined by Annie, Benny, Saoirse, Pascal and Philippe, as they went for a 'private viewing' of the work of the artist in residence.

Arriving with the first of their coffees at exactly that moment, Jason laughingly asked: "Was it something I said?"

Mateo laughed, saying: "No, it was our mum." Emilia added: "If you ever need the room cleared, you can just call on our mum."

Jason laughed and went to get the rest of their coffees and teas.

On his return, Jason began to take the breakfast orders, needing to wait just a brief moment for the group to arrive back to get all their preferred choices, which ranged from a full English to a tower of sweet potato fritters served with avocado and a poached egg, eggs Benedict, eggs Florentine, baked eggs with spiced pepper, tomato and chickpea ragu, French toast with berries and yoghurt, a stack of berry pancakes, baked eggs with chorizo and potatoes, homemade granola with berries and mango and coconut yoghurt, and chorizo crushed avocado on muffins topped with a poached egg. Orders taken, Jason went to have them prepared.

"I love your work, Elena," said Philippe. "Pascal and I have seen it before at a gallery on the First Thursday Bus Tour."

"Thank you," responded Elena. "That was just a few months ago. We would have been in the same room. It really is a small world."

"What's the First Thursday Bus Tour?" asked Saoirse.

Elena explained: "On the first Thursday of every month, over 150 galleries in east London come together and run free events, exhibitions, talks and private views during a special late opening. A bus takes people from gallery to gallery."

"That sounds wonderful," said Saoirse.

"It is," said Philippe.

Pascal smiled: "Do you know what's also wonderful? It's wonderful that we're all here together to celebrate Florian's birthday."

Raising his cup, Pascal said: "Birthdays are a chance to let the good people in your life know how much they matter to you. Today is your day, Florian. Wishing you a birthday filled with happiness and wishing you that all year long."

The group raised their cups and wished Florian a birthday year filled with happiness. "What else have you been up to for your birthday Florian?" asked Saoirse.

"Mateo and Emilia arrived on Friday evening, and we had dinner at my restaurant," replied Florian. "Yesterday we spent the day wandering around Shoreditch. Last night we had dinner at a wonderful Mediterranean restaurant, which I plan on bringing you to. People seemed to know it was my birthday, and many cups and glasses appeared everywhere I went." He laughed, "Before I got a chance to order anything, I found myself at the centre of a toast."

"That's why we love Shoreditch," said Emilia. "We used to help out in Dad's restaurant, bar and coffee shop, so we know lots of people. For us, it's our other home."

"Emilia and I love to visit mum and dad," said Mateo. "And when we do, we love to spend our time wandering around Shoreditch and stopping to talk to people. They always make us feel so welcome."

Jason, helped by Sarah and Jane, arrived with their breakfasts and glasses of their finest champagne.

Glasses raised, everyone wished Florian a happy birthday. He laughed saying, "See what I mean, I'm the centre of a toast, and I don't remember ordering anything. Thank you, dear family and friends, it means a lot to celebrate my birthday with you all."

WorkLife Conversations Assignment

This assignment is designed for you to have WorkLife conversations with yourself. These conversations will take place in your mind as you mull over the questions you're about to pose to yourself. I suggest journalling on whatever comes up for you as you process your responses. From this, you will be able to identify the action steps you need to take to develop and continuously refine your WorkLife learning, development and growth action plans.

You can also use this assignment within your Workplace to have coaching conversations with your colleagues in helping them to develop and refine their WorkLife learning, development and growth action plans.

So make yourself a cup of coffee or tea, ready to begin with:

YOUR BIGGER PICTURE ASSIGNMENT

Start by thinking about your dreams and aspirations. Do this by asking yourself what you will be doing at the pinnacle of your WorkLife – when you're feeling challenged, engaged and not wanting anything else.

You may not have a clear picture at this point, your vision may be blurry, and that is OK. Your goal is to work towards bringing your bigger picture into focus in order to see all of the wonderful details of your WorkLife in a captivating cinematic image – because, after all, you are creating your own compelling WorkLife story. Similar to the film *La La Land*, you will go from black and white images to outline the details, then adding colour to bring those images to life.

Ask yourself the following questions to help you understand your dreams, your aspirations, your bigger picture:

What size of company do I imagine working for?

What industry do I want to be in?

Do I want to be in a very individual contributor-type role or a management-type role?

CREATE YOUR WORKLIFE LEARNING, DEVELOPMENT AND GROWTH ACTION PLAN ASSIGNMENT

STEP 1

From this information, begin to articulate your envisioned future. You are the author of your WorkLife story. Now is the time to start writing your continuing chapters. Each chapter begins with an outline: the key points you have gleaned from answering these questions. Then as you go about your daily WorkLife, continue to reflect on what all of this means. Take whatever clarity that comes to you to add more detail to your outline.

To help you with this, your next assignment is:

GETTING INTO THE DETAIL ASSIGNMENT

You need to actively think about what your WorkLife looks like by looking at what you are doing today and what you want to be doing in eighteen months, then identify what the gaps are in where you want to be.

You can do this by asking yourself the following questions:

How can I improve?
What am I not good at?
What am I afraid of?

Use the information you've gleaned from these questions to:

CREATE YOUR SELF-COACHING PLAN ASSIGNMENT

1. Rate yourself in all the areas you identified. This provides a baseline for improvement.
2. Look for opportunities where you can work on improving the area(s) you identified you want to improve upon; look for opportunities to

become good at what you have identified you are not good at; and look for opportunities to overcome your fear in areas you have identified you are fearful of.
3. Depending on how often you are able to work on these areas, set time aside to assess how you are doing – as a suggestion, once a month is good. As you go through your self-assessment, rate how you are doing now and compare it to where you began. From your re-evaluation, give yourself feedback on how you are doing to help you identify what you want and need to do to continue your improvement plan.
4. Carry on this loop by pursuing opportunities to do what you have identified you need to do, then continue with regular re-assessments, re-evaluation and self-feedback.

DEVELOP A PRACTICE OF CONTINUOUS SELF-FEEDBACK

You need to look beyond your Workplace to detect shifts and changes that might impact your WorkLife learning, development and growth planning. You will need to be aware of your company's growth areas and limitations, as well as changes in the skills that your industry will require. You should also look to good practices across other industries.

DEVELOP A PRACTICE OF INSIGHTFUL SELF-QUESTIONING ASSIGNMENT

A simple way to do this is by having conversations. Below are a few questions that help stimulate good dialogue, which you can pose to people socially over coffee or at events, and online in groups and forums that are of particular interest to you.

Are you optimistic about the industry's future?
Are there specific reasons you feel this way?
Do you see new opportunities?
What do we need to get better at? Faster at? Smarter at?

WORDS OF WISDOM

You then need to consider the implications this information and knowledge have for your WorkLife in terms of revising and fine-tuning your learning, development and growth action plan. While you cannot predict every eventuality, you can prepare.

CREATE YOUR WORKLIFE LEARNING, DEVELOPMENT AND GROWTH ACTION PLAN ASSIGNMENT

STEP 2

From this, craft an action plan to map out in greater detail exactly how you are going to reach your longer-term WorkLife vision for yourself. At various stages, you will most likely identify that you need a new learning opportunity, so you will need to figure out how you will position yourself, so you are in the right place to learn, develop and grow along your WorkLife path.

This will be an ongoing process, and you will use the same strategy you used in your eighteen-month plan to assess and reassess what you want and need to do to achieve your dreams and aspirations.

With this understanding of how you envision your future, what your day-to-day WorkLife looks like, what you want to have accomplished within eighteen months, and ways in which you can strive to achieve this, you have everything you need to take the action needed to start to build your WorkLife learning, development and growth action plan. Think of it as a roadmap to self-actualisation.

ROXANNE
WHITBY STREET E1

4

April

The Case Of Self-Sabotage

Featuring *The Inner Game of Work* by Timothy Gallwey, accompanied by French cuisine

The group felt they were stepping into a little piece of Paris immediately on their arrival at the café-restaurant. Florian told them the design and decor was inspired by the great boulevard cafés of Paris and the artistic and creative heritage of Shoreditch. Pink cherry blossoms, magnolia and wisteria blooms sprinkled with colour from tulips, daffodils and peonies filled the room and gave a sense of springtime in Paris. Combined, this brought a theatrical atmosphere of a French cultural dining experience. As they were taking in the decadent decor, the Front-of-House Manager, Jean-Pierre, greeted them, introduced himself and showed them to their table.

Once seated, their wait staff arrived with a selection of plates and water for the table. Jean-Pierre introduced Cécile and Laurent, letting the group know that together they would be taking care of them this evening. Addressing the group, Jean-Pierre said Florian had let him know that they have enjoyed sharing dishes at the beginning of their meals. He said that while French restaurants will vary in the number of courses they serve, they always serve *hors d'oeuvres* as guests arrive. In keeping with how they enjoy beginning their meal, Chef Lavigne had prepared a selection of cold and warm dishes for them to share. First they had smoked salmon canapés, vegan smoked salmon toasts, *jambon rouleaux de chèvre* (ham and rolls of goats cheese), courgette roulées, *socca* (a chickpea-flour flatbread) and a selection of olives.

"These dishes look amazing," said Annie. "The food is so beautifully presented."

"Here, beauty is both in the room and on the plate," said Florian. "Chef Lavigne, who was once a street artist, combines the rigour of her culinary training with her creative prowess, which is evident in her artistic plating style."

"Thank you," responded Jean-Pierre. "I will share your compliment with Chef Lavigne."

He let the group know that he would bring along the next course in a little while, which would be *amuse-bouche*. Translated from French, he explained, this means 'to amuse the mouth', and that it's served to stimulate the appetite. He said it's complimentary and chosen by the chef. And finally, the third sharing course they would bring along would be the selection of appetisers that Chef Lavigne has prepared for them.

He said they'd come back to take their orders for their remaining courses. He explained that their menu comprised of typical French brasserie food, and while many of the classic French dishes were meat-based, French people also love to eat their greens, served raw as a salad or as a cooked starter side or main dish. He finished by saying that he thought they would appreciate and enjoy the choice of traditional meat and vegetarian dishes on the menu.

Florian asked what he suggested they drink to accompany the dishes.

"Because of the contrasting flavours of the dishes," Jean-Pierre responded, "I suggest a light sparkling wine to complement the livelier ingredients in the dishes."

Benny also asked if he had a suggestion for an accompanying non-alcoholic sparkling wine.

"Yes, that's the great thing about sparkling wines," replied Jean-Pierre. "There are so many wonderful non-alcoholic options. Can I bring you my preferred choices, which are produced in the Limoux wine region? I've selected them because they are crisp, clean and fresh with distinctive apple aromas, making them the perfect accompaniment to your appetisers."

A suggestion to which everyone replied "Yes" in agreement.

Jean-Pierre arrived with his selection of wines as Florian was telling the group that Jean-Pierre is a fellow sommelier.

"I heard there are secret wine societies in France, to which you have to be invited to become a member, and that there are also even more secret, more elite societies for sommeliers, and that nobody can talk about what goes on," commented Benny. "Kind of like what happens in Vegas stays in Vegas, but in a much more sophisticated way. Is that true?"

Neither Jean-Pierre nor Florian said anything to confirm or deny this but smiled and exchanged what seemed to the rest of the group to be a secretly knowing glance. While they all laughed, they were left wondering if they were perhaps in the midst of members of an elite secret society.

Having poured their drinks, Jean-Pierre wished them *bon appétit.*

Glasses filled, Pascal raised his, saying: "*À votre santé*" (cheers), to which the group clinked.

Florian: While I'm not sure if Chef Lavigne has been out on the streets of Shoreditch with her spray cans, French Street artists often feature in the Shoreditch Street Art Tours. And long before French artists painted the walls of Shoreditch, they built them. French Huguenots, a religious group of French protestants, fled persecution in France. Those who settled in Shoreditch built the houses you will have walked past in the streets opposite Spitalfields Market. They are distinguishable by their elegant wooden doors and shutters and have especially high attic windows. These were built for a very specific purpose. The Huguenots were mainly master silk weavers, and by placing their spinning wheel in the attic, they could benefit from natural daylight, allowing them to work as long as possible into the evening. One particular house of note is Dennis Severs' House in Folgate Street. Woven through the house is the story of the fictional Jervis family – Huguenot silk weavers who lived at the house from 1725 to 1919.

Pascal: Yes, I know the houses you mean, but I didn't know the story behind them. It's really interesting to learn about stories of French history and culture. Thank you, *à votre santé*, to my fellow countrymen and women who helped to build our community.

A toast to which they all raised their glasses.

Maggie had chosen this month's case and began to read: The Case Of Self-Sabotage, to which the accompanying book was *The Inner Game of Work* by Timothy Gallwey.

"Tim Gallwey is one of the great teachers of our time. His aspiration is the realization of genuine potential, not miracles, but the gap between that potential and our current performance is often so great that the results are nothing short of miraculous. In this day, when many talk of accelerating learning in organizations but few have actually done it, the words of a master are timely indeed." (Peter M. Senge, author of *The Fifth Discipline: The Art and Practice of the Learning Organization*)

From the back cover:
"Do you think it's possible to truly enjoy your job? No matter what it is or where you are? Timothy Gallwey does, and in this groundbreaking book he tells you how to overcome the inner obstacles that sabotage your efforts to be your best on the job.

"Timothy Gallwey burst upon the scene twenty years ago with his revolutionary approach to excellence in sports. His bestselling books *The Inner Game of Tennis* and *The Inner Game of Golf*... changed the way we think about learning and coaching. But the Inner Game that Gallwey discovered on the tennis court is about more than learning a better backhand; it is about learning how to learn, a critical skill that, in this case, separates the productive, satisfied employee from the rest of the pack. For the past twenty years Gallwey has taken his Inner Game expertise to many of America's top companies, including AT&T, Coca-Cola, Apple, and IBM, to teach their managers and employees how to gain better access to their own internal resources.

"What inner obstacles is Gallwey talking about? Fear of failure, resistance to change, procrastination, stagnation, doubt, and boredom, to name a few. Gallwey shows you how to tap into your natural potential for learning, performance, and enjoyment so that any job, no matter how long you've been doing it or how little you think there is to learn about it, can become an opportunity to sharpen skills, increase pleasure, and heighten awareness."

The Inner Game of Work, by Timothy Gallwey, was originally published by Random House in 2001 (256pp., ISBN 978-1588361295)

The Case of Self-Sabotage

"You sabotaged yourselves through whatever it was that was going on within each of you."

Samantha and Josh's dreams were crushed when they heard these words.

But let's back up a little to:

Samantha & Josh's Stories of Self-Sabotage

Samantha and Josh had been working at A-Z Advertising Agency for two years. Both had joined as college graduates. As part of their graduate programme, they'd both worked for six months at a time in different functions across the company. This was a requirement designed to allow them to understand all aspects of the business more broadly.

The next part of their development plan was to have the opportunity to be part of the team working closely with, and being mentored by, Caitlin, the company's Creative Director. This was an opportunity that was offered just once a year. To be accepted onto her team, they were each required to present their ideas for a new campaign for a long-existing client.

How did they do? They both failed.

Why? Because they both sabotaged themselves. But in very different ways:

Samantha allowed her negative self-talk to impact her self-belief in her own ability. She doubted every single idea she had, and came across as insecure and needy. Josh believed his ideas were the best ideas, and the only ideas that would work. He came across as arrogant and closed-minded.

As part of the process in preparing their presentation for Caitlin, they had first pitched their ideas to focus groups. These groups were made up of experienced professionals across the company. The groups had given feedback on what they liked and didn't like.

Samantha homed in on what they didn't like, completely blanking what they liked, which led her to not believe in herself or her ideas. Her belief was that everyone else's ideas were better than hers. Josh homed in on what they liked, completely blanking what they didn't like, which led him to believe in himself and his ideas. His belief was that his ideas were better than anyone else's.

When they had finished their presentations, Caitlin gave them the following feedback:

"The focus groups were impressed with both of your ideas. The feedback you were given was to help your ideas to be even better. But instead of listening to hear and understand what was being said and learn from that, you both got in your own way. In effect, you sabotaged yourselves through whatever it was that was going on within each of you.

"Listening to the right people – and this includes listening to yourself – is a gift, a chance to learn about how to do better. Listening to the wrong people – and this also includes listening to yourself – particularly the early critics, is a trap. If you're not careful, it can become a place to hide.

"I'm going to give you a second chance. But it comes with a stipulation. To be considered next year, you both need to present back to me what you've learnt from this experience and how you will use this to set yourselves up for success in the next opportunity.

"You both need to reflect on this experience. A question that will serve you well in this moment, and will stand you in good stead throughout your WorkLife, is to ask yourselves: 'How am I complicit in creating the conditions that I say I don't want?'

"I suggest you read Timothy Gallwey's work on the Inner Game.

"I want to see confident presentations that demonstrate both self-belief and humility. I'll meet with you in nine months to hear what you have to say."

And with that, she stood up and left the room.

Although in the moment both Samantha and Josh were crushed by what Caitlin had said, they also sensed there was a glimmer of hope in being given a second chance. There was a lot going on within each of them that they didn't understand, a lot which neither of them knew how to make sense of. The only offering of help that Caitlin had given them was suggesting the book to read. And so in not knowing what else to do, that's what they each set out to do.

Book Wisdom

In researching Gallwey's work, they both ordered a copy of *The Inner Game of Work* – his other work seemed to be about sport and music, and so they both figured this was the book Caitlin was suggesting. In learning how the foundation of the Inner Game idea came about, both Samantha and Josh found it interesting how Gallwey discovered what he went on to coin 'Self 1 and Self 2' – the premise behind his body of work.

It came about through his practice of observing and asking questions, when in his work teaching tennis, one day he "stopped trying to change the students swing." Instead, he started asking questions of himself: "How is learning really taking place?" and "What's going on inside the head of the player when he hits the ball?"

It occurred to him that there was a dialogue going on in the player's head, an internal conversation. That caused him to wonder if all that inner dialogue was really necessary. He asked himself: "Is it helping the learning process, or is it getting in the way?" He knew that when great athletes were asked what they were thinking during their best performance, they universally declared they weren't thinking very much at all. They reported that their minds were quiet and focused.

His next question to himself was: "In the inner dialogue, who is talking to whom?" He called the voice giving the commands and making the self-judgements, 'Self 1'. The one he was talking to he called 'Self 2'. He then asked, "What was their relationship?" The answer that came to him was that Self 1 was the know-it-all who basically didn't trust Self 2, the one who hit the ball. Out of mistrust, Self 1 was trying to control Self 2's behaviour using the tactics it had learnt from its teachers in the outside world. In other words, the distrust implied by the judgemental context was being internalised by the student's Self 1. The resulting self-doubt and over-control interfered with the natural learning process.

Then he asked himself: "But who is Self 2?" "Is it that unworthy of trust?"

His definition was that: "Self 2 is the human being itself. It embodies all the inherent potential we were born with, including all capacities, actualised, and not yet actualised. It also embodies our innate ability to learn and to grow any of those inherent capacities. It is the self we all enjoyed as young children."

He realised that: "All the evidence pointed to the fact that our best performance happened when Self 1's voice was quiet, and Self 2 was allowed to hit the ball undisturbed."

Samantha and Josh were now coming to understand why Caitlin had suggested that they read Gallwey's work on the Inner Game. They both realised they were at the beginning of learning a new way to learn, something they could each work on for themselves.

The short story that Gallwey told about the golfer who complained he couldn't silence the critical voice in his head after hitting one or two bad shots in a round. How he would say to himself: "I'm letting the pressure get to me. I'm getting down on myself when I'm not performing well, and my self-confidence is suffering."

And the short story he told about the basketball player who said the *Inner Game of Tennis* had been like a bible to him for most of the past decade and had significantly enhanced his performance on the court. But recently, he began losing confidence in his shooting, the strongest part of his game. He complained, "I'm talking to myself constantly on the court, and I hate it. I miss the euphoria that comes from being totally immersed in the game without so many thoughts in my head."

Gallwey said he "Felt a great respect for the courage it took for these professional athletes to admit to themselves that their problem was not just technical. They realised they were getting in their own way, and they reached out for coaching."

So did Samantha and Josh.

In the knowledge that the book could serve as their guide to help themselves in getting to where they wanted to be in their WorkLife, they both felt a renewed sense of energy and drive to do what they needed to do, to make this happen.

They had taken all of this learning from the first chapter in the book: 'A Better Way to Change'. Actually, they were only halfway through the first chapter, and already it had evoked a great sense of curiosity within them. They each felt an excited anticipation around where the book would take them in their learning as each chapter unfolded. They knew they were at the beginning of an exciting journey in their WorkLife.

They soon came to learn that they could also access the support of Chris, a coach who worked with people in the company on a consultancy basis, who was experienced in the Inner Game approach. Recognising the positive impact of this support instilled further confidence for both of them in the quest they were both about to embark upon.

From here, some of their chosen paths along their WorkLife journey sometimes crossed and sometimes took different directions, as they each took the learning that was relevant to them in overcoming their personal challenge.

To begin, they both realised they needed to deal with the root problem: Distorted Perception.

They pondered the question, "What would happen if their judgement of themselves and their performance could be replaced by a non-judgemental observation of fact?"

Gallwey suggested a more elegant approach to learning and coaching, which was based on principles that he summarised in three words: awareness, trust and choice.

Elaborating slightly, he made a note to himself on the principles:

(1) Non-judgemental awareness is curative;

(2) Trust Self 2 (my own and the student's);

(3) Leave primary learning choices with the students.

His short, simple description helped them both: "Awareness was about knowing the present situation with clarity. Choice as about moving in a desired direction in the future. And Trust in one's own inner-resources was the essential link that enabled that movement."

Gallwey said that the more he trusted, the easier it was to be aware. The more aware he was, the easier it was to see his choices. And from this, his understanding of each principle deepened. He saw that they were all he needed to form the basis of a new approach to learning and making changes.

Samantha and Josh were both eager and willing to put these three principles to the test. They felt they had found their way forward. A way forward that would help them manage their Self 1 interferences. A way forward that would enable them to learn through experience.

Gallwey described this experience as enrolling in the greatest seminar on earth: the seminar of your everyday life. The price of the admission to this was humility and interest to be a student. At the university of experience, there is a requirement to be both a learner and a doer. Then you must pay attention to the teacher – experience itself.

Gallwey talks about the seminar of experience having an open-door policy. Allowing you to enter and exit when you choose. The learning process begins when you pay attention as a student. You start from your present understanding and move at your own pace. If you forget you are a student and become involved in the drama and trauma of your WorkLife, the seminar goes on without you. You can return at any time and you will always be granted the freedom to be conscious or unconscious, to pay attention or not. And the variety of courses to enrol on is nearly unlimited.

Gallwey advocates for focus of attention to engage in this seminar, to put his principles into play. This is the point from which Samantha and Josh began their quest to gain the learning, knowledge and understanding that would enable the proficiency they wanted in their work. This in turn helped to neutralise the interference of their Self 1 and shift the focus to their Self 2. This then allowed them to be in the moment, a place where they could learn through the experience of doing and enjoy themselves in the process.

The distraction of their self-interference didn't disappear, but they learnt how to manage it by bringing their focus back to being in the moment of what they were doing.

For Samantha, this helped to quieten her self-interference that brought with it anxiety of her ideas not being good enough. She was surprised how creative she could be by simply focusing on the task in hand, which helped alleviate her self-doubt in putting her ideas forward, even in group situations, where she had always held back before because of lack of confidence. She was learning to trust in herself and her ideas.

For Josh, this helped quieten his self-interference that brought with it boredom because of his impatience to push through on his ideas. He was surprised how creative he could be by simply focusing on the task on hand, even during repetitive activities. This allowed him to see more choices, which in turn allowed him to give more input on other people's ideas. He was learning to trust in the learning he was taking from these experiences.

In the one-to-one sessions, Chris defined the Inner Game approach as the facilitator of mobility. His role was to create an environment through conversation, and a way of being, to facilitate learning in a fulfilling manner.

Gallwey said the essential ingredient of Inner Game coaching that cannot be taught is: Caring, not only for external results of desired goals but also for the person being coached. Chris personified this.

In establishing the coach/client relationship, Chris told each of them at the outset that his role was not to give advice or counsel; and that, therefore, he didn't need any detailed background information for the problem at hand. He asked that they simply start thinking out loud about the problem and to allow him to eavesdrop on their thought process. He let them know that he would ask questions or make comments intended to help them clarify or advance their thinking.

He worked with them to help them recognise and understand their own thinking process. He explained he wasn't listening for the content of what was being said as much as he was listening to the way they were thinking, including how their attention was focused and how they defined the key elements of their situations. He would pose questions such as: "What do you consider will be the consequences of your proposed action or decision?" This approach made a significant difference in how they thought.

As a facilitator of mobility, he focussed their coaching conversations on the three principles of the Inner Game:

He facilitated conversations for Awareness by taking them back to an event, sometimes with a very broad question, such as: "What's happening?"

Before narrowing it down by asking: "What are you observing in that moment?"

He facilitated conversation for Choice by asking fundamental questions, such as: "What do you want?"

He facilitated conversations for Trust by asking questions such as: "If you could do it any way you wanted, how would you go about accomplishing this task?" "When have you succeeded in a challenge similar to this?" "At your best, what qualities, attributes, capabilities do you bring to this situation?"

As their Inner Game coach, Chris fostered a non-judgemental environment for Samantha and Josh, which helped to quieten their

Self 1 interference, enabling learning to take place from Self 2 awareness, choice and trust.

Nine months later, helped by the book wisdom of *The Inner Game of Work*, the work they had done on themselves, the learning they had taken from learning and doing, and their coaching sessions with Chris, this is what Samantha and Josh presented to Caitlin:

Samantha

My greatest challenge and consequently my greatest possibilities lie in overcoming the self-imposed mental limitations that prevent the full expression of my ideas and, subsequently, my potential.

Through self-feedback, I realised I need to monitor my negative self-talk because my mind is always listening, and if I talk about all my perceived limitations, if I argue for them, they're mine. If I fight for them, I get to keep them, and so I always have to be careful of my negative self-talk.

My self-image can be an obstacle, probably the greatest obstacle to my growth. By believing my ideas are not as good as other people's, I limit how well I will let myself draw on other people's ideas to develop my own thinking.

Acknowledging my weaknesses has allowed me to behave differently in response to what I've acknowledged. I've taken my inner voices on a journey with me to highlight challenges and obstacles. This allows me to be my own fiercest opponent: other opponents will be small compared to the expectations I have for myself.

Of course, I can't demonstrate I'm right for the project if I only focus on my inadequacies. I have to project confidence, and this is a confidence that I can learn to develop in myself and my ideas through other people and their ideas. I can do this by accepting feedback objectively, making my judgement by observing the facts, and from this, making my decisions.

When I engage in self-sabotage through negative self-talk, then my self-confidence suffers. This leads to a cycle of self-interference, and one that I haven't yet learnt to overcome, but I have learnt how to deal with it and to manage it.

I do this by asking myself the question: "Do I want to do this badly enough, or do I want to give in to the notion that I'm not good enough?" To be part of your team, to have the opportunity to work closely with you, and to learn from you, is my heart's desire. This is an amazing opportunity, and it's my opportunity. So yes, I do want it badly enough, I have to do it, and I am good enough.

Success for me is walking into a room, believing in myself and what I do. Presenting my best self in the knowledge I've put everything I can into my work and being happy with the result.

Josh

I can be my own worst enemy, and I need to get out of my own way and start developing patience. To be patient with myself, to accept that I don't know everything, and my ideas are not the only ideas or necessarily the best ideas.

Self-feedback has allowed me to know that the mental interference that is keeping me from being my best right now will also make it more difficult to acquire new skills. I needed to find a better way and to make a change.

To do this, I looked to behaviours and tactics of people I admire in the world of sports. I posed questions to myself about how they keep their minds quiet and focussed to manage the impact of inner dialogue on their performance. I discovered the art of relaxed concentration to trust my mind's potential to learn and perform.

This practice uses the unconscious rather than the self-conscious mind. It helps to unlearn or suspend the habits and concepts that interfere with my natural learning ability and to trust the innate intelligence of my mind.

I want to be good at my job, and I want to find solutions. I want to find a way to become good. I recognise now that there is no instant solution. I will learn through experience. I will make mistakes, working with and listening to experienced professionals who are passionate about their work will allow me to learn through these experiences and mistakes.

I need to let go of what I think I know because learning any new skill is about the process of discovery that comes primarily from the experience itself. By letting go of my preconceived notions by not resisting new experiences, I can learn far more. I can learn how to deal with the unexpected whenever I encounter it. I'm discovering I can adapt to strange or different concepts only when I'm willing to let go of dependence on old concepts.

George F. Kneller said: "To think creatively, we must be able to look afresh at what we normally take for granted."

I believe there's a way to be humble and confident. Success to me is to turn up in life with humility, confidence, authenticity, with fun and to be myself.

Epilogue

Caitlin was impressed by the sincerity of their self-reflection and what they learnt from this. She gave them both the opportunity to present their ideas for that year's campaign. She asked that they work together on their presentation, saying they each had something different and unique to bring to their work, that they could both learn from and challenge each other.

Samantha and Josh were both relieved and excited to have been given the opportunity again. They agreed to be their own and each other's biggest critics and champions, to hold themselves to the highest standards. To work to come up with new ideas to challenge their excellence.

It worked. They were both successful in Caitlin accepting them onto her team to work closely with her on the new campaign. Their unique WorkLife stories continue.

Words of Wisdom

Taking a long hard look at how you are self-sabotaging is both insightful and painful. It requires you to look in the mirror at who you are, and what you do that at its worse is destructive or at its best is slowing you down, preventing you from fully being who you should be. Master your inner dialogue: what you say to yourself matters more than what the entire world together says about you.

WORKLIFE BOOK CLUB

As Maggie finished reading, Jean-Pierre arrived with their *amuse-bouche*, saying: "Tonight Chef Lavigne has chosen sweet potato chips with goat cheese and caviar. The vegan option is sweet potato chips with cashew nuts and algae."

On eating, Annie summed up the experience, saying: "Such a wonderful flavourful taste in such a small dish."

Jean-Pierre, Cécile and Laurent returned with their small appetiser plates, which included Provençal stuffed squid, vegan and traditional *coquilles Saint Jacques*, a selection of cured meats, mini vegetable quiches and mini quiche lorraines, a warm lentil salad, black olive tapenade, a chicken liver and a herbed mushroom pâté, a fromage blanc spread and breads. Taking their main course orders, he suggested that as they had each chosen something different, they order their wine by the glass. Telling them that he would talk them through his recommended pairings.

They all agreed to this suggestion, and Jean-Pierre once again wished them *bon appétit*.

Saoirse: I did a cordon bleu cooking course. There were six of us on the course, and we would take it in turns to host the evening meal. This meant overseeing the timing of the preparation and the cooking of the various courses being served, as well as the selection of accompanying wines. It was customary for the host to say "*bon appétit*" as a signal that everyone has been served and also that the host was ready to eat. The same applies when eating in a restaurant.

Pascal: Did you do the course in France?

Saoirse: Actually, no, I did it here in the UK at a Cordon Bleu school. It was some years ago now, and the timing of the course here just happened to work better with other things I had going on then. It was quite intense. It was residential, five days a week for three weeks. Each day began at breakfast and ended late evening with dinner, which actually went into late night with drinks. I learnt so much. It was amazing.

Florian: Was there a particular reason you chose Cordon Bleu?

Saoirse: My love of French cuisine was one reason. Another reason was that my partner Patrick and I were planning to live in France. We did the course together because we were toying with the idea of opening a guest house that would serve lunch and evening meals. We didn't do that in the end. Instead, we both focused on our writing and simply enjoyed the French way of life, which we both loved. We lived in France for five years. Our life there was idyllic. I left France for London.

Maggie: What made you decide to live in France?

Saoirse: I once read, "If you really want to understand a place, love it the way it should be loved, maybe you have to live there." And so we did.

Maggie: And why did you leave France and come to London?

Saoirse: I didn't leave France. France left me. Our idyllic life in France left me. Patrick passed away just over a year ago. I couldn't bear to be there without him. Our life in France was idyllic because it was our life together, not my life alone.

Maggie: I am so sorry

The rest of the group echoed Maggie's words.

Florian: I am so sorry for not knowing Saoirse.

Saoirse smiled at the group and thanked them.

Saoirse: You would have had no way of knowing, Florian. I didn't talk about it because it was too raw, too painful. When we met, it was so nice not to have to talk about it. It was so nice to be able to talk about something else, life in general, books in particular. First with you, Florian, and then with all of you when Florian brought us together because of our love of reading and our interest in people's WorkLife stories. Shared discussions over food and drinks was such a nice experience for me. I use the word 'nice' intentionally because I think as a word it's underrated and gets a lot of bad press, but for me being able to describe something as 'nice' is a beautiful thing.

It's one of two beautiful things I've discovered in the last year. Before Patrick died, he was in a lot of pain. Through him, I discovered the first beautiful thing: if you really love someone, you want more for them than you want for yourself. I wanted him to fight his illness, I wanted him to stay. But that was for me. But more than that, I wanted him to go. That was for him.

I was so immensely sad when he passed away, but I was also immensely relieved for him because he had found his peace. He was no longer in pain. But me, I'm in pain every day. I miss him so much.

We met as students, and we had forty wonderful years together. He is part of who I am. He will always be with me, and I will never forget him. But when I have a moment, that's not a painful reminder that he is gone; our chats when we first met Florian, our conversations as a group, our shared experiences of books, stories, food and drinks. The things that I can describe as being nice. That's the second beautiful thing I've discovered.

I left France for London because I wanted to lose myself. I wanted somewhere I could be anonymous. Where no one knew my story, where people weren't always asking how I was or feeling sorry for me. Patrick and I have wonderful family and friends in Ireland and wonderful friends in France, all of whom were well-intentioned when enquiring how I was and wanting to talk about him and share stories. But it was too raw, too painful for me to do that; and so as much as I knew I was surrounded by people who loved both Patrick and me, I couldn't be around them because it was too painful. And so I chose London as a place where I believed I could avoid pain, that although coming from a place of love and concern, was still pain.

Another reason I don't talk about it is because it brings the conversation down. I don't want that to happen this evening. I shared my story because tonight brought up a lot for me. The restaurant, the food, the drink reminded me so much of our life in France. I also shared because I felt I could. I felt I could be vulnerable with you all. Because over the last few months, you've shared your vulnerabilities. That really touched me because to do that requires trust in each other and within the group. I felt privileged to be trusted with your stories, your sharing. I felt privileged to be part of a group that has been so supportive of what people wanted to share. I felt able to share, to show my vulnerability because I trust each and every one of you. I want to thank you for that. But I don't want to make this evening about me or to bring down the conversation. I just felt I needed to tell you. I also feel my story is relevant to the case.

Because I feel in some ways, I have been self-sabotaging: my happiness, my life, my work. I have things I'm not working on because they remind me too much of what I've lost.

I think I've been running away. Running away from people who loved me, who wanted to help with my pain. I didn't want help. While on the one hand, I think I wanted to protect myself from the pain of being reminded of my wonderful life with Patrick by people who had shared many of those moments with us, I think I also wanted to indulge my pain by wallowing in it alone. I think maybe I have been self-sabotaging.

My life in London hasn't been bad. In fact, it's been good. I haven't been unhappy, but I also haven't had the happiness I experienced with Patrick, and in a way, I don't know that I want that. We had a wonderful life together. Our five years in France were idyllic, we were blissfully happy, and in some way, I don't want to be that happy again, because that happiness was my life with Patrick, and I don't want to lose that, because if I lose that, then I lose Patrick.

So to avoid that from happening, I left everyone and everything that was part of that happiness. That's why I think I have been self-sabotaging.

Something more may come up as we continue our discussion, I don't know what will come up, but I feel something stirring within me. I may say more, I may not, but I felt I needed to tell you my story, to perhaps allow you to know where I'm coming from. I know for me when each of you shared your personal story, it helped me to understand more deeply, and I really appreciated that. I felt I wanted to do the same.

The group were silent. As Saoirse looked at each one of them, she saw the tears that were welling up in their eyes. She sensed this would happen, which was why she hadn't shared her story before. Wanting to somehow move the conversation on while letting them know she understood and appreciated their reaction, she continued:

Saoirse: I'm sorry, I know that was a lot. I actually didn't think I was going to say so much. I was able to because of the space you gave me, thank you. I know it's going to be hard to pick up the mood from here. I hope we can.

Florian gave voice to the group's feelings.

Florian: We're all so sorry, Saoirse. Thank you for sharing your story with us in such a beautiful way. The love you and Patrick had for each other was so special. Losing him was so sad.

Saoirse smiled at the group, and thanked them.

Although the group were immensely saddened by Saoirse's story, they wanted to respect her request to pick the mood up. They could see that she wanted to move the conversation back to the case study and book, and so this is what they did.

Annie said the first thing that came into her mind to get the conversation going.

Annie: Caitlin said what she said – the feedback, suggesting they read the work of Gallwey – but that was it. She then left them to their own devices. Was her input enough? Could she have done more?

Saoirse recognised she needed to contribute early to let people know she was OK. If she went quiet, she sensed the group would be concerned about her. She felt she needed to keep the momentum that Annie had started going. And she really did want to bring the conversation back to the case and the book.

Saoirse: When I read the case study, I wondered that too, but then when I read the preface to the book, it explained where she might have been coming from in doing this: "The capacity to adapt and shift our thinking is critical to success – the challenge is how to transform institutions that have been hardwired for consistency, control and predictability into cultures where learning, surprise and discovery are truly valued." I think Caitlin did more to help them by not doing more. In that, I think she gave them the permission to do for themselves. I got a sense the culture at their organisation was one where learning, surprise and discovery are truly valued.

Benny: I also think it has something to do with discovering how to overcome inner obstacles such as fear of failure or self-doubt. Because this is necessary in helping to change your outlook on work. Gallwey talks about how this can transform it to a new and positive experience, and goes on to talk about the realisation of genuine potential – the gap between potential and performance. That discovery needed to come from Samantha and Josh. I agree, Saoirse, I think it was Caitlin's way of pushing or guiding them towards this discovery for themselves.

Pascal: I believe that it is so true that: "The manager or employee who has the courage and commitment to really learn about learning will find concepts and practices that will turn the intention of a learning organisation into a day-to-day lived experience." I loved those lines.

Maggie: What really stood out for me was when Gallwey talked about traditional strategies for learning involving extracurricular activities – training events, special programmes, meetings about creating a learning culture. That stood out for me because he said those strategies reinforce the limiting belief that learning and doing are separate and competing activities. That we become concerned about the transfer of learning – how to take the learning and bring it back into the workplace. He advocates that learning and doing are both parts of a bigger whole. I thought, wow, there is so much truth in that and so much to unpick. I felt both excited and overwhelmed by what that short paragraph opened up to me.

Florian: I know what you mean, Maggie, but then he brought it back to three simple principles: value awareness, consciousness and paying attention to what is happening within and around us. When I read that, I thought, OK, I'm going to be able to see the wood for the trees. Before that I was concerned it was going to be too dense of a read. And he got to that quite early, so that was good.

Maggie: Actually, Benny, I smiled when I read this: "In our Western culture, as soon as you say the words awareness and attention, it is labelled New Age, and the theory is dismissed as a form of Californian dreaming. It's not." Even though I joke and jibe with you about this, I've come to realise it's so not. I think my jokes and jibes are my way of resisting things that are bubbling up within me or around me, that I'm becoming more aware and more conscious of because I don't understand what it is that's happening. I need to figure it out, and I really liked that.

I feel it has something to do with this: "People care about the workplace culture, its relationships, the opportunity to fulfil their potential, and the chance to learn and improve their skills." I'm mulling something over. I'm not ready to share it yet, but I will when I've figured it out.

The group smiled at Maggie. There was something lovely in that moment. None of them ever gave unsolicited advice or rushed in to try to solve a problem that any one of them was experiencing. This was lovely because it demonstrated that everyone believed that individually they each had what they needed within themselves to solve their own problems. It was also a lovely moment because it showed that each of them could say what they wanted to say. When they wanted to say it, there was never any pressure.

There was also an unspoken acknowledgement in this moment that they had been able to move the conversation on as Saoirse had asked. In a quiet, slightly hushed manner within themselves, they each felt a sense of relief that they had been able to do this. They had all felt the need to speak early, in the same way Saoirse had. Now they all sensed the conversation would continue to flow in a way that was natural, with everyone contributing as they always did, because something came to mind that they wanted to say, as opposed to feeling they needed to say something.

Florian: I can understand why they both chose the *Inner Game Of Work* from Gallwey's body of work, in that it certainly seemed the most obvious choice to help them in the challenge they were facing. And although I didn't feel the need to read the other books that were published before this one, I did find it interesting that the principles and methods of the Inner Game came from the fundamental discoveries about learning and coaching from his experience teaching tennis. And that the simple principles and methods of the Inner Game were based on a profound trust in the student's natural capability to learn from direct experience. And that success on this path depends on the participant's "willingness to grant a radical level of trust to themselves".

Maggie: I liked the three principles that helped Samantha and Josh. Although I had more clarity on the first two, I'm still mulling over the third one. What I mean is:

The first one: The Power of Nonjudgemental Awareness. When Gallwey realised that 'should and shouldn't' instructions get in the way. And when the coach is not interested in judging, and an individual is relatively free of self-judgement, and Self 1 type controls, that it helped to reverse the cycle of self-interference. Which, in turn, leads people to feel better about themselves, and they then produced naturally better results.

Benny: Yes, I liked how he described it as first seeming like magic and then realising it was a natural magic, the way learning is supposed to be. I used to coach a football team back home. As a coach, I can really relate to what he said: "My first responsibility is to maintain a nonjudgemental focus, to provide appropriate opportunity for natural learning, and stay out of the way." And how his job was to "help the student to maintain focus while trusting in Self 2's capacity to learn directly from experience."

Maggie: Ah yes, which brings me to the second of the three principles: Trust in Self. He said that perhaps the most difficult thing about this new learning process "was that both the coach and the student had to learn to trust the natural learning process." They both "had to trust that as awareness increased, effective learning and change would take place." He talks about "learning from the inside out, rather than from the outside in." And that "to realise that the final authority and responsibility for learning lies within the individual doing the learning is contrary to much of our conditioning. Yet this principle of trust in oneself is at the heart of finding a better way to change."

I found that powerful and empowering, and I think that's what Caitlin was doing, in effectively leaving both Samantha and Josh to their own devices after directing them to the Inner Game. She was, in effect, empowering them to empower themselves, to take responsibility for their own learning, and to realise and believe that they had what was needed within themselves to do this.

Benny: Yes, again, as a coach, I can relate to that. I knew, as a coach, my actions could either support the players' self-trust or undermine it. I also had to learn to be patient enough to let go of my desire to control the learning, and when I did, as he said, "it took place at its own pace and in a much more elegant and effective way than could ever have happened using a teacher-centred command-and-control methodology."

Maggie: And the third of the three principles: Keep Choice with the Choice-maker. What did that mean for you?

Benny: I can relate to this from when I played football. Over the years, the teams I played with had different coaches. Many used the old teacher-centred approach and maintained most of the important choices during practice games until Doug, who gave the choice back to us, the players. I don't remember him explaining his reasoning behind this, but I do remember that it really worked, and for exactly the reasons Gallwey gives. Because the learning took place within us, the players. We learnt to make choices, and these choices fuelled our learning. We also became more aware of the choices we were making and the reason behind those choices, which, as he says, "was an essential part of the learning process." And "it kept the initiative for learning and change in the hands of the student." It definitely gave me a greater sense of personal involvement and participation. That's what it meant for me. Does that help?

Maggie: Yes, thanks, I understood the principle, but it always helps me when I can put it into context of experiences – other people's or my own, or my wants or needs.

Benny: Which is exactly what Samantha and Josh did. Some of what they took from it was generic, but more of it was specific to their experience, their individual wants or needs. I think that's what Gallwey wanted from his work: for people to adapt and adopt it to serve their wants and needs in the context of their experiences – present, future and past.

Annie: Talking of present, future and past, I liked how he described this: "Awareness was about knowing the present situation with clarity. Choice as about moving in a desired direction in the future. And Trust in one own inner-resources was the essential link that enabled that movement." I related Trust to the past to help me make sense of this. For example, I mean our learning experience to date, our natural attributes, our skills. When he described these as three sides of a triangle, saying each side complemented and supported each other. The more we trust, the easier it is to be aware. The more aware we are, the easier it is to see our choices. I made a mental note to remind myself of that. I also think that was a simple way of thinking about it that helped Samantha and Josh too.

Maggie: And the work environment between our own ears. Our thoughts, feelings, values, assumptions, definitions, attitudes, desires and emotions all contribute to this internal environment. This is, of course, impacted by the external environment or the company culture. Some companies are controlling, but as a company, I don't think A-Z was. The interference or inner conflict Samantha and Josh were experiencing came from somewhere else – something within them, some other external conditioning that had impacted them. Their Self 1 – learning to quieten that internal conversation and trust in their Self 2 voice that can talk about what is real in the external environment they work within.

Cécile and Laurent arrived with their main courses, and as they served their main and accompanying side dishes, Jean-Pierre engaged with them, suggesting the best wine pairing to complement each of their chosen dishes.

He suggested Viognier, a white wine from the Rhône Valley, to accompany Annie's *soupe à l'oignon*, saying this wine brings out the natural, caramelised sweetness of the onions, while adding a lovely, crisp floral character that will complement the cheese and garlic beautifully.

Benny was having *steak frites*. As he liked his steak rare, which according to Jean-Pierre lessens the tannin in any accompanying wine. He suggested a young Cabernet Sauvignon because it is highly tannic and intense and brings a more mellow experience to the pairing.

For Maggie's *le gigot d'agneau*, Jean-Pierre said the tender texture and the tastiness of the lamb required a lighter finer wine with a discreet touch of woody, red and black fruits, suggesting a fruity Burgundy.

The secret to a great *coq au vin*, Jean-Pierre said, is to use the best wine you can in the cooking, and this follows through in the wine pairing. A red Burgundy, he said, was the perfect accompaniment to Florian's chosen dish. Together they embodied the true spirit of French cuisine: a delicious rustic and hearty dish enhanced by the sensual aroma of the wine that classified the land.

Jean-Pierre said that not only is a red Burgundy the best wine to pair with Pascal's *boeuf bourguignon*, it's also the best wine for cooking this dish. Another French staple, from rustic peasant origins, this rich stew braised in red wine, he said, has earned its place as a traditional dish of French haute cuisine. A fruit-driven, full-bodied Burgundy has just enough acidity to refresh the palate for every bite of this hearty dish.

Saoirse's *confit de canard*, Jean-Pierre said, is homely and intense and needs an equally intense wine to accompany it. The perfect pairing is a full-bodied Malbec with robust tannins and powerful dark fruits. It reveals a smokiness that matches the rustic nature of this dish.

As the three of them poured their wines, Saoirse asked what brought them to work in the restaurant industry.

Jean-Pierre said his parents both worked in healthcare, and that the conversations around their dinner table had always been about taking care of people. Their work and those conversations is what inspired him to work in the service industry. He went to catering college and began to learn about food and drink, which he found really interesting. He quickly realised that his interest wasn't in preparing and cooking food but in the hospitality side of the business: welcoming guests, making sure people had a great experience. That's what led him to work front of house.

Cécile said that she was studying International Hospitality Management and that one of the highlights of the course for her is the internship programme. This is what brought her here to London and to working with and learning from Jean-Pierre and the team. She said she thinks her disposition is naturally suited to front-of-house work. The course and the internship programme combined help her to fine-tune her attributes and skills and also develop management expertise.

Laurent said he's also studying International Hospitality Management and that he's more drawn to the management side of things. He loves the academic rigour of the programme. He feels this is enhanced by the combined approach of learning from leading experts in academia and industry practice through the internship. This is also what brought him here to London and to working with and learning from Jean-Pierre and the team.

Ensuring they had everything they needed, the three wished them *bon appétit.*

Florian: Jean-Pierre is greatly respected within international hospitality management for the great work he does supporting both students entering the industry and people already working within the industry. He's done and continues to do great work to champion the people within the industry.

Pascal: That's so good to hear, and his passion is very evident in a subtle way. To use Cécile's word, his disposition is so evident and yet so subtle.

They all murmured in agreement as they each took the first mouthful of their chosen French classical dish. Their choices may have been different, but their immediate reaction was the same, voiced by Benny in his best French accent – "*Superbe*" – met with a resounding "Mmmmmm"... followed by a moment of respectful silence.

Saoirse served herself from the wonderful array of accompanying vegetable dishes.

Saoirse: You know, Annie, summer in France is just the perfect time to be a vegetarian. There is such a variety of Mediterranean vegetables that bring great colour and flavour to meals. Beautifully washed down with a glass of chilled rosé.

Pascal: Ah yes, that's so true.

He laughed and helped himself to a serving of ratatouille.

Pascal: And do you know something else, ratatouille might have been the hero in the story of the film, but in my story growing up, it was the villain of my school dinners. But in as much as I despised ratatouille as a school kid, I now think of it as the hero and undisputed king of French vegetarian food.

Actually, looking back, I now realise how amazing the food we were served at school was and still is. The chef at our school took such immense pride in the food she cooked and served up. Now ratatouille brings back such good memories for me; it's my go-to comfort food. I can't eat it without feeling happy. Philippe describes it as evoking a feeling of sunshine and says eating a plate of ratatouille makes everything all right.

Saoirse: When we had friends to stay who were vegetarian, Patrick used to say, the only limit to eating well as a vegetarian in France is your vegetable tray and your imagination.

Annie: These dishes, this experience, is better than a holiday in Paris, or at least as good as a mini-break.

They all laughed in agreement.

Maggie: Talking about heroes and villains, I think Samantha and Josh's stories began with them being the villains of their own stories, and then they became the heroes of their own individual story and their joint story. And in keeping with your film analogy, I think Caitlin was the underlying hero, or perhaps a better description is that she played the supporting role to both their leading characters. I think Samantha and Josh were both the antagonists and protagonists in this story.

Benny: I agree, and I think we can all be villains and heroes in our own stories. We can play the role of both antagonists and protagonists in our own WorkLife.

Florian: That's why Gallwey's work on the Inner Game is so important. Self 1, Self 2, is a game of opponents we all play.

Annie: The need to manage the conflict that brings about doesn't go away, but there is a way to manage it. Samantha and Josh were able to quieten their self-interference by being focused in the moment of what they were doing. It sounds so simple, but it does take practice.

Benny: Indeed, hence it warranted a chapter of its own, or two chapters – 'The Practice of Focus', and before that, 'The Focus of Attention'.

Maggie: That brings me back to what I was saying earlier about the limiting belief that learning and doing are separate and competing activities. It got a little dense for me again there, but I don't think that's a bad thing. In fact, I think it's the opposite. I mentioned earlier that I feel there's something stirring within me, I don't know what it is yet, but I get a sense that it's something good, some sort of awakening. Gosh, Benny, I think I sound like a California dreamer.

Benny: You know what, Maggie, I'm beginning to think that might be a compliment.

Maggie: Oh, it is, it most definitely is. But I digress. I still haven't figured out what all this means for me, but it's something about: "Shift from a focus on training to a focus on learning, designed around the learner's experience rather than the teacher's expertise." I'll figure it out. I know I will. Sorry, I'm rambling.

The group smiled at her. It was visibly apparent that something was happening to/for Maggie, about which she was excited. They hadn't really seen that in her before, and they knew it was both meaningful and important to her, and they also knew that she would figure it out for herself.

Annie: I liked that he reminded us of the simplicity of Focus – it's simply about paying attention, doing whatever we're doing. And that it's a skill that can be practised through any activity – reading a book, talking and listening to another person, solving a problem, working with others or working alone. And that the most important thing about the practice is that it cannot be forced. Trying hard to concentrate doesn't work. It produces frustration and narrowness of vision.

I think Samantha and Josh both experienced frustration and narrowness of vision, which in turn caused them to lose their focus of attention. The coaching questions he shared that he used with his students were helpful and also very simple. For example, when he saw the focus of attention was lost, he would simply ask: "Where did your attention go?" He said: "The student would reflect for a moment and then express surprise his attention had gotten distracted as if without his permission." And "that just noticing what had pulled attention away was usually sufficient to weaken that distraction and allow for greater focus."

That's a very simple process and great for his students, because he was there with them in the moment. But that would have been more difficult for Samantha and Josh because Chris, their coach, wasn't with them in the moment. So they would either have to catch themselves in that moment and ask the question of themselves, or reflect on it later, maybe by rewinding the moment and ask the question of themselves; or tell Chris about the moment, for him to ask the question of them. It still remains a simple process, but it's most likely not going to be as in the moment as the situation he described with his student. But I guess that's the whole point of the chapter – it's the 'Practice of Focus'. I'm pleased there's an assignment with the case to help develop the power of observation. I'm going to work with that.

The rest of the group said they were also going to work with the observations assignment.

Florian: Yes, the Practice of Focus is definitely ongoing, and as he described in the stories he shared about the basketball player and golfer, there will most likely be times when we think we have a handle on it and be able to manage it for ourselves, with the help of the principles of the Inner Game, and there will be times when we need the support of a coach. Both to stay focused and enjoy learning as Self 2, and to quieten the interference of Self 1.

Benny: There was one story in the book that I so saw myself in. It was the example he gave of Self 1 and Self 2 listening. The small group meeting he was in, where there was a middle-aged manager who provoked his Self 1. Because almost every time she spoke, it was to give advice to someone about something. "If a person was expressing a concern or a problem, she would automatically come up with: Why don't you try doing it this way?" His Self 1 was commenting, "Advice when it's not asked for is just the kind of thing I hate." I can so relate to that. And then, when he shared it with someone else, they acknowledged they had noticed the behaviour but had ignored it because they were interested in other things being said. Going on to say: "Besides, I know her, and in spite of the fact she's a bit free with her advice, she is one of the most intelligent and compassionate managers around." He said he "was shocked. It was as if they had been totally different meetings, and were talking about two totally different people." I've so been there. That's so bad, right?

Pascal: Well, I don't know, is it? There are definitely those kind of people out there, and they drive me insane too. Unsolicited advice, in my book, no matter how well-meaning, is the worst. That did make me wonder about the people who had shared their advice with Samantha and Josh. I know they were experts in their field, but their advice could have played into Samantha and Josh self-sabotaging. The case indicated it was given with good intention, but it could still have caused problems. Giving or receiving advice is tricky. I know Caitlin described it as feedback, and I know the importance of feedback, but there's also a need to know how to give and receive good feedback. That particular part of the story/case study did raise questions for me.

Florian: I think going back to the story shared in the book, when he realised that the meeting he had been in was not the one he wanted to return to and that he had a choice – not whether or not to return to the meeting, but what he would listen for while he was at the meeting. He made a simple choice to listen for what he could appreciate in the group rather than what he could criticise. That was the key point that helped resolve that issue for me. I had the same questions as you did about advice or feedback Samantha and Josh had been given, and I also have the same reaction to unsolicited advice. Now I have a different way to manage it; I have a choice to listen or not.

Annie: And Caitlin did say listening to the right people, including themselves, is a gift, and listening to the wrong people, including themselves, is a trap. So, I think she was on the right track with this.

Benny: Now that you put it like that, I agree. I think I am so automatically incensed by unsolicited advice-givers that I immediately put up my guard and block them out. I'm not there with that yet. That's something I'm going to have to work on. But now that I have the awareness, I can work on nonjudgemental awareness, then trust in Self 2, and then keeping choice with me, the choice maker. It's a simple process, but it's not easy – but that's where the practice of focus comes in, right?

In a chorus-like response, the group nodded their heads and said "Yes", as much to themselves as to Benny.

Maggie: Has anyone ever worked with an Inner Game coach?

Another group response. This time they all shook their heads and said "No".

Benny: No, but the experience I mentioned earlier, with our coach Doug, was somewhat similar, and while I certainly haven't practised it exactly as described in the coaching I've done, I think I have practised some of the principles. Certainly not in a way that was as finely tuned as described in the book – more loosely, I think it would be fair to say. But I think it is something I would like to learn and model in my work.

Florian: I think I would like to learn and model it in my work too. It comes across as being simple yet really effective in the case study for Samantha and Josh and the stories in the book too. But I think similar to the principles we've discussed as being simple, that doesn't mean it would be easy. I think it would definitely require the Practice of Focus.

Pascal: I agree. It would require quietening the Self 1 interference to allow Self 2 learning. I also think it would be quite good to learn, but I'm not sure how it would work in my line of work.

Maggie: What is it a management consultant does again?

Pascal gave her that all familiar 'Really' look over his signature Clark Kent styled glasses.

Maggie: I'm joking, I'm joking.

Which was true. However, she was actually wondering something else, but she wasn't cheeky or brave enough to ask, even in a joking way. She was wondering if Pascal's attire this evening was to represent the French flag, as he was wearing a blue suit with a red tie, red pocket hankie, matching red-rimmed glasses and a white shirt. She was convinced it was, but she thought it might be disrespectful to ask.

Pascal: However, in my volunteering work as a business consultant, I think it could be really helpful. And also, I really like the concept presented that learning and doing are both parts of a bigger whole. Because that's the only way it could work for me, and I think that's the way it would work for me, as opposed to the old way of extracurricular activities – training courses and then the worry of the transfer of learning. Just as you mentioned, Maggie, that really struck a chord with me too. I think there's so much power in learning and doing, or learning by doing.

Annie: I think Caitlin opened up that way of thinking for Samantha and Josh. We talked about the feedback they had both been given by people in their company, and we learnt how that led them to self-sabotaging themselves through what was going on within each of them. We also learnt that on being given a second chance, they agreed to be their own and each other's biggest critics and champions, to hold themselves to the highest standards. To work to come up with new ideas to challenge their excellence. We experienced their shift in thinking, which I think was to do with being excited to learn and do, whereas they started, I think, from a place where that wasn't the case. They began from a place of disconnected learning and ended up at a place of connected learning.

Gallwey summed that up for me when he talked about how in the workplace, that people working together can either excite Self 1 doubts and fears or quiet them. And "how if a worker is viewed as being less than competent, it tends to reinforce self-doubt, increase self-interference with the worker's potential, and thus fulfil a self-fulfilling prophecy for those who are looking for and expecting to find the perceived deficiency." That's what Caitlin meant when she said listening to the wrong people, including themselves, is a trap, and could become a place to hide.

Gallwey also said, "In a work team where the individual members view one another with mutual respect, encourage appropriate risk-taking, and value one another's capabilities, the internal dialogue has less of a chance to interfere, and workers perform better than when alone." I think Caitlin was setting them up for success when she asked that they work together, and I also think this was her way of rolling out the principles of the Inner Game within the workplace. She was in effect initiating the spreading of the learning and doing by people who were learning and doing. I think her role as hero – which, yes, could be described as underlying – or playing a support role, was also quite profound.

Saoirse: That is so true, Annie, and it brings me to the presentations that they both gave to Caitlin. When I first read the story, I thought, what are they going to be able to say to turn this around, but they both found a way. And they both did it in a very simple yet meaningful way for each of them. A way that expressed their awareness of the situation and their way forward, trust in themselves to do this, and that they recognised that the choices they will make are their own. I thought what they both said was both profound and simple. It was their truth, and Caitlin saw that. That, for me, was a lovely moment for all three of them.

Annie and Saoirse's words were a fitting summary of what they had all taken from the epilogue.

Jean-Pierre arrived to enquire if they were ready for their cheese course, letting them know he had prepared a selection of French cheeses for them, which included a selection of artisan vegan cheeses. He suggested Sauvignon Blanc, Champagne, Burgundy and sweet Bordeaux wines to accompany the cheeses, letting Benny know he had selected the perfect non-alcoholic wines and champagne from each region for him.

"I've never had four wines with a cheese course before," commented Maggie. "Please tell me it's not going to be the same for dessert, or is this dessert?"

Jean-Pierre said the cheese course in France comes before the desert. That cheese is not eaten as a desert and that a French cheese course is divided into four groups: beginning with simple and moving towards more complex cheeses. The wines are served in smaller glasses. Their compact size help accentuate the distinct flavours of the cheeses.

"Thank you, I love these little nuggets of learning," said Maggie. "But I need to say this, and I hope it's OK. A cheese course with four wines, even if they are smaller glasses, will definitely need to be my final course. I have to go to work tomorrow."

The rest of the group echoed Maggie's sentiment, with Annie adding that she though they might need a strong coffee to balance things out. There was a further echo of consensus on that.

Jean-Pierre smiled and departed soon to return with Cécile and Laurent carrying their selection of cheeses and accompanying wines, which Jean-Pierre introduced to an attentive table of six very enthusiastic wine connoisseurs and cheese fanciers in the making:

"First, we have *crottin de chèvre*, a goat cheese produced in the Loire valley, and a vegan goat cheese which has a cashew nut base served with a Sauvignon Blanc. The cheeses are both earthy and tart. The crisp, fruity notes of the wines draw these flavours out.

"Next, we have *brie*, a soft-ripened cheese that comes from the Brie district of France, and a vegan brie which has a coconut milk base served with champagne. The mild buttery notes of brie make it a perfect partner for the toasty flavour of champagne.

"Then we have *livarot*, a soft, pungent, washed-rind cheese from the Normandy region, and a sun-dried tomato vegan cheese served with a Burgundy. The nutty taste of the cheeses melt in the mouth and release flavours of saltiness. The flavours of red berries from the full-bodied wines enhance the cheeses with hints of spice.

"Finally, we have *roquefort*, and a vegan blue cheese served with Bordeaux sweet wines, a non-alcoholic rosé and a Sauternes. The pungent smell and sharp tanginess of the cheeses are perfectly matched with the honey flavours of the wines."

"I think rosé-coloured glasses may be the key to Learning and Doing or Learning by Doing," Maggie was quick to observe. "*À votre santé*."

Words that may have been spoken in jest, but the simplicity and profundity of that moment they were sharing resonated with each of them.

Following their lesson in French wines and cheeses, Jean-Pierre, Cécile and Laurent prepared their coffees.

Saoirse: Our cheese and wine experience reminds me of when Patrick and I ran the Medoc Marathon through the vineyards of Bordeaux. Along the route, there were twenty-three wine stops also offering cheeses and other specialities, such as oysters and steak. That's what we loved about the French way of life – they combine wine, food, sports, health and fun. Every year is a different theme and runners are expected to wear fancy dress. We learnt and loved a lot about the French way of life. A beautiful life is created by bringing simple pleasures together, fun and engaging in-the-moment experiences that create magical memories.

The group smiled at Saoirse, and Pascal said that he and Philippe had also run the Medoc Marathon, and that it holds great memories for them, too, for all the reasons Saoirse had said.

EPILOGUE

As they sipped on their espressos, which most definitely served as the perfect digestif to finish their meal, they reflected on the single most important learning they had taken from the evening.

Maggie: I want to create moments of magic where suddenly you believe anything can happen.

Benny smiled to himself and resisted the urge to call out Maggie as a California Dreamer. She had been pensive in speaking her words, and he sensed there was something deeper occurring within her.

Benny: Every step back is a step forward. We all have the power within us to turn negative things that happen in our WorkLife into something positive by first taking that step back, learning from it and then trusting our chosen step forward.
Florian: We need the awareness that can be evoked by a simple question. Great questions can be simple and profound.
Pascal: Learning and doing is the way it is meant to be.
Annie: We all have those inner voices of Self 1. They're not going to

go away, but we can learn to quieten them by turning down the volume of their interference.

Saoirse: The pursuit of self-protection can lead to self-sabotage.

Florian: Thank you again for trusting us with your story, Saoirse. I know I'm speaking for the rest of the group in saying we want to be sure you're OK, but we don't want to do this in a way that is in any way upsetting for you. How can we do that?

Saoirse: Do you know I think I am going to be OK. I wasn't sure if I would be before I shared my story, and I didn't know what else this evening would bring up for me, but I'm feeling OK, so thank you all again. I really think I'm going to be OK, but if I'm not, I'll let you know. Is that OK? And I know I've used the word OK a lot just now. I'm not sure if it was intentional. It just seemed to happen. But that's actually a pretty big deal for me to be able to use that word because it's been a long time since that word has been part of my vocabulary, and it's a good word to be able to use. So, I think I'm going to be OK. I know you all care, and that means a lot, and I appreciate it so much. I think it's best if I just take it one day at a time and if I need anything I'll let you know, is that OK?

Smiling and holding her gaze as she looked to each of them, they all assured her that was OK.

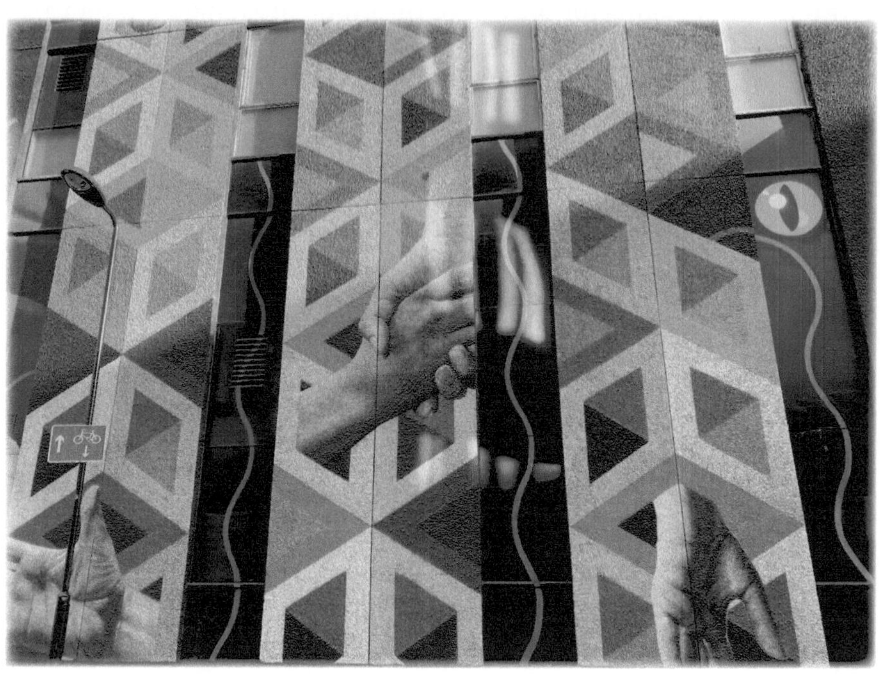

Interlude 4

Developing Your Power of Observation Assignment

Featuring the First Thursdays Art Bus Tour and accompanied by a nightcap

The group met at the Whitechapel Gallery to join the First Thursdays Art Bus Tour. Florian had suggested they do it together for a couple of reasons: 1. He knew it had piqued Saoirse's interest when she first heard about it; 2. Following on from Saoirse sharing her story, he and the rest of the group wanted to find a way to check in that she was OK, that wasn't in any way intrusive. Something they could do, that was active in an interesting and fun way, where the group didn't feel the need to ask directly how she was, and Saoirse didn't feel the need to tell them. Florian felt this was a nice way to show they cared, so did Saoirse and the rest of the group.

Annie had asked if they could talk through their experience of working through the Developing Your Power of Observation Assignment if time permitted. She had found sharing the experience of the other assignments really helpful. Florian suggested they could do it over a drink on their return to the Whitechapel Gallery while experiencing their 'After Hours' reception. Everyone agreed.

While they waited for the bus to start their tour, Florian shared the

history of the Whitechapel Gallery, beginning with a quote from The Independent: "If anywhere, this is the place to promote a new belief in the good of art." Then a quote from the gallery itself: "Our history has always been our future."

He said the Gallery was founded in 1901, with the purpose of bringing great art to the people in East London, Britain and the world. That it has a history of firsts and has always had a connection with politics, society and world events – driven by the desire to share the wider context of art. He told the story of how in 1939, the Stepney trade union approached the Gallery about a Spanish artist who wanted to raise consciousness about the Spanish civil war. The artist was called Picasso.

As always, the group loved Florian's interesting snippets of their neighbourhood history, which they expressed as they boarded the bus, ready to be taken to the first gallery on their tour:

The Art Pavilion, Mile End Park.

The information pack had shared that the building is buried in a grass bank and has a glass frontage that overlooks a small lake. Earth-roofed and close to Regents Canal, its secluded yet accessible location makes it the ideal space for exhibitions and installations.

During the twenty-minute journey to their destination, Florian shared the history he had gleaned about this community-orientated gallery. He told them how the gallery hosts a varied line-up of exhibitions that are free to all. It supports local artists through its flexible and adaptable space-hire initiative. The natural lighting through the stunning glass wall and its unique architecture creates the perfect setting for artists to showcase their work.

Maggie said Mile End Park had been her playground as a child. Wanting to understand its history, she had learnt it had been created on industrial land devastated by Second World War bombing.

Pascal shared that having previously visited the gallery with Philippe, they had discovered the park follows the Regent's Canal from Victoria Park to Limehouse Basin. He said, walking the Regent's Canal route was something they enjoyed doing at weekends.

Annie said Mile End Park is one of her favourite London parks to walk in and explore. She said that the meadows and woodland throughout the park support an amazing variety of wildlife, including birds, butterflies and bees. She said she loves that there is wildlife everywhere.

At each gallery on the tour, guests are welcomed by the artist or curator, who gives a brief introduction to the exhibition before people take their time to wander and appreciate the artist's work on display. Each tour lasts for two hours and visits three galleries. Each stop is between thirty and forty minutes.

The next stop was:

Raven Row

Once again, on their journey to this non-profit contemporary art exhibition centre in Spitalfields, Florian shared the history he had gleaned. He said the gallery stands on the part of Artillery Lane that was known as Raven Row until 1895. The gallery was constructed within domestic rooms of adjoining houses (numbers 56 and 58), which had been built around 1690 on land that was previously a weapons practice ground. In the Middle Ages, it was the site of the monastery of St. Mary Spital, the largest hospital in Europe. In the 1750s, the buildings were transformed into luxury shops in the Rococo style by Huguenot silk merchants. In the 1800s, the weaving economy in Spitalfields collapsed, and the area became impoverished. In the early twentieth century, 56 and 58 Artillery Lane housed many families who worked in the local food markets.

Benny said that the gallery is funded by its founding director, Alex Sainsbury. Sharing his story, he said the supermarket heir grew up surrounded by his family's fabulous art collection and that he always knew he wanted to do something artistic but struggled to know what that was, until he found his calling in the shape of the grade-one listed building, which had sat empty for twelve years. With the help of architects, he spent four years restoring it before it opened in 2013, and Raven Row became part of London's visual culture.

The final stop was:

Public

This contemporary art gallery in Middlesex Street, located in the heart of Shoreditch with a diverse international programme, focuses on emerging artists.

Florian shared that the small gallery showcased an impressive monthly rotation of inspiring artists. He said that it was the first newly built art gallery in London since the opening of the Hayward Gallery in 1968. The street is home to the five-centuries-old street market, Petticoat Lane, and is also home to Middlesex University. The area has an incredible history, and there are plans to commission a cultural programme to help people who live, work and study in the area to celebrate their Petticoat Lane heritage and presence. He said the area has gone through two rough decades, which began with the decline of traditional street markets and saw it appear on the Heritage at Risk register. A study by the London Assembly in 2008 called for steps to be taken to protect Petticoat Lane from developers and the rocketing rents that were forcing out street traders.

Saoirse said she loved how Florian brought together snippets of history and current-day happenings. She said the tour had reminded her of the beautiful community of people they're all part of, from Whitechapel to Mile End to Spitalfields and Shoreditch. A community group of creative enterprises, stallholders and businesses. She particularly loves the diversity of the streets of Shoreditch and how they retain their history while welcoming contemporary life.

The rest of the group agreed with Saoirse's summation of their evening and their neighbourhood.

On their arrival back at the Whitechapel Gallery, the group were

welcomed by the After Hour's team with a drink of their choice – a soft drink, a beer, or a glass of red or white wine. Finding a comfortable space, they raised their glasses in acknowledgement and appreciation of a lovely evening discovering and rediscovering the richness of the culture on their doorstep and a short bus ride away. Brought together through the power of art.

Maggie: I think our evening was perfect for bringing together everything presented in the Developing Your Power of Observation Assignment. I pride myself on having strong powers of observation. I need to. It's a skill that's crucial in my work. But tonight felt different. I think the assignment helped in my appreciation of art – noticing detail and connecting it to a bigger story: the artist's story, and their world and also how their work and story fits into the wider world. I'm not sure what that means in the context of my WorkLife. I'm going to follow the step of Developing a Practice of Continuous Self-Feedback, as suggested by journalling, to stay in contact with my thoughts and the world around me.

Saoirse: As a writer, I've always journalled to stay in contact with my thoughts and also as a way to try to understand how other people think. The people I've written about as a journalist and a blogger. It helps when I interview people to know how to ask good questions and how to take their answers and turn them into an interesting story. A story that expresses who they are, what they care about, what they stand for and what they stand against. What stood out for me most in the assignment was the step 'Develop a Practice of Insightful Self-Questioning', and the proposed questions to ask of oneself:

Where am I now?
Where have I come from? What's next?
Then what?

These aren't new to me. As a practice this step has served me well throughout my WorkLife. It's a practice I dip in and out of. The reason it stood out for me was it served as a reminder to revisit the practice of insightful self-questioning.

Benny: I liked the Words of Wisdom in the assignment: "Implement ideas in real life, develop a practice of doing, stay observant, stay curious." This stood out for me in a similar way to what you've just described, Saoirse. It's a practice I've followed throughout my WorkLife, that has served me well. It's a practice that I dip in and out of also. The assignment served as a reminder to revisit the practice.

Annie: The assignment was new to me. I don't think I've ever practised observing. Not knowingly, anyway. So I started at the very first step: Re-Wind/Replay Your Day. As suggested, I took a two-minute event from my day – it was a brief interaction I had in a coffee shop. Then I replayed it in my mind, observing myself when I was in that moment, along with everything else that was going on around me. It felt strange the first time I did it. I couldn't really get into it. I've repeated it a few times now – same situation, my brief daily interaction in a coffee shop. It's becoming more accessible in that I'm beginning to be able to get back into the moment. I don't think I'm quite there with it yet, but I will continue as I believe it is a helpful skill.

Florian: I started with that step as well. The two-minute event I took from my day was from our daily team meeting. I meet with my team at the beginning of each shift by way of checking in with everyone, addressing anything that needs to be addressed. We have well-oiled processes in place that help things to run smoothly, but it's always important to check in to make sure everyone is OK. When I replayed it in my mind, I focused on everything else that was going on around me. Like you, Annie, I found it strange the first time I did it. I couldn't really get into it either. I've also repeated it a few times now – same situation, our daily team meeting. I'm beginning to get back into the moment more easily, but I also think I'm not quite there with it yet. I'm going to continue because I want to be able to pick up on what's going on around me and within people. I mentioned before that I support a culture of openness, where people can say what they need to say. I know that's not always easy for everyone, and I want to be sensitive to emotions that might be holding people back.

Pascal: I'm familiar with the steps of the assignment. They have served me well in my WorkLife. It's a long time ago now, but I began as the assignment suggests by taking one moment from my day, replaying it in my mind at the end of the day. Then building on that one moment to many moments.

Then as in the assignment I focused on the step 'Building Your Power of Observation' by asking myself whatever question I thought was most important to make sense of what I observed throughout my day and how it applied to my WorkLife. For me, that usually meant trying to understand what was going on within the minds of my clients. Quite often, this opened my awareness to their unspoken concerns. Concerns that needed to be brought out into the open and addressed in order to proceed in a way that was in the best interest of all parties. The assignment helped me develop my intuition and put my gut instincts into the context of what was going on around me. This gave me the confidence to voice whatever that was, which in turn helped to ease the process of the merger, take-over, or whatever situation was happening. Because it demonstrated my ability to understand people's concerns and my desire to move beyond those in a way that best served the wants and needs of all parties.

Annie: Wow, that's so fascinating to hear how the assignment can and has helped you all in your WorkLives. I don't know that I'm ever going to need it in the same way as you all have, but knowing that it has helped you all in ways that are both different but overlap too, I'm definitely going to continue with it. Thank you. Cheers to the power of observation.

The group laughed and raised their glasses in a toast to the power of observation.

Developing Your Power of Observation Assignment

Now it's time for you to develop your power of observation with your nightcap of choice.

Finely tuned powers of observation is a powerful technique to keep your WorkLife real. It will enable you to be acutely aware of everything that is going on around you, and it will allow you to know how to harness that for your good.

So, make your nightcap of choice, ready to set to work with your first assignment, designed to help you to begin to develop your power of observation by taking notice of one moment from your day.

RE-WIND/REPLAY YOUR DAY OBSERVATION ASSIGNMENT

A Day in The Life of... Drumroll... You!

To begin to develop your power of observation, take something that happened in your day. I like to suggest a two-minute event, but it can be shorter or longer. It could be a brief interaction you had in a coffee shop or in a meeting. It could be something you observed as you went about your day without interacting with anyone. It could be a moment when you were at home alone doing something.

Now replay that in your mind. The idea is to observe yourself when you were in that moment, along with everything else that was going on around you.

Simple? Yes! The power of observation really is that simple.

* * *

Your second assignment is to help you to develop your power of observation by capturing more moments from your day.

DEVELOPING YOUR POWER OF OBSERVATION ASSIGNMENT

The power of observation becomes more and more powerful the more observant you become as you go about your daily WorkLife.

Find something to capture every day. Begin with one moment, building to many moments.

Maybe there will be days when you think there is nothing to observe because they are very normal days. But actually, normal days are great days because they force you to be a little more mindful, a little more aware, a little more creative.

* * *

Your third assignment is to help you to make sense of what you observed throughout your day and how it applies to what you want to achieve in your WorkLife.

BUILDING YOUR POWER OF OBSERVATION ASSIGNMENT

At the end of your day, ask yourself the question that you consider is the most important you can ask in that moment, by way of making sense of what you observed throughout your day and how it applies to what you want to achieve in your WorkLife.

If you cannot figure out what your most important question should be, ask:

What is the most important question?

Write down your response in your journal, and then let it go.

The next morning sit down and journal any answer to that question, anything that comes up through your stream of consciousness. Self-expression in your journal will help you to tap into your power of observation, to turn your WorkLife story into a work of art.

DEVELOP A PRACTICE OF CONTINUOUS SELF-FEEDBACK

Continuing to journal is an effective way to keep in contact with your own thoughts, not only for self-expression and self-knowledge but for observation of the world around you. Taking down your thoughts before they escape you is a good way to sharpen your observational skills.

DEVELOP A PRACTICE OF INSIGHTFUL SELF-QUESTIONING

To tighten your self-feedback loop, ask yourself the following questions:

Where am I now?
Where have I come from? What's next?
Then what?

WORDS OF WISDOM

Implement ideas in real life, develop a practice of doing, stay observant, stay curious.

London Borough of Hackney
Crooked Billet Yard E2
Oi!
Can we
have
our art
back?

Meeting of Styles

5

May

The Case of Crushing Feedback and the Healing Power of Voice

Featuring *The Vocal Arts Workbook: A Practical Course for Developing the Expressive Range of Your Voice* by David Carey and Rebecca Clark Carey, accompanied by Italian cuisine

Italian food was on the menu tonight, and that menu was all about the shared experience. The Italian restaurant Florian was taking them to was built on the philosophy of sharing great Italian food with the people you choose to spend time with.

Tucked away on one of the many side streets of Shoreditch, the restaurant was situated behind a brick wall. On booking, guests are given a secret code to tap into the door entry system to get in, which adds to the sense of clandestineness. As the group stepped inside, they were immediately struck by the relaxed feeling of warmth it emanated. Sofia, one of the co-creators, welcomed them and showed them to their table.

As they took their seats, Saoirse commented that the restaurant had a lovely personal feel to it.

"Thank you", responded Sofia. "What's important in our restaurant is the feel, as much as the look. We want people to feel comfortable in our environment, a place where you can be yourself."

"It does look lovely too," said Saoirse.

"Thank you," replied Sofia. "We wanted to create a dining room that's reminiscent of a family dining experience rather than a fancy restaurant."

Luca, Sofia's co-creator and boyfriend, came over to greet the group, bringing a jug of water, and on introducing himself, he handed them the drinks menus.

"I love your selection of cocktails and wines," said Florian. "I'm always curious to see what's new that you've added to your list."

"Thank you," responded Luca.

Addressing the group, Luca said they create their cocktails beginning from a base of seasonal herbs, fruits and edible wild flowers, which they grow themselves, and also source from both Italy and within the UK. From this base they develop the cocktails to alcoholic or non-alcoholic drinks. He said their wine list is growing slowly as they take time to personally select the best Italian wines, from north to south. Their motivation is to combine renowned wineries with emerging local producers. Every brand they represent tells a story of the Italian wine culture.

As always, the moment Saoirse hears the word 'story', her curiosity is piqued, and opening the menu she asked how they discovered and selected their wines.

Sofia said they visited Italy as often as they could. They pick a region, and roam the countryside for a few days, visiting wineries and tasting their wines, getting to know the people behind each brand, learning about their stories. Luca added that it's important to them to work with suppliers who share their principles, which is to bring the best of Italian food, drink and culture to the people they serve here in their restaurant. They are always in the pursuit of excellence, and they select who they partner with based on this. Whether that's individual suppliers, small or family enterprises or bigger companies, they need to share their passion and purpose to constantly strive for quality in their products and produce.

"This is evident in the food Sofia, Luca and their team create," said Florian. "They pay special attention to preparing dishes using seasonal produce. For this reason I asked them to prepare a selection for us to share and experience together to begin our evening."

They all thanked Florian, Sofia and Luca. The group loved and appreciated how much care and attention Florian put into creating the wonderful experiences they shared each month. He was living true to his promise of taking them on a culinary tour of their neighbourhood and they were learning so much along the way.

"Roaming the countryside visiting vineyards," Pascal said. "What a wonderful way to discover and select your wines."

Sofia smiled and said yes, telling the group that they discover so much more along the way. And how on a recent trip they took a walk after dinner, and behind their hotel there was a slope that fell away toward a landscape of olive and lemon groves, lying hazy in the evening light. Early next morning, in the glistening sunlight, they went in search of the owners and growers to discover their stories, and now they bring their produce to their restaurant.

Luca asked if they would like to taste those olives and lemons, going on to say that for their *aperitivo* they would bring olives and cheeses. He suggested a negroni or a prosecco to accompany their *aperitivo* and *antipasti*, for which they'd prepared charcuterie platters with cheeses, olives, bread, fruits, vegetables, cured meats and seafood. He finished by saying their selection of cheeses included vegan.

Maggie asked what the difference was between *aperitivo* and *antipasti.*

"The *aperitivo* begins the meal," said Luca. "Small dishes accompanied by a drink. We say in Italy *'L'appetito vien mangiando'*. Eating awakens the appetite. *Antipasti* is considered the starter and will consist of the dishes we've prepared for you."

Looking through the drinks menu, Benny asked which non-alcoholic cocktail he would suggest.

"We've created a blood orange, bitter lemon and tonic cocktail," responded Luca. "Which presents an intense orange peel aroma, packed with citrus note, giving a perfect sweet and sour balance."

"Oh yes please," said Benny. "That sounds wonderful."

"What's in a negroni?" asked Maggie.

"Gin, vermouth and campari, garnished with orange peel," answered

Luca. "It's stirred not shaken and built over ice. It also offers a pleasant mixture of bitter and sweet."

"Oh yes please," said Maggie. "That sounds like the perfect drink to awaken my appetite."

The others laughed, saying they too would like a negroni.

Luca said they would bring along their *aperitivo* now and come back with their *antipasti* a little later. Letting them know the next course they serve is pizza, of which they make two kinds of pizza: margherita and marinara. He said they'd come back to take their pizza, accompanying salads and drinks orders.

"Sofia and Luca's pizzas will take you to Naples, the birthplace of pizza," said Florian. "There, pizza making is an art. Neapolitans will rarely order anything other than a margherita or a marinara pizza."

"Thank you," said Sofia. "We remain true to Neapolitan tradition in making our pizzas."

"What is the tradition?" asked Annie.

Sofia said that the golden rules of *La Vera Pizza* – the Neapolitan Pizza Association of Naples – are that pizzas can only be cooked in wood-burning brick ovens; the crust has to be soft and light; and the *pizzaiolo* (pizza maker) must serve their time as an apprentice mastering the art.

Leaving and soon returning with their dishes and drinks, Sofia and Luca gave a brief description of the olives and cheeses in their *aperitivo*, which included lemon-infused olives and olives marinated in olive oil, a smoked vegan cheese, an almond cheese spread, mozzarella balls, a creamy burrata and an Italian flat cracker bread. They then wished them "*Buon appetito*".

Benny tasted the olives.

Benny: I think I can taste the glistening sunlight.
Maggie (laughing): Oh Benny, you really are a California dreamer

She raised her glass in a toast to Italian glistening sunlit mornings and hazy evenings, to which they all said *salute*.

Annie had chosen the case this month and began to read The Case Of The Crushing Feedback and The Healing Power of Voice, to which the accompanying book was *Vocal Arts Workbook: A Practical Course for Vocal Clarity and Expression* by David Carey and Rebecca Clark Carey.

"I find the book both refreshing and remarkable since it teaches, not by telling you what to do, but rather by first making the reader aware of their own personal bodily responses to breathing, tension, resonance etc., and to the whole process of making sound in their everyday life. In a most imaginative, and often humorous, way, it arouses our curiosity as to how we each make sound and speech in the variable circumstances of our lives." (Cicely Berry, theatre director and vocal coach)

From the back cover:
"This practical workbook helps actors to fully develop expressive voice skills to communicate thoughts and feelings with precision and power. At the heart of the book are practical projects, with examples, which enables you to: connect your breath with your voice; meet the demands of your performance; use your voice expressively with pitch and range Each chapter consists of an introductory Framework; Explorations; Exercises; Follow Up work; Suggested Texts; and Further Reading: a unique, student-centred approach not found in other voice books. The *Vocal Arts Workbook* is a complete learning programme drawing on the work of a wide range of practitioners to be used at home, as a course text, or as a way to integrate 20-30 mins of voice work into an acting class."

"Voice is about not having to live in the silence of the lonely imagination, instead sharing our thoughts and sculpting sound so that not only is meaning conveyed, but also the essence of who we are. It is about our possibility. So there is not a person on the planet who will not benefit from making sure that their voice is being true to its master, the inner self." (Fiona Shaw, actor and theatre director)

Vocal Arts Workbook, by David Carey and Rebecca Clark Carey, was originally published by Methuen in 2008 (224pp., ISBN 978-0713688245)

The Case of the Crushing Feedback and the Healing Power of Voice

"You have: 1. hard glottal attacks; 2. breathiness; 3. too much rise and fall; 4. not enough variation; 5. too monotone – you need more light and shade; 6. you're too softly spoken – you're not reaching all four corners, or the back of the room; 7. you need to drive it more; 8. you need to get out of your head..." There were more, but Aisling lost count after 8.

Aisling was absolutely crushed by this feedback. She was ready to walk.

But let's back up a little to Aisling's story.

Aisling was doing a Foundation in Drama course. She was doing this in the hope that it would help her overcome the crippling fear she had when speaking in public and also the woodenness that took over her body and movement – or rather lack thereof. This was important to her in her personal and professional growth and development in her WorkLife.

This involved attending drama school every Saturday over the course of the school year. The day was made up of three classes: 1. Movement; 2. Voice; 3. Acting. She had successfully auditioned to get a place on the course. For the audition, she was required to deliver a short monologue from a contemporary play. Her audition piece was a monologue from *Dancing at Lughnasa*, a play by Irish dramatist Brian Friel. She'd chosen this because it was set in Ireland and played to her Irish accent.

When they began their voice class, the students were required to deliver their audition pieces again, and they were given feedback on this. This was the baseline from which, over the course of the year, they would work to improve upon. Aisling got great feedback from her voice teacher, Jane. Actually, she had always gotten great feedback on her voice – unsolicited feedback. People would say to her: "You've got such a lovely voice", both in person and over the phone. She's softly spoken with an Irish lilt. She's been told her voice is "warm, welcoming, calming, interesting. It puts people at ease. Her voice lets people know she's interested in them."

At the end of the first term, they were required to give a short recital of a poem. Aisling chose a passage from *The Ballad of Reading Gaol* by Oscar Wilde – one of her favourite poems by one of her favourite poets. She put a lot of work into preparing her piece, not just learning the lines but understanding the meaning behind them – understanding what was going on for Wilde at that time in his life. He had always been a man who has intrigued, inspired and influenced her. She really enjoyed all of this preparation, and although nervous delivering her piece to an audience, which was made up of her fellow classmates (she was still working to overcome her crippling fear of speaking in public), she was quietly confident because of the work she'd put into it, and also because of the good feedback she'd received on her audition piece.

The following week the class all sat around in a circle as, one by one, they each received feedback on their recital. Aisling's came at the very end of the class of twenty students. Waiting for performance feedback would normally have been something that would have caused her to become more and more anxious as the time went by, especially feedback that was going to be delivered in front of a group of people. But because of the good work she had put in, and because of the good feedback she had always received on her voice, the quiet confidence she had helped to alleviate the anxiety she would normally have felt. So, when her time eventually came, she sat up eagerly awaiting feedback, which she believed was going to be mostly positive with constructive elements to help her improve. Instead, this is what came her way:

"You have: 1. glottal attacks; 2. breathiness; 3. too much rise and fall; 4. not enough variation; 5. too monotone – you need more light and shade; 6. you're too softly spoken – you're not reaching all four corners, or the back of the room; 7. you need to drive it more; 8. you need to get out of your head..." There was more, but Aisling zoned out after 8.

Then one of her classmates began to chirp in his tuppence halfpennyworth. She gave him a look that said, "Kick me while I'm down, why don't you?", which he was completely unaware of, and he continued making his points, which she also blocked out. There's only so much feedback a girl can take. She needed just one thing she was doing well, but that wasn't forthcoming. Aisling was ready to walk.

She didn't walk. She didn't leave the class. She saw the course through. But she did give up. She developed a couldn't-care-less attitude. She did what she needed to do, no more. She lost interest, really.

As part of their final performance, they had to work in pairs to deliver one of Shakespeare's sonnets. Aisling was paired with Jon, a wonderful young actor who had a really powerful, strong voice. The pairing was quite clever on Jane's part. Jon and Aisling complemented each other. He brought his range down to the softness of her voice, and she brought power to her voice to reach his strength. They also worked well as a double act, drawing out the wonderful underlying humour of Shakespeare, getting laughs in all the intended places from their audience.

Aisling got a distinction on her end-of-year voice exam. But she didn't believe it. She didn't think she deserved it. She thought the teacher gave it to her to be nice and that everyone got a similar grade (which actually wasn't the case) to make the college look good.

Aisling had been crushed by the feedback she had received. This caused her to lose confidence in her voice, and the impact went much wider and much deeper. She lost confidence in herself. The purpose of doing the course was to overcome her anxiety when speaking in public, to become surer of herself and less wooden. To a large extent, she had achieved this through the acting and movement classes.

The acting class, in particular, was good because it required the students to be vulnerable. Vulnerable because, week in week out, they were required to work with and perform to their fellow classmates. Aisling still doesn't know why, but the teacher always focused on performances that portrayed negative traits and emotions: i.e. greed, anger, jealously, shame, fear, and so on. It was heavy going, and there were times when the students would have appreciated being able to work on something that portrayed positive traits and emotions. She thinks the teacher really wanted to push them and to stretch them to really push themselves. He would say that the Foundation Year in drama was designed to allow students to know if they wanted to follow through with further training towards a career in acting, to know if they had what it took. His feedback was always tough. He would say it's a tough world out there for actors. This was his way of preparing the students in knowing if this is what they wanted, in knowing what to expect. He was, in effect, toughening them up for the tough world that actors have to face and navigate.

He worked primarily with Stanislavsky's system, which required the students to search for inner motives to justify action and the definition of what the character seeks to achieve at a given moment.

All of this actually helped Aisling get over her crippling fear of speaking in public. She felt that having done everything that was required from her in the acting class week in and week out, with performances that demanded being vulnerable. She felt if she could do that, she could do anything. And the movement class helped her overcome her woodenness. She was a lot more grounded, relaxed and free in how she moved. So she had achieved what she had set out to achieve through the Foundation in Drama class.

But she had lost confidence in her voice, the most fundamental requirement of speaking in public. The feedback had completely crushed her belief that she could speak to an audience in a way that would engage them. Being crushed took the confidence she once had in her voice away.

Three years later, Aisling did Acting and Performing for Radio and Voice Over classes. These involved learning about: working on scenes, sound effects, monologues, commercials, audiobooks, voiceovers and all kinds of microphone techniques.

Her reason for doing the classes was because she wanted to develop a podcast, and she also had an idea for a radio programme. Aisling's intention wasn't to speak on the podcast or radio show herself because she didn't think her voice was good enough. She wanted to get an understanding of what was involved so she could direct other people.

The classes were amazing. The students had so much fun, and they learnt so much. Each week they'd either use the bigger studio to perform a short radio play (they each had their individual roles, including creating sound effects), or they'd record monologues or duologues in the smaller booth. Each week they were given an assignment to prepare. They either had to write a specific piece, or they had to research a written piece that fitted in with the focus for that week – e.g. commercial, audiobook, monologue, breaking news story. They explored voice types from seductive to suspenseful and many, many more.

Their performances were recorded each week and then played back. They'd listen, give feedback on their own work, get feedback from each other and from David, the teacher. David quickly noticed that Aisling struggled to recognise anything good in her work, and she was dismissive of the good feedback coming from him and her fellow classmates. He gently challenged her on it, and she opened up about what had happened in her voice class. He and everyone else in the class were genuinely shocked. They were actually slightly outraged on her behalf. They all chirped in to say what a great voice she had. David sensed Aisling wasn't believing what they were saying, and he was right. She thought they were just being nice.

So he had them all put it in context: for example, that week Aisling had chosen a passage from a suspense thriller, and one of her classmates mentioned how her breathiness really brought that alive. He played back the recording from the previous week, when she had chosen the L'Oreal 'Because You're Worth It' commercial, and pointed out how the softness of her voice was quite seductive.

Aisling began to recognise and believe what everyone else was hearing in her voice. Slowly over the remaining weeks of the courses, her confidence in her voice returned. She recognised what was good and also what she could improve upon. This took her back to the textbook she had for the voice foundation class:

Book Wisdom

The Vocal Arts Workbook: A Practical Course for Developing the Expressive Range of Your Voice by David Carey and Rebecca Clark Carey

Aisling returned to the eight points of feedback and began to look at them objectively, for example:

1. Hard glottal attacks: She was tightly clamping shut her vocal folds before any breath got to them;

2. Breathiness: She was letting a little bit of breath escape before closing her vocal folds.

The book has exercises to help connect the voice and breath to overcome these challenges. It's also filled with exercises to overcome the remaining six points of feedback Aisling had been given by her voice teacher.

Of course, Aisling knew when she had received the feedback that the book had the solutions to overcome all of these points. But because she had received only negative feedback, she was totally crushed, and instead of working to overcome them, she gave up.

This book brings together all the factors that are needed to find one's own authentic voice.

The restored confidence Aisling felt caused her to ask herself what she had learnt from the situation and how she could manage differently a situation that had such a negative impact on her self-esteem and self-confidence, should she ever encounter something like this in her WorkLife again. She began to journal on these questions. She decided she needed to take control by giving herself feedback. Constructive feedback that would enable her to build herself up, not crushing feedback that would knock her down. From this through journalling, she gave herself the following self-feedback:

"I believe so much in the power of effective feedback. I also believe there's an effective and ineffective way of giving and receiving feedback. I've never liked the feedback 'sandwich', because the crux of what needs to be said and heard can be lost within what is said around it – the dressing that surrounds it.

"I believe feedback should be given context. For example, when the teacher said I had glottal attacks and breathiness, she could also have drawn my attention to particular words on which this happened, e.g. in the English language, words beginning with a vowel tend to cause these problems. Of course, I could have found this out for myself by simply reading the textbook, but I didn't have an awareness I was doing this until I got the feedback; and because I hadn't received feedback to this effect when I performed my audition piece, or throughout the first term, when I must have been doing it, I struggled in knowing what to do. I actually couldn't hear myself doing it. This, to me, would have been constructive feedback. I also think it should have been limited to no more than three points. Three is a good and achievable number to work with. Any more makes it too challenging.

"My teacher David and my classmates did put the feedback in context, e.g. how my breathiness brought the suspense needed for the story I was reading, how the softness of my voice brought the seductiveness needed for the commercial voiceover. David gave me feedback on my pacing, which helped with many of the other points of feedback my voice teacher had given me. For example, speeding up, slowing down, pausing, helped overcome points 3 (too much rise and fall), 4 (not enough variation), 5 (too monotone – needing more light and shade – different parts are different in tone and mood) and 7 (needing to drive it more – pace).

"He did exercises with us that drew awareness to working with our diaphragm, which helped with point 6 (being too softly spoken and not reaching all four corners or the back of the room); and he made the class fun, which helped with point 8 (needing to get out of my head). I prepared well for the class, undertaking the weekly assignments. Then I let go by being present in the moment, which took me out of my head. I had fun and enjoyed the moment."

Epilogue

Because of Aisling's renewed confidence in her voice, she continues to work on improving it. She does this by working through exercises in the *Vocal Arts Workbook*. Sometimes she records herself speaking so she can actually hear how she sounds. She then gives herself feedback on what's good about her voice and areas that she needs to work on to improve.

The questions she continues to ask herself in WorkLife situations – good, bad and challenging – through journalling are:

What have I learnt from this?
What does this mean in the context of my WorkLife?
What do I want and need to do next?

She then devises a plan to make what she has identified happen.

The learning Aisling took from her situation led her to create a WorkLife that allows her to combine her knowledge and experience of WorkLife learning and development with drama-based techniques by collaborating with performing artists. Their work enables individuals and teams to be more active, spontaneous and flexible, freeing their minds to use their imagination in being inventive and original. The intrinsic nature of their work helps foster creativity, team spirit and emotional intelligence. Aisling works with so many interesting people, helping them manage, develop and transition their WorkLives, and she works with an amazing team of artists in delivering the work.

Words of Wisdom

Sometimes your greatest challenge can become your driving motivation to get you to where you want to be. That has certainly been true for Aisling. Beginning from a place of wanting to overcome her crippling nervousness when speaking in public, and her woodenness, followed (eventually!) by wanting to embrace what was good about her voice and to work towards improving what wasn't has led her to where she is in her WorkLife.

WORKLIFE BOOK CLUB

Maggie: I'm pleased you chose this case, Annie. Last month I was toying with this and the case I chose. It could have gone either way, and it would have been the next case I would have chosen, when it's my turn again. Now I don't have to wait. I'm pleased about that. I'm also pleased that we get to meet Aisling again. I like that the *Learning Through Reading* series has stand-alone cases where we get to meet new characters, and also stories of continuation. I like that Aisling's stories are both stand-alone cases and also give a sense of continuation, in that we get to learn more about her backstory and how her WorkLife is continuing too. So, thanks, Annie, your choice this month has given me a lot to be pleased about.

Annie: You're welcome Maggie, I aim to please.

Sofia and Luca replenished their drinks and brought along their *antipasti*, which included tenderstem broccoli with garlic and chilli, oven-roasted asparagus sprinkled with salt, chargrilled avocado with chilli vinaigrette, mozzarella with parma ham and marinated black truffle, calamari served with garlic aioli, vegan baby mozzarella balls served with sweet cherry tomatoes, a selection of Italian breads and olives, and fresh strawberries.

"I love that you have vegan mozzarella," said Annie. "It makes me so happy as a vegetarian pizza eater to see it on the menu."

Sofia said that they source their vegan mozzarella from a traditional cheese-making family. That one of the sons who joined the family business in recent years wanted to marry the family business tradition with his own vegan principles.

Taking their pizza and salad orders, the group continued with their sharing experience, ordering both the margherita (with the vegan and non-vegan mozzarella) and marinara pizzas. Together with a mixed salad, a rocket and parmesan salad, and an avocado, vine tomato, red onion salad in a balsamic and pomegranate dressing.

Saoirse asked what the best drink was to accompany pizza and Luca said that many Italians like a beer: "Peroni is crisp and clean and doesn't overpower the pizza. The sweetness contrasts perfectly with the saltiness of the cheese on the pizza. The alcohol-free Peroni works well too. Others like a light-bodied chianti. It brings fruity and smokey flavours to the tastebuds and brings out the best in savoury food."

"I've really enjoyed my cocktail," said Benny. "I might have another one of these. Or is there a different one that's a better accompaniment for pizza?"

Luca said they have a bittersweet apple and rose shrub cocktail, which has a sharp fruit note, and a rich, velvety feeling in the mouth, and when served with soda water creates a wonderful warmth when paired with pizza.

Benny said he'd have that.

Annie and Maggie both ordered Peronis, and Saoirse, Pascal and Florian chose the Chianti.

Orders taken, Sofia and Luca left the group to their discussion.

Benny reached for the charcuterie platters.

Benny: This really works, these different combinations together, the different foods and the cocktail. I wouldn't have thought it would have done, I wouldn't have thought of putting them together, but it really does work. The different tastes really complement each other.

Saoirse: It's the same for the negroni.

Pascal: I thought that about the book choice this month. It's different to the combination of case/book that we've experienced being combined before, in that it's a workbook with lots of exercises to do, as opposed to telling a story. I suppose we got the background to the people who wrote the book and the people who wrote the foreword. But that was it really, in terms of telling a story or having stories woven into it, but yet, it did work, I think.

Maggie: That was partly my reason why I didn't go with it last month, but yet I was really pulled towards it. I sensed it would be good, a good combination, but I also questioned how it would complement the case study, how it would play out in the discussion, which like the meal we're about to share, we'll experience together.

Annie: The reason I chose this story was because of the accompanying book. I'm fascinated by voice and especially by breath. As a child, I had a stutter, and even though it was more or less under control by the time I hit my teens, or I had found a way of managing it, it's held me back at different times in my WorkLife.

During my school days, I would never speak up in class. Even when I was with my friends, I would hold back. I'm quite reflective anyway, and I like to think things through rather than just blurting them out. Nowadays, people like to label that as being introverted, but to me, it's just that I'm reflective. I actually don't understand why people need to name or label everything. Because all it does is group everyone together, and we don't get to see what makes people who they are.

But my stutter has also played into me holding back. Growing up, other kids would laugh. I don't think they were being deliberately cruel. I was different, they thought it was funny, and yes, as we grow up, we know that it's cruel behaviour to make fun of or laugh at someone because they're different, but that's something some people need to learn.

It was through voice work that I managed to be able to control my stutter. When I started secondary school, we had a wonderful singing teacher who encouraged me to be part of the choir. I resisted initially because I thought, there's no way I'm going to stand up in front of people and stutter my way through a song. She was persistent but gentle in her encouragement. We had a singing class each week as part of our curriculum, and so I had to attend that. The choir was an after-school activity. We had a choice in doing that or not. Anyway, through the weekly singing classes, I began to notice I wasn't stuttering when I was singing in the same way I stuttered when I talked. I knew it was because of the breathing exercises she did with us, and I knew I wanted more exposure to those, and so I joined the choir, and it really helped me in managing my stutter.

But it continued to flare up, at times when I was tired or if I was nervous about something. And so, it continued to hold me back. Once, when I was at university, I was asked to host a chat with a visiting techie, whose work and thinking is much revered in the tech world, my world, or at that time, the world I aspired to work within. But my anxiousness that my stutter would flare up caused me to say no. Someone else stood in to help me; she figured it was low risk, or mistakes that could be made were relatively low, and that it would be good public-speaking practice – and that she'd get to spend extra time with the visiting techie.

She covered for me and my insecurities. That's what I had allowed my stutter to do, to cause me not only to feel anxious but also insecure. As I watched her do an amazing job, I knew I had a choice. I could only take on tasks where I knew I would succeed, or I could take risks that would challenge me to grow.

To help me, I volunteered for a charity organisation that helped people with stutters. I was mainly behind the scenes doing whatever was needed. I helped with social media campaigns that allowed them to show their work and impact up close and personal through engaging video content. This was designed to help raise awareness of their fundraiser events, which raised money for the great services that were provided.

There were voice coaches who equipped people with the technical skills to manage their stutter, which in turn gave them confidence because it's a real problem for people – children and also adults. I got to be part of those classes by way of giving whatever assistance was needed. I learnt so much.

I think we've come a long way for sure, but I also think this kind of judgement is still happening. I would love to see more companies offering support, by way of a voice coach to their people, to overcome challenges they may be facing and also to help them make the most of their voice because voice is so important in everyday communication. But if that help is not available, the great thing about this book is that it allows people to be their own voice coach in making the best of their voice.

Maggie: Thank you for sharing your story, Annie.

The rest of the group acknowledged their thanks to Annie for sharing her story.

Maggie: I can relate to how we can be misrepresented by how we speak through a story my mum shared with me.

My mum was a little girl when she arrived in the UK from Jamaica. When she began school and walked into the classroom, she said it was the first time she felt different. Her name was different. Her accent was different. She also held back from speaking up in class because when she did, the other children would laugh at her, and in the playground, they would mimic her. She had to adjust who she was to fit that room, that playground, and a big part of that was losing her accent. She did that by listening to how the other children were speaking. As she grew up, she became obsessed with perfecting her voice. She went to a weekly class at a drama school as a teenager, mainly because of the voice class, because she wanted to work on her Received Pronunciation.

Benny: Received Pronunciation?

Maggie: I thought someone might need clarification on that. I did, and I looked up the Wiki explanation, which is: The word 'received' means accepted or approved, in relation to its 'pronunciation', as in 'received' wisdom.

My mum has a beautiful voice, a voice that people want to listen to, both because of how she sounds and also because of what she has to say. My mum is a very wise person, and she's done really well in her WorkLife.

She went on to be a primary school teacher. This allows her to share her wisdom with young people in their formative years. She keeps a close eye on any child that is being singled out for being different, whether it's because of their name, or their accent, or anything else. The school she works at works hard to embrace differences, and my mum plays a big role in that.

She facilitates the children in telling their stories, the stories that make them who they are, the stories that make them different and unique and also the stories that show how all of them are also the same – their likes and their dislikes, how they love their families and also how at times they're annoyed by them, the TV programmes they enjoy watching, the books or comics they enjoy reading, the games they like to play.

My mum does this because it's something she would have liked her teachers to have done when she was young. Because she believes children are really intelligent, they love to learn, and in learning about each other, their backgrounds, their cultures, it helps them to understand, accept and respect each others' differences and similarities. This, in turn, helps to prevent the laughing at people because they're different, that my mum experienced. As you said, Annie, I don't think children mean to be cruel when they practice these behaviours, but these are cruel behaviours, and the best way to help children understand that is to help them understand each other.

Mum also volunteers at a refugee centre, helping people learning to speak English. I know she drives home clarity on pronunciation, because as you say, Annie, people are misrepresented by how they speak, and to get the jobs they deserve, it's a hurdle they need to jump before they even get onto the playing field. My mum strives to do this in a way that people don't feel they have to do this by having to change who they are to fit a room, as she did, but in a way that the room fits who they are, or that there's a space in that room for them. She does this by helping them tell their story in their interviews in how they answer the questions, and also in their presentations if that's a required element of the interview process. She helps them to tell their stories clearly and concisely in a way that allows people to see who they really are and what they can bring to the role and the company. This, in turn, instils confidence in the people she works with.

And food plays a role in the interview work my mum does. She'll bake something or bring along a dish, and talk about it in a way that allows the people she works with to understand her background. She encourages those people to do the same. She says food is a brilliant device because interviews can just feel awkward and formal, whereas if you share food with someone, it makes it more relaxed, and it opens up so many doors to great stories and a greater understanding of people.

Florian: Your mum's story is so interesting, Maggie. Is that why you were pulled towards this case and book?

Maggie: Partly, but there was something else too. There's been a lot stirring up within me over the last few months. In our first meeting, I told you how I was asked to be part of a steering group for inclusion and diversity in our organisation and that I said no because I felt while I was chosen to be an advocate, I was also being stereotyped as someone who would have an agenda because I'm young, I'm black and I'm a woman.

That didn't sit well with me; I didn't want to be part of anyone else's agenda. And while I know I made the right decision based on what I was asked to do, I felt there was something I could do, and maybe even should do – and 'should' is not a word I use very often. And that feeling just wouldn't go away.

The truth is I was being presented with an opportunity, an opportunity to give a voice to young, black women, and I turned it down flat, and that's the thing that just wouldn't go away. OK, being part of someone else's agenda wasn't right for me, but neither was the fact that I had turned it down flat.

The case and the book caused me to think about my mum's story and reminded me of how she had to work so hard to have a voice that is heard and listened to, and here I had turned down an opportunity to give a voice to people who perhaps have also struggled having their voice heard and listened to.

I also shared with you that an important part of my grandparents keeping their Jamaican culture alive was through sharing their food. Another important part was in sharing their music. They both sang and played in a band. That was how they met, through their love of Jamaican music, song and dance. When they arrived here, they played at clubs in London – Brixton and Soho. Their music gave voice to their culture, a voice that was oftentimes silenced outside of the clubs.

My grandparents' generation helped to rebuild Britain after

the Second World War. They were invited here to do just that, and yet they were often met with intolerance.

I chatted with them both recently, and they said life was hard at times, but it was also good. They had good jobs. They were able to provide for their family. My granddad worked for British Rail, and my grandmother worked for the NHS. They were immensely proud and thankful to have had those jobs, to have played their part in rebuilding Britain. They were also immensely proud and thankful for having kept their culture alive through everything they shared – their music, their food, their customs. I asked them what was most important in keeping their culture alive, and my granddad said, "it's really about the combination of cultures, because it's all British culture. Britain has always been a place of migration and a movement of people and mixing, which is one of the beautiful things about the UK as a whole; and London, in particular, is one big melting pot of cultures."

The answer to what I could do and what I should do came to me through my granddad's words. I want to find a way to give everyone in our organisation a voice, not just young, black women because that's discriminating against everyone else. That's what I was struggling with, and that's what my conversation with my grandparents allowed me to see. I've broached it with my boss, and he's on board, and we're going to talk through the idea with other people in the organisation and see how we can develop it from here. I've named the project 'Voices of the Met'. And that's why I was drawn to this case and book, Florian.

Florian: That's amazing, Maggie, and good luck with 'Voices of the Met'.

Florian and the rest of the group raised their glasses to a chorus of, "Well done Maggie, good luck, and here's to 'Voices of the Met'."

Sofia and Luca arrived with their pizzas, salads and drinks.

On tasting her wine, Saoirse said: "I quite like this, but for some reason, I wasn't expecting it to be chilled. However, I have had chilled red wines in France, and I like them."

Sofia said that lighter-bodied red wines are best served chilled for optimal taste as the temperature helps to keep the acidity down, creating a smoother finish to the aftertaste effect.

Looking around, Pascal said: "I just love how bright and fresh your restaurant feels. From the art on the walls to the beautiful flowers throughout. I feel as though I've stepped into a garden, but one that has beautifully decorated walls. You really have created a space that exudes a simple yet happy feeling."

Luca thanked him, and said: "Sofia and I were born in different parts of Italy, but we both grew up in the countryside. When we had the idea to open our restaurant, we immediately knew we wanted to capture the wonderful memories we both had growing up. Our playgrounds as children were the fields, the streams, the rivers, the woods and what lay within them that would capture our imaginations. We laugh and say that mother nature was the second mother to both of us. We both just have this great love affair with nature. We love flowers, and we love art that depicts nature and humanity's relationship to nature."

Saoirse asked where the concept of their menu came from, and Sofia responded that their food reflected where they came from, and also their dreams and aspirations.

"That's really inspirational and great that you've been able to combine what's important to you," commented Saoirse.

Sofia thanked her.

"Did you fall in love over your love of food?" asked Maggie.

"The first time she stayed over, I cooked for her three eggs, two asparagus, five cherry tomatoes with my heart," said Luca. "And we had this small but very beautiful brunch."

"That's so romantic," said Maggie.

Sofia continued: "Then he said to me: 'When I see you eating, I don't want to hear anything. I just want to see your expression, seeing you're connecting with the food, without you having to have a dialogue about it.'"

She laughed. "He was trying to be romantic but what he was really saying was that he doesn't like to talk while he eats, which is OK because I don't either."

"Phew, that was good," said Maggie. "You could have ruined your lovely romantic moment!"

They all laughed.

Checking they had everything they needed, Sofia and Luca wished them "*buon appetito*".

Pascal: How Sofia and Luca told their story, the way in which they were able to bring everything together – where they came from, their dreams and aspirations. To achieve this, they, in effect, connected the dots.

Annie and Maggie, both of your stories are helping me to connect the dots, too, as it were. The book to the case study, to our conversation, through the stories you're sharing, which is helping me to put everything in context of people's WorkLives and, in turn, the connection to, and importance of voice. I think this passage from the book is connected and helps to understand this more deeply: "Voice is about connecting both our primitive thoughts and our sophisticated ones to a mechanism that can communicate. Having a voice in the world, whatever that world is, is the gift we inherit and one we can develop. Voice holds our self-esteem, confidence, comfort and control. It is a physical activity: we 'draw breath' and speak."

Saoirse: Yes, your stories are helping me to make those connections too, and I think these lines from the book are relevant to the stories you've shared: "Each time we speak, we reveal our nationality, disposition, attitudes, background, idiosyncrasies, familial traits and mannerisms. We carry our lives and childhoods in our voice, and this is an important part of the armoury of any artist or any person who wishes to be heard." I'd never given much thought to it before, but that's so beautifully put and serves to make me more aware; and also as Cicely Berry says, "the book teaches through enhanced awareness, and instructs through clear specific exercises – refreshing and imaginative."

Maggie: Yes, that line stood out on the page for me.

Annie: Me too. Actually, it had me at the front cover: "A practical course for vocal clarity and expression."

There was a sudden unified silence as they began to eat their pizzas. Annie summed up what was a mouth-watering collective experience, saying: "I've never been to Naples, but if this is how they eat their pizza,

I'm booking the next flight. No wonder there are only two types of pizza. Who needs more when both of these are so sublime."

The group murmured in agreement through pizza-filled mouths.

The hushed sound of attentive eaters prevailed for a little longer. The pizzas had earned their respectful silence, which after a few moments Maggie broke.

Maggie: I totally get why Luca and Sofia don't like to talk when they eat. I didn't fully understand earlier what he meant by connecting with the food. I do now. I just want to savour every last bite and not talk about it.

She was met with another group murmured agreement as they each savoured their last bites.

Florian: I love how the margherita got its name. The story goes that a Neapolitan *pizzaiolo* was commissioned to make pizza for the visiting King Umberto and Queen Margherita. Her favourite was the one that represented the colours of the Italian flag – tomatoes, mozzarella and basil – or in the order from the flag pole – green, white and red.

Maggie nearly choked on her pizza when she realised that once again, it seemed Pascal's attire complemented the colours of the flag of the country of the food they were eating. He was wearing a dark green suit with a white shirt, and his red tie, red pocket square, and red Clark Kent styled square glasses had come out again. So far, his attire had matched the colours of the Spanish, French and now Italian flags. His pinstripe suit in a deep blue background with fine stripes of red and white, worn with a white pocket square and his signature glasses in the same blue as his suit, Maggie believed represented the flag of the United Kingdom, on the evening they had enjoyed British pub food. And the green suit he had worn with a white shirt, orange pocket square, and what seemed to Maggie to be a pin in the shape of a wheel with spokes in a navy blue that was set off by the navy blue-rimmed glasses he wore for their curry evening represented the Indian flag. Although Maggie found this fascinating, she didn't say anything, as she thought it might be rude, and she didn't want him to think she was in any way being disrespectful of his dress sense, which she actually thought was fabulous.

Looking around the room and noticing how the wait staff were interacting with their customers brought Florian's mind back to the case.

Florian: Annie, you talked about insecurity. How does that play out in lack of confidence in voice? I ask because I meet so many people for whom English is not their first language, especially in the hospitality industry. I wonder how that impacts them and if perhaps it's something I can be part of in creating a way to help them.

Pascal: You read my mind, Florian. Annie and Maggie, both of your stories are so fascinating. I work across industries, as you know, and I recognise that voice plays such an important role in people's WorkLives. I'm also interested in understanding the challenges people encounter. It may be that I, too, can play a part in helping people in some way.

Annie: Security is how stable your confidence is, and insecurity is the opposite where your confidence is unstable. In WorkLife, if people are insecure, making one mistake can bring their entire sense of competence and worth crashing down. Being secure means your confidence isn't easily shattered; you can fail without feeling like a complete failure, which is important because failure is a stepping stone to success in so many jobs.

Insecurity itself is not a problem. The problem lies in how we cover up deficits rather than facing and dealing with them effectively. The first mistake is becoming paralysed by them, which is, in essence, what happened to me. The fear that I might stutter on stage, and not be able to facilitate the discussion was real, and it paralysed me. I needed to find a reason to push past that paralysis, and for me, that reason was that I really wanted to grow, personally and professionally.

I think it was the same for Aisling: she wanted to overcome her crippling fear, which could also be described as a paralysing fear when speaking in public. That was her reason for undertaking the Foundation in Drama course. Pushing beyond her paralysis was important to her in her personal and professional growth and development.

The second mistake insecurity can cause is that it stops you from trying hard enough. You don't give it your best shot because you're afraid you'll find out you don't have what it takes. That was true for me when I said no to facilitating the conversation because I would have been crushed if I'd discovered that about myself. Whereas for my classmate, because she was secure within herself, that thinking didn't factor into her decision. She was open to learning, even if it meant it didn't go perfectly or she made a mistake. I was closed to learning for the same reasons. I think it was the same for Aisling. She said she gave up and developed a couldn't-care-less attitude. I think maybe she was afraid she'd find out she didn't have what it takes. The thing is, we won't know if we have what it takes to be great until we make a real investment. So we just have to rise to the occasion and be worthy of the opportunities we're given. Florian and Pascal, introducing people in your industries to the self-coaching course presented in the book could help you create a way to help them. Bringing in voice coaches to work with people is also something you could perhaps encourage.

The assignment that's included with this case (Finding Your Unique Story and Making it into a Powerful Presentation), could also be helpful, because it helps people use their own stories to communicate with power and impact, in the same way Maggie's mum does in helping people tell their stories in interviews.

Florian: Thanks, that's really helpful to know and understand. I'd never given it much thought before. But as you say, voice is so important in everyday communication, and communication is so important in our industry because we have so much face-to-face, and one-to-one communication.

Pascal: Yes, thanks, Annie, that was really helpful and has certainly given me a lot to think about.

Benny: And pursuing validation backfires. I sense that was what Aisling was doing. She wanted validation from the teacher, and I understand why, but the thing is, not all teachers are made equal. There are good teachers for sure, and I think David was one of them, but there are also teachers that aren't so good, or who may be good at teaching their subject, but not so good in giving feedback. I think Jane was one of those. Feedback requires a different skill set.

I agree with you that Aisling was struggling with insecurity. She said she had low self-esteem. I think that was in relation to how she rated herself as an actor or a speaker, and this meant her confidence in her ability was low.

And here's the thing. If you base your self-esteem on other people's approval, your confidence will always be unstable, and that's emotionally exhausting.

A better approach to managing self-esteem is to stabilise your self-esteem by making it less dependent on external validation. The starting point is to decide whose approval really matters to you.

My friend Sharlene does stand-up comedy. She said, starting out, she used to be crippled with fear going on stage and that she still gets nervous because she never knows how the crowd will react. I asked why she does it because I just couldn't imagine putting myself through that.

She told me it has always been her goal to perform in theatres, and she's doing that now. And that it was only when she did it all the time that she wasn't afraid of it anymore. She's fine with being nervous because she says that keeps her on her toes and prevents her from becoming complacent.

That was true for Aisling too. The acting class helped her overcome her crippling fear of speaking in public. The vulnerability required each week, in the work she was required to do – she felt having done that, she could do anything.

But then came the crushing feedback that wasn't something she had prepared for, and that had a lasting negative impact for her.

Sharlene has found a way of managing feedback that would have crushed her before – a bad reaction from the audience. If that happens now, she tells herself: "I'm just not for them, and they're just not for me. There are plenty of people who I am for." She said adopting that attitude didn't happen overnight and that she had to work at it.

She said she learnt to focus on how she wanted her life to be instead of how others perceived her. By shifting her goals from external image to internal mastery, she was able to move from a place of proving her competence to a place of improving her confidence.

She shifted her focus to having stand-up sessions that are successful so that people come out to see her do what she loves because that's what she wants her life to look like.

Sharlene says you might not be able to ignore everyone else's opinion altogether, but you can change how you want to be seen, and that makes it less likely that she'll become discouraged. She said that is really important because when she started out, when she did well, she thought it was because she was young and she was lucky, but never because she was good. It was similar for Aisling: she thought she received a merit because everyone got one to make the school look good; and when she got good feedback in the classes she went on to do, she thought people were just saying that to be nice. It took David's intervention to put the feedback in context to shift her thinking, and through this her confidence in her voice was restored.

Now Sharlene says she knows she works really hard and that she can feel confident about that. She describes it as a shift from extrinsic to intrinsic motivation: to pursue excellence in a task because you enjoy it, to focus on activity for its own sake instead or results or awards that might follow from it. That's what Aisling did when she went back to the textbook she'd had during her voice class.

Florian: Yes, but it did take Aisling a long time to get there. The foreword says, "Teaches not by telling but by making the reader/student aware of their own personal body responses to breathing, tension, resonance etc. and to the whole process of making sound in their everyday life." I was wondering why Aisling didn't have that, why did she need feedback to tell her that – which it didn't directly, but that was what was behind the feedback. I suppose I'm wondering if she could have taken more responsibility.

Saoirse: I sensed it was because she was a student. She was learning. Because she had always gotten good feedback on her voice previously, she didn't know she had these problems. She said she couldn't hear what she was doing wrong. But I get what you're saying; maybe she should have been able to feel it or have more awareness. Or maybe it could have been observed earlier by the teacher. In the classes she went on to do, because their work was recorded and played back, she could hear it, but it still needed the intervention of the teacher for him and her fellow students to put it in context. I think perhaps it's similar to what we've been saying in our discussion. It helps to understand things – learning more in context. On a slight aside, has anyone worked through the accompanying DVD to the book? I will, but I haven't yet. I'm also going to work through the accompanying assignments to the case about 'How to Find Your Unique Story and Make it into a Powerful Presentation'.

Pascal: I haven't yet, but I will. It's something I would like to build into my day, little and often.

Benny: That's my plan too.

Florian: And me.

Annie: I've begun to.

Maggie: Me too.

Saoirse: But Aisling did get there in the end. Through her journalling on what she had learnt from the situation and how she could handle a situation that had such a negative impact on her self-confidence and self-esteem, should she ever encounter something like that in her WorkLife again. I think it was just that she didn't see it coming, and then it knocked her for six – or in her words, it crushed her.

Pascal: Cicely Berry says, "The message that underpins the work is that good breathing not only produces a good voice, but also feeds the actor in their exploration of character, and in the truth of that character. In other words, to breathe deeply is to think deeply." I think Aisling was doing the deep work in thinking deeply, in her exploration of Oscar Wilde, understanding him, his life, the meaning behind the lines, but I don't think she was making the connection to good breathing, to good voice. She does seem to have missed a crucial step, which I think was down to lack of awareness. I don't think she can have been the only person to have done that. Maybe the importance of the book needs to be driven home more.

Maggie: It also takes time. That's what my mum says, and her awareness of her voice being different was immediate from her first day in the classroom and playground. Even with that awareness, she still had to work hard, and most importantly, to listen hard.

Annie: That's true. I had to work hard too. I think I used to be more visual than auditory, and learning visually was perhaps easier for me. I had to work to be more auditory in my learning.

Pascal: That's a good point. I think I'm naturally more auditory, and perhaps that's why I didn't fully appreciate why Aisling was struggling to hear the aspects her teacher pointed out to her.

Saoirse: I really love the poetic yet inspiring descriptions: "We need voices to be able to perform better than our natures and yet to reveal our natures. We are asked to be the conduits of big thoughts – bigger than normal conversational usage – and so voice work is as much about tuning into our own possibilities as it is about gaining vocal skill. It also has a philosophical dimension and, through it, we open up the possibilities for the listener to be touched more profoundly." That really arouses my curiosity about sound and speech in everyday life.

Florian: True, but can I bring the conversation to the crushing feedback aspect of Aisling's story. I feel we've talked a lot about the healing power of voice but not about the crushing feedback.

Aisling said she always got good feedback on her voice. People would say she had a lovely voice. And that's nice, but doing a voice class is not about having a lovely voice. It's about building on that. Aisling did the drama course to overcome her crippling nerves when speaking in public, and her woodenness. The acting and movement class helped her to achieve what she set out to do. I think because she'd always been told she had a lovely voice, that she wasn't as focused on that. Maybe that's why the feedback was so crushing; she wasn't expecting it because she didn't think there was anything wrong with her voice. I do think it could have been handled better, but I also think it was what she needed to be told. I think there's responsibility for both parties in giving and receiving feedback.

Saoirse: It was the sheer volume of it. Aisling said she lost count after eight points of feedback, and that there was more – and then her classmate chirping in too – and it was delivered in front of her class. I know that was the same for everyone, but what came her way would have crushed anyone. Yes, she needed feedback, but not by the truckload. I don't know how anyone could take responsibility for taking on so much, all in one go, and it did need to be put in context. That was the difference in the other class she did – and then she did take responsibility for receiving the feedback she was being given. I think she deserves credit for not walking, for seeing it through. She said she developed a couldn't-care-less attitude. Did Jane see this? David saw that she wasn't taking the feedback on board that was coming her way, and he approached that. I think it's back to what you said about there being good teachers, and David was one of them, and there being teachers who may be good in their subject matter but are not equipped in managing a good feedback process.

Pascal: For their end-of-term piece, Jane did pair Aisling with another actor, Jon, and Aisling did say that the pairing was clever because they complimented each other – the strength of his voice and the softness of her voice. So, I think the teacher was aware of what was going on, the different challenges each student was facing, and I think as a teacher she was trying to help. But I also think she needed to be better at handling the feedback process.

I have actor friends who say they had teachers who absolutely crushed them at drama school. They said some of them had the same thinking as Aisling's acting teacher: it's a tough world out there for actors, and they were preparing them for that. And Aisling seemed OK with the feedback from her acting teacher. I think she was open to constructive feedback.

My friends also said that there were teachers who treated their students as they had been treated when they had been at drama school: a bullying type of approach. But my friends said there were other teachers who didn't take that approach, who were nurturing in the way they handled feedback, which in turn helped them to grow in their learning and development – perhaps similar to David – and that those teachers got more out of their students and the students got more out of themselves.

Florian: "Voice is about not having to live in the silence of the lonely imagination, instead of sharing our thoughts and sculpting sound so that not only is meaning conveyed but also the essence of who we are. It is about our possibility." That passage from the book is about voice, but I think it's also connected to feedback. I think feedback helps us realise our possibilities, and it's really key in helping our learning and development. I think after her experience in her voice class, Aisling retreated to a lonely place. It took her a long time to come back from this place, to realise her possibility.

There are two sayings: "There is no such thing as a bad student, just an unresourceful teacher"; and "When the student is ready, the teacher will come."

I think both are true in relation to Aisling's story. I think as a teacher, Jane was resourceful or equipped in her subject, but not in giving feedback. I don't know if Aisling was ready when she began David's classes, but I think because of the environment he created, she became ready.

Benny: That reminds me of two sayings: "Those who can, do; those who can't, teach." Which implies that professionals who seek success in their field, and fail because of lack of ability, resort to teaching. Sharlene said that's a phrase that's bandied about a lot in performing arts about 'failed' actors, turned teachers.

Pascal: Ah yes, I've heard that from my actor friends too. I think that's because it comes from their world. It's a line from a George Bernard Shaw play, *Man and Superman*.

Saoirse: Really! I love George Bernard Shaw, but what was his thinking in saying that? Do you know what the context was?

Maggie: I actually know the answer because I, too, was curious. I asked my mum, which is where I first heard the line. It's a line that, without context, can serve to infuriate teachers. Shaw was suggesting that teachers that do not know or have not learnt their discipline are an embodiment of the failed artist in Dickensian novels, who would resort to teaching to put bread on their tables. Teaching was considered to be the only apparent outlet available to them, as they had failed in their art.

Benny: That's interesting and brings me the second saying, by Lee Lecoca: "In a completely rational society, the best of us would be teachers and the rest of us would have to settle for something less because passing civilisation along from one generation to the next ought to be the highest honour and the highest responsibility anyone could have."

Maggie: That's exactly the comeback quote my mum uses in response to the first. How funny.

Benny: That is funny, but it's also a very true response. I get where you're going with this, I think, Florian. The ability to be a good teacher requires certain skills, and the ability to give good feedback requires certain skills. Not everyone is equipped; some people require help in developing those skills.

Florian: Yes, that is where I was going with it, but I was struggling in getting there. I was labouring with the crushing feedback aspect in bringing everything together. You helped me connect the dots. Thank you.

In wanting to know how to help people in my industry by introducing them to the self-coaching course in the book and perhaps more specifically in bringing in voice coaches to work with people, I needed a better understanding of why one teacher worked for Aisling and why one didn't.

What makes for a good feedback giver and a bad feedback giver. And also the responsibility of the student in giving themselves feedback as directed in the book, and also in receiving feedback when working with a voice teacher or coach.

Pascal: Yes, and in relation to what you said about David creating the right environment, I think this sentence from the book is relevant: "Work on the voice, in particular, is work on the self, and learners need to feel that they are free to work without fear of judgement." The environment David created was conducive to this, the environment Jane created wasn't.

Maggie: So, was David the hero of the story, and was Jane the villain of the story?

Benny: I think David was the hero of the story. And to a degree, Jane was the villain – but not necessarily evil, more ill-equipped or lacking resourcefulness.

Annie: Or to stay with the title, crushing feedback was the villain and the healing power of voice was the hero.

Saoirse: Maybe Aisling was a villain in her own story too. "Often we are our own worst enemies when it comes to vocal expression: we judge, censor and constrict ourselves;" and *Vocal Arts* was the hero, in this wisdom and direction: "An inquisitive spirit that is open to play and discovery is also vital in voice work. Allow yourself to explore beyond how you usually use your voice and, more significantly, how you feel you 'should' use your voice. Actively seek to discover and enjoy possibilities in your voice, your body and yourself that you may not have experienced before."

Saoirse laughed.

Saoirse: I could wax lyrical about the truth held in the poetic language of the book.

Pascal: Me too, and it's so true that "Acting is the art of transforming both the ordinary and the extraordinary so that it can be heard in a poetic way so that it lodges in the listener's minds and haunts them after the event." That's true for actors, and it's also true for speakers, presenters, all communicators in everyday WorkLife.

Florian: It's also true that "When we think about the arts, most of us think about music, painting, sculpture, literature, dance, drama. Speaking can also be considered a form of art. The vocal arts are so commonly practised, though, that sometimes we forget how powerful they can be. The voice and the words we speak are fundamentally a product of our whole selves – our thoughts, our feelings, our body and our soul – and so have the potential to affect us deeply as both speakers and listeners. To develop our vocal artistry is to develop our ability to affect and contribute to our common human experience."

He laughed

Pascal: The poetic language of the book is mesmerising for sure. And it's so true. "Even if you never aspire to act professionally, the work can open the door to your expressive potential as a human being." Everything about the book draws me in. I'm going to work with the workbook for sure.

The rest of the group acknowledged their agreement.

Arriving with dessert menus, Luca asked if anyone wanted "*dolce*".

"I know I shouldn't," said Benny. "But when in Rome, or whatever part of Italy your deserts are about to take me to..."

"I don't know if I can eat any more," said Annie.

"As we say in Italy, *l'appetito vien mangiando*," said Sofia. "The appetite comes while you are eating. Perhaps something light and palate-cleansing, a *sorbetto* or *gelato*."

Annie said she though that was a good idea.

"Ooooh, *tiramisu* and *panna cotta*," exclaimed Maggie. "I always find it so hard to choose between them. Ooooh, and summer fruit pudding, this really is too difficult a decision."

Luca suggested that they bring them a selection of smaller plates, so that she wouldn't have to choose.

"Si, grazie," said Maggie.

The rest of the group laughed and echoed Maggie's seal of approval on Luca's suggestion.

"After that, I'll definitely only be able to manage a coffee," added Annie.

"Ah yes," responded Sofia. "A strong espresso is served after *dolce*."

"And finally..." began Luca.

"And finally!" interrupted Annie. "Don't tell me there's another course after that, *per favore*!"

Luca laughed and said, "I didn't know you all spoke such perfect Italian. The final course is *digestivo*. To finish your meal, we serve *limoncello*, a drink that aids digestion. We have a non-alcoholic version, Benny."

"When in Rome, eh Benny!" Maggie said.

Benny laughed in agreement.

Continuing, Luca asked if they would like to have their deserts, coffee and *digestivo* in their garden.

"Oh, I didn't notice a garden," Maggie said.

Luca smiled and said that was because it's a secret garden.

EPILOGUE

The doorway to the secret garden was hidden behind a wall of climbing plants. As the group stepped through the open door, they felt they were entering an oasis of beauty and calm. The garden was where Sofia and Luca grew much of the fresh fruits, vegetables, herbs, plants and wild flowers they used in their kitchen in preparing the food and drinks they served.

As they settled into their garden armchairs, which were plumped with soft cushions, they draped themselves in the warm blankets that lay on the tables next to their chairs. Breathing in the scent from the wild flowers wafting in the breeze accompanied by the gentle sound of water trickling from the garden fountains intensified their sense of serenity in the midst of their bustling Shoreditch neighbourhood.

As they sipped on their *limoncellos*, Saoirse turned to Florian.

Saoirse: Is there an Italian connection to Shoreditch?

Florian: Yes, it's the oldest connection of all. The Romans built London in 47 AD. They also built the first roads in Britain. London remained under Roman authority until 410 AD.

And there's a further connection to the world of drama, to the world of vocal arts. Romeo – or the first actor who is said to have played him, Richard Burbage – is buried in the crypt where Shakespeare placed the final scene of his tragic play. That crypt is in Shoreditch church, which by a curious twist of fate stands on the site where all Roman roads joined, perhaps even to the city of Verona, and to Juliet's balcony, where she uttered the most poetic words of all: "O Romeo, Romeo, wherefore art thou Romeo?"

They all laughed

Saoirse: How very poetic, Florian. As we say in Ireland, you certainly know how to spin a good yarn. Really interesting, too. Where do you get all these facts?

Florian: That particular story is from the Shoreditch Church website. And you're right, Saoirse, I did put my spin on it. There's so much history and interesting facts about our neighbourhood. I pick them up from everywhere, really. Reading about, listening to, stories that have been handed down through the years, steeped in the history of our neighbourhood, many have been spun that's for sure, but with interesting tales/truths woven into them, and many have been stretched, with a few far-fetching tales/truths, that's for sure too.

Tonight's case, book, discussion, stories being shared served to remind me to look for the poetry in ordinary things. That's the beautiful thing I'm constantly being reminded of in our Book Club each month: through the case, the book, our discussion, the stories shared during our evening – ours, and the people we talk to in the restaurants. I share snippets of history, but really together we're making what will be history one day. Our Book Club is perhaps the start of a tradition. Saoirse, last month, you said: "Traditions are the stories that families, friends and communities write together." That really stuck with me and made me think that those are the stories that will go on to be the stories that people in time will share: the stories that are part of the history of a community, a city, a country. That's my learning from this month's Book Club.

Saoirse: Maybe one day we'll be written into the history books, or whatever the modern equivalent of the blog of that time will be, or our stories will be shared around the tables of future generations. All the snippets we're sharing, stories, facts, sometimes even trivia. There's a writer I like, Seth Godin, who says, "Trivia isn't trivial. In fact, it's a building block of our culture, a shared, safe secret, a shortcut to belonging. And creators of culture get to invent new bits every day." I really like that.

I'm 58. I said to a young(er) friend once – living in Shoreditch, there's all the cool hippies, and then there's me, heading to the blue-rinse brigade. He looked at me quite puzzled, and then it dawned on him what I meant, and he asked, do you mean hipsters?

She laughed.

Saoirse: I really was showing my age. I don't think he had any idea what I meant by the 'blue-rinse brigade', and I didn't elaborate. There's an Irish saying that if you crack a joke and people don't laugh, don't attempt to explain it, just move on, fast. I think I might already be part of the history, or maybe I'm the new old.

What I mean is, remembering something Maggie said that struck me, when you start to rethink your job as a set of skills you have, you can, in effect, work anywhere. I've done it. The next generation is more willing to change industries than any previous generation. And age isn't a discriminator. I'm living proof of that. That makes me the new old and makes all of us part of a generation that are doing things differently, which of course, every generation does. Like other generations gone before us, our stories will perhaps feature in future history publications. I'm taking the long road to say what I'm taking from this month.

I, too, was unsure about the combination of the case and the book, or rather the type of book. My learning this month is to be open to where things can take you. Because there's learning in every thing, every experience, every situation, and that learning can provide you with a pathway, so even if I think a particular story and accompanying book doesn't apply to me, I understand there is a path to follow – whatever you want to do there is a clear path to it. Once you understand those steps, it becomes much more intuitive, and perhaps it even gives you the courage to get started because that's what you need most the courage to get started. Aisling needed courage to get started, and to keep going, or to pick herself back up when she got knocked down. I loved that she journalled and then gave herself feedback on the questions:

What have I learnt from this?

What does this mean in the context of my WorkLife?

What do I want and need to do next?

Because that led her to the work she's doing now. All of that long-winded answer is what I'm taking from this month's meeting: be open to where things can take you, and have the courage to take the first steps.

Pascal: That's actually helpful, Saoirse, as have been the stories shared tonight about learning: Aisling's, yours Annie, yours Maggie and your mum's, your friend Sharlene's, Benny. That's how we learn most of the foundational and fundamental things that we know, the things we remember and care about. It's not through simply being exposed to them but through effort and failure. That's why tests aren't nearly as useful as projects. Aisling prepared for a test in her voice class, but that wasn't nearly as useful as the preparation she was required to do each week in the classes with David, producing a piece of work, a project, working individually, in pairs or as a group. And just about anything worth learning is worth learning the hard way. I'm still mulling things over, but all of those points are really helping me to gain clarity on my learning and also what I can do with it to make an impact in some way – through enabling good feedback and good vocal practices.

Maggie: Through books, stories, conversations, the arts, including vocal and culinary arts, you grow and discover and make connections. That's what learning is about. That's what I learnt this month.

Benny: Feedback can be crushing, and the power of voice can be healing. And so can life. We will all experience crushing and healing moments. Because life is a river, and it carries you into your future whether you like it or not. There will be crashing waves, and there will be calm waters. There will be rainy days when you won't want to get out of bed, and there will be days when you wake up, and you see that the sun is shining, and you go on. Those are the stories that make us who we are.

Annie: When I think of the times in my life when I took myself away from people, when I needed time apart from everyone to reflect on what I needed to do to achieve what I wanted. Whether that was not to let my stutter or fear of failure that caused me to fear situations to hold me back, I think if you use your apartness to hone your creative skills and unique talents, doors can open up for you. You just have to take that brave step out of your comfort zone. It's scary for sure, but the consequences of not doing it are far scarier.

The openness in which Annie had shared her vulnerabilities and how brave she had been in overcoming them brought a respectful quietness to the moment. They had been on a journey together over the last five months, and the stories they had shared about their WorkLife experiences – the good, the bad, the ugly and the challenging – had brought a closeness to the group, such that Annie's words served as a reminder and reinforcement within each of them.

The respectful quietness lingered on, as each, lost in their thoughts, soaked up the calming ambience of their surroundings and the comfortableness of each other's company.

Interlude 5

Finding Your Unique Story and Making it into a Powerful Presentation Assignments

Featuring Alternative London Bike Tours Accompanied by Cake and Fizz

Bikes and helmets were at the ready for the group as they joined the Alternative London Bike Tour for a Sunday afternoon ride through the streets of Shoreditch, Brick Lane, Hoxton and Hackney to experience the street art that is part of their community heritage.

Saoirse had suggested doing it ahead of her birthday celebration and invited Elena and Philippe to join them. She said two hours in the saddle with a street artist as their guide would give them an insightful perspective into the artists behind the work while also learning about the different histories and cultures of East London as they pedalled their way. On their bikes, they could go off the beaten track to discover exclusive hidden-away pieces. Not to mention working up an appetite and a thirst for what was, in Saoirse's book, the best cake and fizz experience in London.

Except they weren't going to have to wait that long – well, not for the fizz anyway. Florian had brought a very special bottle of champagne (Veuve Clicquot La Grande Dame 2012 by Yayoi Kusama), to honour

Saoirse's special day, and also her love of bringing simple pleasures together to create memorable experiences. Saoirse (and everyone else) was immediately blown away by the beauty of how the bottle was presented. The case and the bottle were adorned with iconic symbols – an opulent flower decorated in playful colours, surrounded by polka dots (Yayoi Kusama's signature patterns) reimagined to symbolise the vibrant sparkle of champagne bubbles.

As the group marvelled at the beauty of the design, Florian said the collaboration connects the work of two inspiring women – Madame Clicquot, an iconic producer of French Champagne, and Kusama, a world-renowned artist.

Florian: Despite the 150 years that separate them, parallels can be drawn between the lives of Madame Clicquot and Yayoi Kusama. Determined and successful women, they were fighters, pioneers, entrepreneurs, modern women – writers of their own stories – characteristics that are united in the optimism and creative power of the flower. An artwork created by a *grande dame* of art in tribute to a *grande dame* of champagne.

While they waited for the tour to start, Florian filled their champagne flutes (needless to say, he had brought along a suitable special fizz for Benny too).

Florian: Through her creation, Kusama sent a beautiful message to the world. A message that symbolises vital energy, love and celebration of life. A message that represents the path that has brought us here today, ready to embark on and explore new paths together. Our desire, Saoirse, is to honour your special day and our collective special relationships through a celebration of life, love and vital energy.

The group raised their glasses in a toast to Saoirse.

Saoirse (smiling): Thank you for your beautiful words, Florian, that represent the beauty of the gift from all of you, and thank you for the beauty of presence that each of you has brought to my day.

Saoirse raised her glass.

Saoirse: To the beauty of our friendship, and the beauty of life.

Smiling back at Saoirse, the group raised their glasses to the beauty of their friendship and of life. And with that, it was time to get on their bikes to embark on and explore new paths together.

Alternative Tours was founded by a collective of local artists and creatives. People who live in and love their neighbourhood, who have been actively involved in the East London community for many years. They know its social history, architecture and street art like the backs of their hands. Cycling is their primary mode of transport for getting around London, and so not only do they know the coolest places, they also know the best, safest and most interesting routes to get people there.

They say: "Local street artists and creatives came on board to shape our collective and to generate a realistic London income to fund their creative endeavours. We are proud to have provided a platform for so many young creatives to go on to achieve great things."

At a relaxed pace, the group cycled along quiet roads, venturing off the beaten track into parts of East London they hadn't experienced before. Their ride took them along London's scenic canals, along tow-paths that provided green corridors through the city and interesting waterside scenery – including canal-side communities of new building developments and old disused buildings, displaying interesting works of street art, murals and hidden gems.

Along the way, they were regaled with entertaining and interesting stories about the street art, the artists, the history of the street art and the history of the area. Learning how the street art in the area changes all the time gave the group an awareness of the research required to have the most up-to-date knowledge to provide such a unique experience.

On finishing the tour, as the group made their way for cake and fizz, they did so with a much deeper appreciation of street art and graffiti. As well as a much deeper insight into the current challenges their community faces as they move into the future. Along with all of the exciting things that people are doing to keep their amazing neighbourhood unique.

On their arrival at the cafe-restaurant, as they made their way to their table, to their left they walked past communal tables of late afternoon

market-goers, visitors and locals, all experiencing the daily-changing lunch menu which embraces the freshest of seasonal produce. And to their right, a bar of attentive guests who were taking in a cocktail-making demonstration by two of the bartenders.

Their waiter, Aaron, brought along their drinks menu, letting them know they could choose their cake from the selection displayed towards the front of the premises, and he'd be back to take their orders. The patisserie area also served as a takeaway for their delicatessen of Mediterranean salads and a shop with shelves filled with quality store-cupboard ingredients and hamper-ready foods.

Having manoeuvred their way on their bikes through narrow alleyways and, in parts, bumpy terrain, it was ironic that the major challenge of their day was the one they were now facing – to select their cake of choice.

They were presented with a selection that included: rolled pavlova with peaches and blackberry; Middle Eastern millionaire's shortbread; pistachio orange cake; chocolate chip and pecan cookies; lemon drizzle cake; red velvet gold leaf cake; knickerbocker glories; chocolate sponge cake; blueberry lemon cheesecake; coffee and walnut financiers; fig and pistachio frangipane tartlets; rum and raisin cake with rum and caramel icing; flourless lemon, polenta and pistachio cake; hot chocolate and lime puddings; lime meringue cheesecakes; passionfruit and pistachio cake; cookie-based s'mores; lemon and mascarpone tart; baked rhubarb tart; summer berry cake; hazelnut and ricotta cake; rosewater and walnut cake. The variety seemed endless.

Needless to say, it really was a difficult decision for each of them to make. But sometimes, life is about making difficult decisions. And so they each faced their challenge head-on (eventually) and were quite ruthless (in the end) in ruling cakes in or out until they filtered it down and made their final decision. Decisions that weren't based on anything (remotely) measured – other than, "well it's always good to leave something to come back for". Words of wisdom passed on by Benny.

Aaron took their cake and fizz orders – which had been a decidedly easier decision to make, at least when guided by Florian. Remaining in the company of the *grande dame* of champagne, they chose glasses of Veuve Clicquot rosé. Florian said the sunset hue and indulgent berry aromas made it the perfect pairing to their luxurious cakes while also signalling the importance of their celebration. Benny was pleased there was an equally special and well-suited rosé to his sweet treat. Remaining in France, Florian suggested a glass of Perle Rose de Chavin, saying the delicate aromas of rose petals and elegant palate would be enhanced by the sweet freshness of his sumptuous cake.

Before he left to prepare their orders, Aaron smiled and thanked Florian for another wonderful lesson in wine pairings. Addressing the group, he said he, and his fellow wait staff, regularly attend Florian's masterclasses in wine pairings. He said they are incredibly educational, interesting and great fun too. Returning his smile, Florian said he was most welcome and hoped to see him soon at another class.

While they were waiting for their orders, Florian told the group that the masterclass in wine pairings is a collaboration between sommeliers and chefs to teach people who appreciate good food and wine, how to create restaurant-quality food at home, and understand how to pair it with the best wines to complement the dishes. He said the initiative is in support of their industry – local restaurants, wine and food suppliers, and schools providing culinary arts programmes.

Maggie: Wow, just wow, I have learnt so much today – about street art, about parts of our neighbourhood I had never experienced before, about our community – the challenges and opportunities. Now learning about this wonderful initiative is just the icing on the cake or the bubbles in the champagne.

Right on cue, Aaron returned with their cakes and drinks. Raising her glass, Maggie led a toast to the icing on the cake, the bubbles in the champagne, the perfect day with good people and the happiest of birthdays to their good friend Saoirse, to which they all clinked glasses.

A moment of silence followed as they entered a sugar-induced delirium. Florian had shared with them that food has a greater impact on wine than wine does on food, and with sweet flavours, the rule is to generally go sweeter with your champagne. His suggestions most definitely made for a decadent cake and champagne pairing. They each savoured the indulgence of their shared scrumptious experience – it was a birthday celebration, after all.

Pascal: This really is as wonderful as you said, Saoirse. Philippe, I can't believe we haven't been here before.

Philippe: Me neither, but I have a sneaking suspicion we'll be back again soon.

A sentiment the rest of the group agreed with through cake-filled mouths.

Annie: I just love how they've made so many of the cakes vegan-friendly while retaining the wonderful decadence of the original creations.
Benny: This experience captures the essence of what birthdays are meant to be about – indulgence to the highest order.

Another sentiment the rest of the group agreed with, through cake-filled mouths. A few more moments of silence followed as they savoured the last moments of their indulgence.

Annie: Our experience today also captured the essence of the assignment that was part of our last case: Finding Your Unique Story and Making it into a Powerful Presentation. In that, the assignment begins by saying: "Truly great stories and presentations live on in the hearts and minds of audiences the world over. That's a fact. Everyone has an innate storytelling ability. That's another fact. You just need to think about a time when you were with friends (or strangers!) in a bar or other social setting to know that you're a natural-born storyteller. Why is that? Because when you're in a friendly setting, you can be yourself, and you'll use really direct language (no jargon) to make sure what you say is engaging."

We've heard so many stories today, along our tour, and before that, when you shared the story about the *grande dame* of art and the *grande dame* of champagne, Florian. Aaron introducing us to the story of the masterclasses, and you providing the backstory to the initiative. These are stories that will remain with me because they were so interesting and part of what made them so interesting was that they were told so naturally.

I haven't worked through the assignment yet, because, while I've become more confident in social settings, I still haven't completely overcome my fear of speaking in public and my belief in myself that I can do that by telling a story that will interest people.

Addressing Elena and Philippe, Annie shared she had a stutter growing up, and how at times it has held her back from putting herself out there if it required any form of presentation. She said she'd recently given talks at schools, and that's definitely helped, and that today's experience of interesting stories shared in such a natural way is giving her the impetus to continue to push through the barrier she created for herself.

Maggie shared with Elena and Philippe that the introduction to the assignment goes on to say: "These experiences show that we all have that innate sense of what makes a good story, but we tend to forget that a great presentation is simply a great story, and we can also at times struggle to express our natural and true selves."

Maggie: I also held back on starting the assignment because I struggle to express my natural and true self. The social interaction of our Book Club has helped me for sure, but I still don't feel confident in my ability. I agree, Annie, our experience today was a masterclass in the lesson of naturalness and how that makes a story interesting.

Saoirse: I haven't worked through it yet either because the assignment is in two parts: first, discovering your unique story; and second, turning it into a powerful presentation. I wanted to do it in the context of an actual situation, so I was holding off until that point.

Pascal, Benny and Florian said they were holding off for the same reason.

Elena: It sounds really interesting. Is it something we could do together? I'd really like to experience it.

Philippe: So would I. I find it fascinating when Pascal tells me about the different assignments you've been experiencing together. I'd really like to experience that too.

Annie: I'm not sure if it's something we could complete together. I think it will take time and reflection to complete the second part of the assignment. But I think we could start the first part for sure. Shall we give it a go?

She was met with a group "Yes, let's give it a go."

Setting the stage for Elena and Philippe, Saoirse said the first assignment is to help people to find their story from what is important to them. And that the process of doing that is going to a social setting and working through five steps.

She said to help people work through the assignment, it uses the working example of the protagonist in the story of the case that they had discussed in their last Book Club: The Case of Crushing Feedback and the Healing Power of Voice.

Briefing them, she said the protagonist's name is Aisling and that her area of work is people development. She works with a team of performing, visual and literary artists to deliver training programmes that combine learning and development strategies with skills and techniques from the Arts. Saoirse said they would learn more about Aisling's story throughout the five steps, as she shares how she used the steps to find her story.

And so, with Saoirse reading the steps of the assignment, the group began to work their way through the:

Five Steps to Finding Your Unique Story Assignment

STEP 1: BEGIN BY THINKING ABOUT WHERE YOUR PASSIONS LIE

What topics are you most likely going to be talking about?
What are the things that excite you?
What are the subject matters that make you feel you have something to say?

For example, Aisling is passionate about learning and development – her own and other people's. She's also passionate about the Arts, and this is what excites her and what she's most likely going to be talking about – and she happens to have a lot to say on these matters.

* * *

Saoirse: I'm passionate about finding out about the people behind what interests me, whether it's music, beer, gin or coffee. I'm passionate about it in a way that helps me understand the importance of what people do, whether as individuals or as part of a company, and the importance of this to their community. Because community to me is a place of togetherness, a place where everyone feels included. It unites us, it provides the opportunity for connection, collaboration, shared experiences, and it also benefits our wellbeing and our happiness. I'm passionate about finding out the stories that make all of this possible and then sharing them.

Annie: I'm passionate about technology. As an industry, it's shaping the world we live in today. It inspires and drives the way the world functions and lives.

Elena: I'm passionate about landscape art because I want my work to represent the beauty of our natural world. I'm passionate about family – my immediate family, Florian, Emilia and Mateo, and also our extended family in Spain. I'm also passionate about my home country of Spain – the land and the culture.

Florian: I'm passionate about my industry and the role it plays in bringing people together over shared experiences of food and drink. I'm also passionate about my family, my home country of Spain and also my adopted country – the UK.

Philippe: As an art curator, I'm passionate about preserving art in the sense of safeguarding the heritage of art. I'm also passionate about selecting new work, and I'm passionate about connecting with artists. With Pascal, I'm passionate about making the most of our life and time here in London, and I'm also passionate about spending time with family in France.

Pascal: Yes, those are passions Philippe and I share – embracing our life here in London and with our family back home in France as much as we can. As a management consultant, I'm passionate about working with businesses to solve problems that help to improve their performance and enable growth.

Benny: I'm passionate about bringing ideas to the table and ensuring these ideas are brought to life – through compelling visuals and storytelling. I'm passionate about leading a team of creative thinkers. And I'm passionate about playing an integral role in building and maintaining a great company culture that lives and breathes our core values: curiosity, respect, teamwork, and employee health and wellbeing.

Maggie: I'm passionate about the safety and security of the people I serve. I'm passionate about helping to solve problems through good communication. I'm passionate about making a difference.

* * *

STEP 2: LOOK WHERE YOU SPEND YOUR TIME

What is it you do outside of your work when your time is valuable? Where do you choose to spend it?

For example, Aisling is always learning, whether listening to podcasts, reading or taking a course. Together with visiting galleries, museums, going to the cinema and theatre is where she chooses to spend her time. As learning and the Arts are her work, this is what she does daily and at weekends for both work and leisure.

* * *

Saoirse: I spend my time talking and listening to people – at music festivals and events in my areas of interest – gin, beer, coffee. And also here within our neighbourhood – workers and business owners, anyone I can have a conversation with really.

Annie: The passion and drive of the tech sector are infectious, and because of that, I also spend time learning – mainly reading. I actually love the idea of being able to learn so much and still not know enough because of the ever-changing nature of the industry.

Elena: I spend my time discovering new landscapes and returning to old, familiar landscapes, and I spend as much time as I can with my family.

Florian: I spend my time involved in initiatives that help the people in my industry. I also love to spend as much time as I can with my family.

Philippe: I spend my time discovering new artists – that's part of my work, and it's something I also do outside of work. Outside of work, I also choose to spend my time with Pascal, living our best life together.

Pascal: I spend my time providing pro bono management support to help businesses in their community to grow – it's also part of my work because I'm very much involved in the non-profit social enterprise arm of my company, and it's also something I do outside of work. And, of course, I also choose to spend my time with Philippe, living our best life together.

Benny: I spend my time reading, and I spend my time going to galleries and exhibitions. Similar to Aisling, learning through the arts is so powerful for me. It fuels my creative thinking.

Maggie: I also spend time reading. I like running and boxing, and I like to spend as much time as I can with my family.

* * *

STEP 3: LOOK WHERE YOUR SPEND YOUR DISPOSABLE INCOME

What are the things you spend your money on? Your interests or hobbies.

For example, this is also where Aisling spends her money: learning and the Arts. She did the courses in acting and performing for radio and voice-over classes, which were so interesting and great fun. Other recent spends include West End theatre tickets and tickets to art galleries and museum exhibitions.

* * *

Saoirse: I spend money on music festivals and also learning-type events – for example, events that have talks, demonstrations or classes about gin, beer, coffee. I've always bought loads of books. Reading plays an integral part to being a good writer.

Annie: I don't actually spend money on my interests – well, not a lot anyway. I subscribe to a couple of publications, but a lot of what I read is online for free. Because of my love of reading, I buy a lot of books, but I don't consider it to be a lot of money. Someone once asked me if I ever feel guilty about spending so much money on books. I said no because every time I buy another book, I remind myself that I just purchased one to five years of that person's life for £10 or £20. Oh, and I love walking, and I suppose that could be classed as a hobby, but that's free too.

Elena: I spend money on travel that takes me out of London into the countryside, where I can paint, and also trips back to Spain to see the children and to paint landscapes there too.

Florian: I spend money on books – they are my go-to place to learn. I also spend money on trips back to Spain to see Emilia and Mateo, and also the team that work with them at our vineyard and winery, who I also consider to be family.

Philippe: I spend money doing things with Pascal – experiencing as much as we can on our weekends. Activities, culture, food and drink. Just like today, really.

Pascal: Yes, that's the same for me. I don't spend anything related to my work, outside of work, really, other than books of course. I spend on the things Philippe and I like to do outside of work.

Benny: I spend my money on books and galleries and museum exhibitions.

Maggie: I spend money on books too, but I don't necessarily consider it a big spend. I like to have good gear for running and boxing. I pay for quality, but then it lasts, so I don't consider that a big spend either.

* * *

STEP 4: THINK ABOUT YOUR STRUGGLES

In tough times, what did you do?
What kind of uncertainties did you feel?

For example, Aisling changed her WorkLife from investment banking to WorkLife coaching and learning practitioner, going to university as a mature student. That was a struggle because it was a juggling act initially. She worked to bring in much-needed income while studying and gaining practical experience to launch her new WorkLife. She felt great uncertainty about whether she could make that transition and if she could make a living from it.

There have been many tough times, getting things started and keeping them going. She's gotten through those by persistence, determination and a positive attitude – she keeps on going because she believes her work has a positive impact in helping people develop, and working with learning and the Arts makes it easy to remain positive.

* * *

Saoirse: Life as a freelance journalist and writer is by its very nature a struggle. There have been many times in my WorkLife where I faced the uncertainty of being able to keep my head above water. I've gotten through those by continuing to do what I love and what I know I'm good at: writing. I've been flexible and adaptable to the changes in my industry. For example, the move from print to online publications.

Annie: When I wanted to change from working at a tech startup to working in cybersecurity within government, I initially struggled to get a job. One reason was that the work was different, and I didn't have experience in the area I wanted to transition into. And although I believe my experience demonstrated I had the aptitude and transferable skills that would enable me to do the job, it took time for someone to recognise that – and not necessarily take a chance on me, but to see my ability and potential to connect where I was coming from to where I wanted to get to.

Elena: Starting out as an artist, I struggled to make ends meet. Florian and I were already a couple when we graduated from university. Starting on our life together, we both needed to have jobs that would help us sustain ourselves and to save for the life and family we wanted to start together. My work as an artist didn't afford that. So I took the best job I could. I helped run a small art gallery. The pay wasn't great, but it was good enough.

Moreover, it gave me great opportunities. I helped put on shows, promoting artists and selling their work, and building relationships with people in the industry. I got to display my own work in the gallery, and every year I got to show it as part of a local artist's collective exhibition, which ran for a week in August and a week in September each year. This meant we had two very different audiences: in August, visitors and holidaymakers; in September, our local community. Over time, my work generated interest, I began to sell more and more paintings, and I began to receive commissions for my work. I also went on to teach a class at the art college I had attended, and when we moved to London, I continued my teaching at an art college here. So despite it being a struggle to get started in my work as an artist, by being persistent, consistent and determined, it eventually happened for me. In time, my art supported me as an independent artist and helped to support my family too.

Florian: I have faced so many struggles as a restaurateur, many of them financial. At times caused by external influences – a downturn in the economy that brings about a change in people's disposable income, and as a result, their behaviour. They are forced to tighten their belts, and one of the first things they cut back on is eating out because they simply can't afford it. Rising rent is something else that is outside of our control. These are just two of the many challenges that have brought and continue to bring struggles for me to do the best for the people who work with me, our customers, our community and our industry.

Philippe: I struggled with finding the right balance between the commercial and non-commercial dimensions in today's market-driven contemporary art environment. I believe no matter what crazy price art can demand from wealthy investors, art is needed by society. The struggle or conflict I experienced comes from the responsibility I have to the artist – creating demand for their work can help launch their career. I wanted to do that in a way that wasn't denying the public of their talent, which happens when viewings are for private investors.

Pascal: When I first began my work, I struggled with inner conflict – who I was as a corporate citizen and who I was as a citizen of the world. My two personas, as it were, weren't aligned. I felt my role was all about the bottom line, but I wanted my role to also be about greater corporate responsibility.

Benny: I struggled with the status quo of my industry – the accepted practice of too often pushing creative teams too hard on speed and volume. There's the old adage in my industry that you can choose quality, speed or cost, but not all three. Sometimes two, but never all three. So we say the most important thing is quality creative, but then we measure on speed and efficiency. This didn't sit well with me, but I struggled to know how to change it.

Maggie: I struggled with not wanting to stand out for being a young female black police officer. It wasn't about wanting to fit in. It was more about wanting to be accepted as someone who is good at what they do – not good for someone who is young, or good for someone who is female, or good for someone who is black.

* * *

STEP 5: DISCOVER YOUR EUREKA MOMENT

What was the moment you had your greatest realisation?

For example, there was a further struggle that led Aisling to discover her 'Eureka' moment. Once qualified, while individual WorkLife coaching came easily to her, group workshops and presentations didn't. She was so incredibly nervous that she would be physically ill before talking in front of people. She was also very inhibited and not her natural self, and to top all of that off she became very wooden!

To overcome this, she undertook the Foundation year in Drama along with several shorter acting courses and a year-long directing course, which led her to be Assistant Director on a production of *Hamlet* that went on to be performed at the RSC Open Space in Stratford-upon-Avon (that's Aisling's claim to fame!)

This was when she had her 'Eureka' moment of how the techniques, structures and methods of theatre making are significant in the world of people development. The unique skills sets performing artists have had to develop in their craft brings learning alive. This excited Aisling because she knew with her background in learning and development, she could collaborate with artists to create meaningful learning programmes.

* * *

Saoirse: My 'Eureka' moment was when I realised the world was open and receptive to reading 'nice' stories. There was still a place and demand for breaking news stories that brought with them big emotional reactions – shock, alarm, fear, excitement. But now, there was also a place for small emotional reactions: everyday life kind of reactions – calm, gratifying, easy-going, pleasant. Those are the stories that enabled me to monetise my blog, which helped the financial uncertainty of my work, and also connected me to people – individually and within companies and communities. That was the beginning of taking my WorkLife in a new direction.

Annie: While I was going through the struggle of getting into a new role and sector, I had the realisation that this was more of a challenge for women in tech. I couldn't figure out why then, and I still can't now. Because it's still a problem or a challenge within my industry. It's gotten a little bit better, but it's still no way good enough. There's a major gender imbalance, which seems so illogical because it's such an important and fascinating industry.

I don't know if that realisation can be described as a 'Eureka' moment because it didn't set me off on a path to change my world. But it is something I want to share – not to discourage men from entering the industry, but to try to encourage more women to consider a WorkLife in tech. I've mentioned it in the talks I've given at schools, really by way of raising awareness of this fact, and by way of encouragement as I mentioned. This may lead me to do more, but I'm not sure what that 'more' looks like. Yet.

But I have a sense it's going to be part of a chapter of my WorkLife. For now, that's enough for me to know. I'm going to take it as it comes. I first had the realisation a few years ago, and while I haven't done anything specific about it, it also hasn't left me, and so I sense when the time is right, I will do something.

Elena: I don't know that I had a 'Eureka' moment. For as long as I can remember, I had a purpose and a passion for painting. It's been the driving force of my life all of my life. It directed me to art school, then to work at the gallery, and eventually to being a landscape artist and teacher.

Florian: I also don't know if I had a 'Eureka' moment as such. Retaining staff, customers and suppliers, while a known challenge within our industry, thankfully has not been a challenge for us. I believe this is because I started from a place of seeking out the highest quality people to join my business and the highest quality produce from our suppliers. I have always treated people well, which in our industry, among other things, means fair pay – a fair wage to the people who work with me and a fair price for produce to our suppliers.

Together we provide quality food and drinks to our customers, as well as providing excellent customer service and creating a wonderful experience. We want our customers to return, and we want them to recommend us to their family and friends. However (and there is a however, because this didn't come without a struggle, which is back to a financial struggle, or rather a struggle of slow growth), to pay my employees and suppliers fairly, our prices needed to cover that while also earning a fair profit for the business. The quality of the dining experience is reflected in the price. That's the reputation we had to build, and it took time, and so we experienced slow growth, but I was OK with that because I knew I was in this for the long haul. So, I didn't have a 'Eureka' moment. I had a desire to treat people fairly.

Philippe: I did have a 'Eureka' moment. When I was conflicted between the commercial and non-commercial dimensions of my world, I had the realisation that my role is to be helpful to artists and what they want. The choice between commercial and non-commercial is their decision, not mine. My role is more that of an enabler. It sounds so obvious, but I was so caught up in the 'commercial/non-commercial' mindset, I just couldn't see it. The wonderful thing is once I was able to resolve the conflict I was experiencing, I was then able to move on to taking a more explicitly activist role as well. That's what I'm really passionate about. I want to give voice to artists who, because of their background or upbringing, don't always have the opportunities to be part of the discourse. My passion for discovering new work has connected me with so many wonderfully talented artists to whom I can give a voice in the art world. Using a curatorial platform for advocacy and activism is a responsibility and an honour.

Pascal: My 'Eureka' moment came as my confidence in my competence to do my work grew. While I have always done good work, starting out I needed to learn the ropes, some of which takes time – it takes time to be practised, experienced, accomplished and skilful. With time as my proficiency grew, so did my confidence in myself and my work. My 'Eureka' moment was recognising the responsibility to be a good corporate citizen was my responsibility, and that who I am as a good corporate citizen isn't different to who I am as a good citizen of the world, or is shouldn't be. There is no need for inner conflict. In the same way, there is no need to have two personas. I am one and the same person in my WorkLife – in and out of work. It was this realisation that led me to be a founding member of a non-profit social enterprise arm of the company I worked at then, and an active driver of greater social responsibility at the company I'm with now.

Benny: My 'Eureka' moment came through observation that set me on a path to change the status quo in my industry. I observed that creative teams were increasingly taking on new responsibilities outside of traditional roles. This indicated the increasingly strategic partnerships that individuals and teams have on a business. I also observed that they weren't getting quantitative feedback on the performance of their work. So I set about establishing a new status quo – one that is about partnership. In-house teams planning for the current year and beyond consistently asking themselves,

"How can we be better partners?" And getting feedback from colleagues, collaborators and clients. This information is vital to meeting business objectives. It's also crucial in understanding the different inputs from different teams. With this understanding comes respect for what can be realistically achieved (in time, volume and cost), which has helped alleviate the practice of pushing individuals and teams too hard.

Maggie: I don't know that I have had a 'Eureka' moment either, or maybe it's something I've been experiencing lately. I don't fully recognise what this is. Yet. But I feel a shift in my thinking about what I don't want to stand out for. I'm still not there with it, but I'm beginning to question within myself how I can use what makes me different to help others.

* * *

That's how Aisling found her story, and it has helped establish her company brand and in business and networking situations helping her to talk about what she does. It's also helped develop presentations and pitches for work.

But what about presentations? How can you adapt your unique story to help you deliver a great presentation that people will want to listen to?

You need to think about the single purpose of your presentation, the one principle that is most central to what you want to accomplish.

Let me demonstrate with a presentation Aisling is currently working on. This is part of an application process for funding to deliver community projects.

First, a little further background:

As well as working with the Arts in the workplace through people-development programmes, Aisling is also passionate about bringing the joy and benefits of the Arts to the community. This includes retirement homes and to people who are living with dementia and Alzheimer's.

Here's how Aisling's Story/Presentation is shaping up:

MAKING YOUR STORY INTO A POWERFUL PRESENTATION ASSIGNMENT

"My love of the Arts came from my parents, music, song and dance, film and theatre.

"Sadly, towards the end of my mum's life, she developed dementia, which progressed quite rapidly. She had to go into a retirement home as she required round-the-clock care. As a family, we felt we'd lost her: dementia took away aspects of her personality and parts of her memory, she just wasn't the same anymore, and it was heartbreaking.

"When we went to visit, she always knew us, but as soon as we left, she wouldn't remember we'd been there. We also couldn't have a conversation with her because she just couldn't remember things, and she'd become frustrated and agitated. It was too upsetting for her.

"Every couple of weeks, a singer would go into the home and have a sing-song with the residents, and when she did, my mum would sing along, and she'd remember every single word of every single song, and she'd talk about it for days afterwards. It lifted her mood immediately, and she was so much happier and calmer.

"This is why I want to work with a team of performing artists, to create a programme of events bringing music, song and dance to the lives of people who live with dementia and Alzheimer's. I know the joys, benefits and wellbeing it will bring."

Aisling's One Purpose: To help people understand the immediate and lasting impact these programmes will have on people's lives.

Wish her luck!

* * *

Saoirse: My One Purpose is to discover, uncover and share the stories of the people who make up our community – stories that may on the surface appear to be everyday stories, but underneath they are stories of inspiration.

Annie: I believe my One Purpose is to share why tech is such an important and fascinating industry for both men and women.

Elena: My One Purpose is to share my journey as an artist. In particular with my students who are preparing to embark on a WorkLife in art, as well as fellow artists who are struggling to establish themselves in their chosen field. I want to share the importance of persistence, consistency and determination in carving out a WorkLife true to their purpose and passion.

Florian: My One Purpose is to continue to support and promote the people in my industry.

Philippe: My One Purpose is to use my curatorial platform for advocacy and activism, to give voice to talented artists who deserve to have a voice in the art world

Pascal: My One Purpose is to be a good citizen of the world and an active driver of greater social responsibility within my workplace and community.

Benny: My One Purpose is to advocate for building and maintaining a great culture at my company and within my industry. One that lives and breathes important core values: curiosity, respect, teamwork, and employee health and wellbeing.

Maggie: My One Purpose is to use what makes me different to help others.

* * *

The group enjoyed working through the first part of the assignment together. The five steps helped them to discover or rediscover their unique story. They were pleased with how the steps helped put everything in context and enabled them to identify their One Purpose easily. They felt they had what they needed to develop this into a presentation. This was something they wanted to do alone, at a time when they had an actual presentation to prepare for. That, they believed, would allow them to take their unique story and turn it into a powerful presentation because it would give them the context to focus on what they wanted and needed to say.

FIVE STEPS TO FINDING YOUR UNIQUE STORY ASSIGNMENT

Now it's time for you to complete the assignment with your accompaniment of choice.

A reminder of the Words Of Wisdom shared earlier:

Truly great stories and presentations live on in the hearts and minds of audiences the world over, that is a Fact. Everyone has an innate storytelling ability, that is another Fact.

You just need to think about a time when you were with friends (or strangers!) in a bar or other social setting to know that you are a natural-born storyteller.

Why is that? Because when you are in a friendly setting, you can be yourself, and you will use really direct language (no jargon) to make sure what you say is engaging.

These experiences show that we all have an innate sense of what makes a good story. But we tend to forget that a great presentation is simply a great story, and we can also at times struggle to express our natural and true self.

Step 1:

Begin by thinking about where your passions lie.

What topics are you most likely going to be talking about?
What are the things that excite you?
What are the subject matters that make you feel you have something to say?

Step 2:

Look where you spend your time.

What is it you do outside of your work when your time is valuable?
Where do you choose to spend it?

Step 3:

Look where you spend your disposable income.

What are the things you spend your money on? Your interests or hobbies.

Step 4:

Think about your struggles.

In tough times, what did you do?
What kind of uncertainties did you feel?

Step 5:

Discover your Eureka moment.

What was the moment you had your greatest realisation?

MAKING YOUR STORY INTO A POWERFUL PRESENTATION ASSIGNMENT

Next, you need to think about the single purpose of your presentation, the one principle that is most central to what you want to accomplish.

SALADS
READY

SPITALFIELDS

6

June

The Case of Having to Deliver Bad News

Featuring *The Power of a Positive No* by William Ury, accompanied by Afternoon Tea

The summer sun was shining on the streets of Shoreditch, and the group soaked up the late afternoon rays as they made their way to celebrate Benny's birthday over afternoon tea. They were meeting earlier for this month's Book Club. They had booked the 5 pm serving, which, although it seemed to be late for afternoon tea, it was, according to Florian, within the timeframe of this long-held British tradition.

Telling the group of its origin, Florian said it dated back to 1840, and to Anna the Duchess of Bedford, who introduced the idea to combat her late afternoon hunger pangs, at a time when it was customary to have two main meals per day: breakfast in the morning and dinner at around 8 pm. The tradition began with tea, bread and butter and cake being brought to Anna's rooms. Then she began to invite friends to join her, and the practice moved into her drawing room. Before long, all of fashionable society was drinking tea and eating sandwiches and cakes in the afternoon – a trend that was to evolve to become a national tradition.

The newly founded boutique hotel had made the afternoon tea ritual their own. Inspired by the British tea rooms of old, it served a traditional spread that was reimagined with a modern twist, and the late afternoon sitting often rolled into evening drinks.

Florian had told the group the story of the founders: Aisha, Mollie, Darius and Ben, all of whom had all grown up in the East End of London, and had been friends since their schooldays. Aisha had gone on to study Economics, Mollie Hotel Management and Hospitality, Darius Business and Management, and Ben Marketing. Their studies and earlier work had taken them out of London and away from each other. But they had always stayed in touch, catching up when they could. It was one of those catch-ups that led to what they all thought at the time was a crazy idea. That was to move back to London and open a hotel together. It was an industry that interested all of them simply because they loved socialising, and they loved how hotels were hubs that brought people together. Having each worked around the world, they appreciated how a great hotel showcased a city and its communities, serving both visitors and locals by providing great experiences, whether that was an overnight stay or a shared meal, a place to work from or to have a drink at the bar.

Where would they do this? That wasn't the crazy part of their idea. They instantly knew it had to be Shoreditch, simply because that's where they loved to socialise when in London, and that's where locals, Londoners far and wide and visitors to the city flocked to. It was London's hub of social activity that was also steeped in arts, culture and history, making it a great part of town for people across all walks of life and life stages to visit for a short stay or to stay awhile.

No, where they would do this wasn't the crazy part of their idea. The crazy part of their idea was how they would do this. How could they, with very little capital between them, finance such a venture? The solution came to them through a British investment crowdfunding platform, where they ran an extremely successful crowdfunding campaign, quickly hitting the target amount they needed to buy the hotel that had come on the market, which was ripe for refurbishment.

That was how their collective acorn of an idea began, and it's been bearing fruit ever since as they continue to grow. In growing, they strive to honour the traditions and history of the neighbourhood and the legacies of those who have gone before them; and in so doing, they're creating their own history and legacies. They're writing themselves and their neighbourhood into the history books. The derelict building was the starting point for the perfect partnership – between the four young friends, and between them and their community.

The group loved that story, as they loved all the interesting nuggets they were discovering together on their culinary tour of their neighbourhood.

From the moment they stepped through the thick red velvet curtain into the tea room, they were struck by an ambience of a lovely, old world that seemed to whoosh around them. The dedicated English tea room had a quiet elegance and a sense of timelessness – a quintessentially British afternoon tea affair with tables dressed with crisp white linen, floral china and silverware, surrounded by snug velvet red armchairs. A gently lit glass-ceilinged room with a wonderfully scented aroma from the beautiful fresh flower arrangements that filled the room. Suited wait staff roaming quietly around and tunes from bygone eras played by a pianist created the perfect backdrop for a special experience.

As they took their seats, their waitress, Charlotte, arrived with a big jug of homemade lemonade, saying the sweet and sour flavours of real lemonade are perfect to hit the spot in a way that nothing else seems to do on a hot summer's day.

Having introduced herself, she asked if they had been for afternoon tea at the hotel before. On learning they hadn't, she let them know that they served a traditional British afternoon tea with some modern twists and a vegan afternoon tea. Saying their tea would begin with finger sandwiches, followed by scones, and then a selection of sweets, she gave them their tea menu, which had quite an extensive range of blends. Charlotte let them know that both she and their tea sommelier, Ruben, could answer any questions they had in helping to select their choice of tea.

Annie said she would like the vegan option, which pleased Charlotte, who said she was vegan, and it makes her happy when guests order this. Smiling at the rest of the group, who all ordered the other option, she said both are wonderful, and she has that on good authority from their previous guests. Enquiring if they would like a cocktail to begin, she was met with a resounding yes, and she handed them their drinks menus, leaving them for a moment to make their selection.

Raising his ice-cold glass of lemonade, Florian led a toast to Benny.

Florian: A toast, dear friend, you've touched us with your New York energy and vibrancy and a little Californian dreaming thrown in. All of us are better for knowing you, and we are truly thankful for you being a part of our lives. Happy birthday Benny, we wish you a wonderful birthday month of celebrations and many years of a life filled with happiness.

They all clinked glasses to a chorus of "Happy birthday dear Benny".

For once, Benny was lost for words. Florian's words, together with the heartfelt warmth that was emanating from the group, really touched him. All he could muster up in response was a quiet, equally heartfelt thanks.

Benny sipped on his lemonade.

Benny: Wow, this is definitely sunshine in a glass.

They all laughed.

Maggie: Cheers, dear Benny, our California dreamer

To which they all clinked glasses. Benny picked up his drinks menu.

Benny: Wow, such an extensive range of non-alcoholic cocktails. This really is exciting.

Saoirse: There are certainly some interesting concoctions on here, quite interesting infusions that play on blends of tea. That's really quite innovative.

Charlotte returned to take their cocktail orders, which included a non-alcoholic Long Island iced tea, a sweet tea vodka lemonade mojito, a green tea martini, an earl grey, a royal tea cocktail and a chai whiskey sour, then went to have them prepared at the bar, which was an intimate space bookended by two small seating areas.

Saoirse: While we're waiting for our drinks, I'd like to share something new that I'm doing, something that I'm just beginning.

There are a whole lot of people living in Shoreditch. Over the last few months, we've come to know some of them together, and I've come to know some more by taking time to explore and to stop and talk. These are the people who make the neighbourhood what it is, the people who make it such a great place to eat and explore. Many of these people are very far from the place they once called home. Some have been displaced. But Shoreditch is home now, even if they're just passing through.

I want to work with people in their communities, to tell their stories, to get their stories out there, to remind people what happened. I want to help people to speak up and speak out. These stories need to be told. People need to know what they did and continue to do in order to survive.

Hearing peoples stories that illuminate a place, that's the journalism I want to be a part of. I want to give a platform to people who would be usually ignored, who would be forgotten, to give people who wouldn't have a voice otherwise, an opportunity to shine.

There are big stories, and there are small stories, and inside those small stories there are hundreds of more small stories, and it's a willingness to let those stories be told and find the best storytellers to tell them. To begin, my idea is for that to be me, and in time to enable other people to tell these stories, individuals themselves through speaking or writing, or through theatre and bringing in other people to help tell these stories.

I want to find and write about the little off-the-grid places throughout our neighbourhood. I feel I'm at the intersection between food and drink, culture and history, and I feel I got to this point by kind of cobbling together a way to travel, write, learn, eat, drink and live my WorkLife.

I believe every meal and every dish has a story, often a very personal one, often a story of hardship, separation, difficult times, but also stories of good times, happiness and hope. And when somebody cooks for you, they're saying something. They're telling you something about themselves, where they come from, who they are, what makes them happy.

And I also want to write about the wait staff, because we need to all hail the waiter, the career server, that great disappearing species of proud well-trained specialists, members of the service industry, who can trace their roots back to the great hotels of Europe and beyond. I want to write their stories into history. And not just the front-of-house stories, but the back-of-house stories, too – the chefs and everybody who is involved in sourcing, and preparing the food, and the stories of the founders, creators of the places where people love to share experiences and stories over a shared meal. The out-of-house stories too – suppliers from near and far.

Over the past year, I've been writing for myself, and I think there is a time and a place to write for yourself. That, for me, is in my journal. But when I'm writing to share work, I'm writing to connect to other people. I differentiate writing for others by thinking about it as a gift I'm trying to make for someone that's given – given freely.

That's important because I have to be able to let my writing go because part of making a gift is when the time comes, it's not yours anymore. And that can be a really hard part of writing. Sometimes I really want to hold on to the stuff that I'm working on and not let it go and not let it become someone else's.

Patrick and I both had restless bones, and we were not the kind of people who sat back. We were much more about getting the most out of life and seeking fresh challenges. That was part of the attraction for us, to each other, to life and to our life together. I've realised that this last year, it wasn't that I was running from something, but that I was running towards something. I didn't know what that something was, but now I'm beginning to.

The books we've read together, our shared discussions and, as importantly, our shared experiences eating, drinking, listening to each other's stories, and the stories of the people we've met along the way – the people in the stories, and the people in the restaurants – has gotten me to this place. It's the beginning of something new, and I don't know where I'm going with it or where it will take me, but I sense it will be an interesting and wonderful journey on which I will learn and grow through the stories I'll uncover and the experiences I encounter along the way.

Charlotte's arrival with their cocktails was the perfect timing for Saoirse to raise her glass.

Saoirse: Thank you all for helping me to get here.

To which they all clinked.

Florian: If you need me to make any introductions to people in food and drinks, let me know.
Maggie: You might also like to meet my mum, who, as you know, helps people to tell their stories. She may be able to introduce you to people as well, and I know she'd love to meet you.
Pascal: I meet lots of people through my work who I think it could be good for you to meet, if you would like that.
Benny: Actually, I could help in that way too.
Annie: I'm not sure I can make introductions that would help you, but I would love to help in any way I can.
Saoirse: Thank you all. I was kind of hoping you might make the suggestions you have and want to help out.
Florian: To your new adventure, Saoirse – in your writing and your next WorkLife chapter.

Once again, they all clinked glasses. Benny took the first sip of his cocktail.

Benny: This is absolute pleasure in a glass.

He wasn't met with any arguments to that, just sipping noises of complete agreement.

Pascal had chosen this month's case: The Case of Having to Deliver Bad News, to which to accompanying book was *The Power of a Positive No* by William Ury. He began to read the story.

“In *The Power of a Positive No*, I have tried to identify the fundamental practical principles that apply across cultural contexts and across arenas of life from personal to professional to societal. I trust you will be able to adapt these principles to your particular relationships for your own benefit and the benefit of all those around you.” (William Ury)

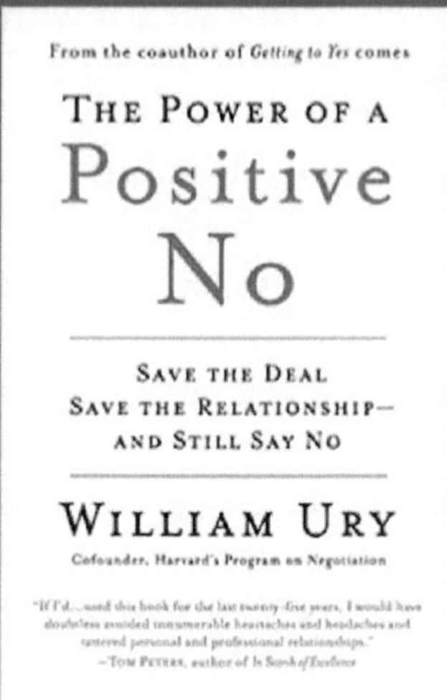

From the back cover:
“The most powerful word in the language is also potentially the most destructive, and for most people is the most difficult to say. Yet when we know how to use it correctly, it has the power to profoundly transform our lives. That word is ‘No.’

“In this wise and insightful book, the author of *Getting to Yes* asserts that, although you may be able to say Yes, you cannot get to the right Yes until you know how to say No.

“Each of us faces the dilemma at least a dozen times a day of whether and how to say No to a request or demand, inappropriate or abusive behaviours, or simply the status quo. People are concerned about spoiling relationships with bosses, losing the deal with clients or upsetting family members.

“*The Power of a Positive No* provides a simple, proven five-step solution to this everyday dilemma. It offers an innovative framework that will help you use the constructive power of ‘No’ in a way that is positive, powerful and productive, not destructive.”

“I see *The Power of a Positive No* not only as a negotiation book but as a life skills book, for all of life is a dance of Yes and No. Each of us every waking hour is called upon to say No, whether to friends or family members, to our bosses, employees, or co-workers, or to ourselves. Whether and how we say No determines the very quality of our lives. It is perhaps the most important word for us to learn to say gracefully and effectively.” (William Ury)

The Power of a Positive No, by William Ury, was originally published by Hodder in 2007 (272pp., ISBN 978-0340923801)

The Case of Having to Deliver Bad News

ABC Property Association had gone through a major downsizing and restructuring process due to the economic crisis. Two-thirds of the company employees were going to lose their jobs. The company had decided that the fairest approach in deciding who would keep and who would lose their job was to have everyone interview for the job they were already doing. This meant people were competing against their colleagues for one in three of them to remain in their role. Morale that was already at an all-time low, continued to be destroyed day in day out as the interviews took place, and the subsequent decisions were made as to who would keep and who would lose their job.

Arnold's position in the company meant he had responsibility for managing this restructuring and for delivering the bad news to the people who were losing their jobs. This was causing him a lot of pain and anxiety. He knew all of these people individually. He knew their backgrounds and their circumstances, and he knew how bad the job market within their industry was and how difficult it would be for people to get a new job.

In preparing for the first two conversations he needed to have, he met with Tom, a colleague and fellow manager whose way of looking at things was always something that Arnold had valued. Tom imparted these:

Words of Wisdom

- Prepare what you are going to say from a place of empathy and humility, with regard to both the situation and what you're going to do next;
- Don't sugarcoat the truth, instead say what you have to say, and phrase it in a way that people know you respect their humanity;
- The more sensitive the issue, the more rapidly emotions can escalate. See things from each individual's perspective, not as "you in their shoes", but as them. Do this by really listening to their responses and allowing them to tell their story.

This really helped Arnold. He wanted to navigate this difficult situation that people found themselves in through no fault of their own with dignity for everyone impacted. He believed it was important to be open and honest about bad situations, and he always strived to take a straightforward approach in saying the toughest stuff.

This is not something that always came easily to him, especially at the early stages of his WorkLife. Actually, even before that, when as a student he somehow found himself leading fellow students in a summer internship based abroad. He was part of a team who were teaching English as a foreign language to young teenagers who aspired to go on to university to study Business.

The behaviours the team experienced from the employees at the school they were teaching at were bad, really bad. They were undermined at every given point, ridiculed in front of their students. It was demoralising for everyone, and it was like that from day one. But Arnold didn't speak up, he let it slide, and before long, it had snowballed out of control. Arnold began to believe that he was chosen as leader because he was considered to be a soft touch. This wasn't true, however he was completely out of his depth. He also didn't want to fail in his first leadership role. But inevitably he felt he had failed.

Arnold felt he had failed his team and himself by not speaking up sooner, by not saying what needed to be said, by not speaking the truth. And when in time he tried to speak up, to say what needed to be said, he was called a whiner and told that leaders don't whine.

These weren't good people, and this was a very bad situation and one that came close to destroying Arnold's WorkLife. Because it took time for him to let go of it, it took time for him to learn the lessons from it, and it took time for him to regain trust in himself as a leader.

Over time he did recover. He did learn lessons from it, which in turn allowed him to move on and rebuild his self-trust in his leadership abilities. Over the years, he learnt through many sources and resources – people, training courses and books that helped in being able to say what needed to be said.

Arnold had to learn to listen to his emotions. Fear of failure as a leader had caused him to avoid speaking up, and in so doing, he had suppressed his underlying anger evoked by being treated so badly. He also felt a sense of guilt for letting his team down. He had to learn to become aware of his emotions, and in so doing, he was able to take control of them rather than let them take control of him.

Another lesson Arnold learnt from that summer internship experience was to always uncover the underlying motivations in knowing what to say No to in the future and what to say Yes to.

To do this, he had to learn how to uncover his interests. He came to understand he had said Yes to the leadership position because he hadn't known what he wanted. He hadn't clarity on what his interests were. His Wants: desires, aspirations and concerns. He had thought of it only as a summer internship and hadn't felt the need to overthink it, other than that. His learning was that he wanted to say Yes to leadership roles in companies that valued their people and treated them well and No to leadership roles in companies that didn't.

Arnold learnt he needed to probe even deeper into his underlying motivations to find what lay underneath those Wants to get to his Needs. He came to understand that beneath the anger he had felt and suppressed was a basic need for respect. Arnold learnt that respect was his greatest motivator.

To be in a position to recognise when his Wants and Needs were under threat, Arnold's lessons in listening to his emotions allowed him to recognise them: Fear alerted him to a possible threat; Anger would tell him that something in the situation was wrong and needed to be corrected; Guilt alerted him to be sensitive to important relationships. By paying attention to these emotions, he learnt to listen to his feelings rather than react to them. This helped to fine-tune his ability to take control, rather than being controlled by his emotions.

The next lesson that Arnold learnt was the importance of uncovering his values. The principles and beliefs that guided his WorkLife. For Arnold, that was: treat everyone fairly. This value gave him strong motivation to be able to say No to people, companies and situations that didn't live up to this core value for Arnold, and Yes to those that did.

Book Wisdom

The book from which Arnold had gleaned this learning was *The Power Of A Positive No* by William Ury. This was the book from which he had also gleaned the lessons of The Three Gifts of a Positive No when he worked to rebuild himself and his WorkLife, following the devastating summer internship.

"According to the sages of ancient India, there are three fundamental processes at work in the universe: creation, preservation and transformation. Saying No is essential to all three processes. If you can learn to say No skilfully and wisely, you can create what you want, protect what you value, and change what doesn't work. These are the three great gifts of a positive No."

As Arnold began to develop his WorkLife and rebuild his self-trust in his leadership abilities, in creating what he wanted, he had to learn to say No to competing demands for his time and energy, in order to create spaces for the Yeses in his life, the people and activities that mattered the most to him. Arnold learnt the paradoxical secret of this gift is: "you cannot truly say Yes until you can truly say No." It took many lessons from saying Yes too readily before Arnold accepted this gift. Lessons learnt from missed opportunities that he couldn't say Yes to because he hadn't been able to say No to proposals that ended up taking over and draining his time and energy.

In protecting what he valued, Arnold had to learn to say No to threats to his personal happiness. That for Arnold was quality time with his family, being there for the important moments with his girlfriend who became his wife and in time their children. Again, this wasn't straightforward as he was building his WorkLife. Long hours and travel would have accelerated his advancement in the company. At first he said Yes, but this took a toll on his and his family's WorkLife happiness. It had the same impact for many of his colleagues, which in turn negatively impacted the success of the company. This was because they couldn't retain their people.

Arnold had to work to find a way to create a culture where people could say No that wouldn't impact their WorkLife opportunities. Again, this took time, but over time, working with his team, he created a workplace that wasn't a fixed place. Arnold led on what was a pioneering project at the time to enable working from home, which alleviated time travelling to work and trips away from home. He found a way to say a positive No to demands that would have negatively impacted his and his colleague's happiness by saying Yes to finding a way to retain people. Which, in turn, positively impacted the success of the company. This was because people felt that their WorkLife happiness was valued, which made them feel valued. These happy and valued people were motivated and driven in their work and wanted to remain part of a company that was driven by a happy workforce. It became known in the company as the loop of happiness, motivation and drive.

In changing what no longer worked, Arnold had to learn to say No to his addiction to smoking. At university, cigarettes had become his coping mechanism to stay on top of his course load while working a part-time job to pay his university and living costs. In effect, cigarettes replaced food – the need to buy it and the time to prepare and eat it. He needed the money to go towards other costs, and he needed the time to stay on top of his course load.

He continued this behaviour in his first job. This was because he found the work to be a steep learning curve and required long hours on his part to stay on top of things. While he now had money to buy food and even to have it delivered, he denied himself the time to eat it. He had developed habits that were not only bad but were also self-destructive and very soon began to impact his health. His wake up call was when he caught a cold, which got in on his chest, and he developed a really bad chest infection. He struggled with his breathing, and that frightened him. He learnt to say No to cigarettes to get to a higher Yes. That was his health and wellbeing.

Fast forward to his current situation, and on re-reading the book, he gleaned the following wisdom:

"When No means bad news for the recipient, it can be hard to deliver. A fact-based approach can help the recipient accept the No."

"Sometimes blunt candour is called for."

"The employee may not like hearing this, but in the end, he may learn something useful and, in any case, it serves him better than the boss being evasive. Being honest and straight with people can work well if you accompany the candour with empathy and respect."

"Be hard on the problem, not the person."

This also really helped Arnold in preparing for the first two conversations he needed to have.

For his conversation with Dom, Arnold knew that he needed to stick to the facts, to let Dom know what the decision had been based upon. Knowing Dom, he believed he would respect the process and recognise that it was fair.

For his conversation with Rob, whose performance of late had caused serious concerns, he knew he needed to be honest and straight in saying what needed to be said. He also knew he needed to say this with empathy and respect.

By way of further preparation, Arnold asked himself the following question:

How can I ensure I understand and respond to the needs, viewpoints and perspectives of everyone I need to deliver bad news to?

The answer that came to him was:

• He needed to prepare well for each conversation by way of knowing each person's individual circumstances. This would allow him to think about the support he could offer, over and above the redundancy financial package.

• In the meetings, he needed to give people the space to say what they needed to say, and he needed to listen well in order to truly understand what was being said.

This is how Arnold began his conversation with Dom:

"Dom, I'm sorry to tell you we have decided to give the job to Ben. Our decision was based on the fact that he has had more experience interacting with stakeholders on eco-policies. Your work with the company has been exemplary, and it was a difficult decision."

Even though Dom was disappointed, he appreciated the way in which Arnold had delivered the news. Because it was fact-based, Dom said he recognised the decision had been made objectively.

Dom went on to share with Arnold that he was considering undertaking a university course. His reasons were two-fold:

1. He believed it would take the economy, the industry and the market time to recover, time during which he believed it would be difficult to secure a new position, and so he was planning on taking time out to do a masters in eco-design;

2. He'd had a keen interest in eco-design for a long time but never had the time or the disposable income to invest in doing a masters. He believed together with his experience and knowledge of the property industry, this course would allow him to hit the ground running when the economy did improve, and as importantly, it would allow him to make a positive impact to environmental housing.

Over and above the redundancy financial settlement Arnold was able to give Dom, he was also able to offer him further support with university fees. This was part of an ongoing programme the company had with the local university. On top of this, he told Dom he would be able to offer him work experience as his course progressed.

This is how Arnold began his conversation with Rob:

"Rob, you didn't get the job. We had some concerns about your performance. I understand how difficult it is to find any positivity in a situation like this, but the truth is your negativity has had a serious impact on your performance."

Although this was hard for Rob to hear, he knew it was the truth, and he needed someone to speak the truth to him. Arnold had delivered these words with empathy and respect, and Rob appreciated that. He opened up to Arnold about how he was feeling, about how he was struggling every day to get through the day. He was worried about himself, and he was also worried how he was going to survive financially being out of work. But instead of asking for help, he'd reacted negatively and pushed people away when they'd showed concern.

Arnold was in a position to make sure that Rob received the help and support he needed. He arranged for him to meet with a career counsellor to help him manage the emotional and practical elements in moving his WorkLife forward during this time of uncertainty.

Epilogue

Arnold took time to reflect on both conversations by way of giving himself feedback on how they had gone. He acknowledged what he had done that had allowed the conversations to go well, which was:

- The way in which he had prepared;
- The way in which he had delivered the news in saying what he had to say;
- The way in which this had given Dom and Rob the space they needed to say what they needed to say;
- The way in which by really listening, he was able to offer both of them the individual support they needed over and above the redundancy financial settlement.

He also acknowledged what he could have done better, which was:

- He could have taken time to talk to Dom about what he wanted rather than automatically have him go through the interview process. He now knew that Dom would have opted out of this and would have welcomed knowing about the extra support Arnold was able to offer at an earlier stage in the process.
- He knew he needed to have had an earlier conversation with Rob. He knew Rob's behaviour was out of character, and now he realised it was a cry for help. Had Arnold taken the time to speak to him earlier, he could have helped to alleviate some of Rob's anxiety and concerns.

WORKLIFE BOOK CLUB

Adjusting his dark blue Tom Ford glasses, Pascal took a sip from his cocktail.

Pascal: Another interesting case that requires our skills of detection.

He laughed.

Pascal: That's what I always feel at the beginning of each evening, and I'm always curious as to where the evidence and our analysis and interpretation of it will take us.

They all laughed in agreement

Maggie: It does at times feel as though we're applying forensic psychology in our deductions.

It hadn't escaped Maggie's attention that Pascal was wearing the colours of the Union Jack again. His pinstripe suit and matching accessories was, she believed, a nod to the flag of the country where the tradition of afternoon tea had originated.

Charlotte, accompanied by two of her fellow wait staff, brought the first of their afternoon-tea stands down a flight of steps from a faraway corner of the room, almost 'off stage', and set them down on the table. It was clear the first act was about to begin as the selection of sandwiches took centre stage.

The traditional-with-a-modern-twist option included coronation-chicken-filled brioche rolls lined with pineapple and coriander, in a nod to Brick Lane; smoked salmon with herb crème fraiche on a dark pumpernickel bread; honey-roasted ham and cheese (which was from a local cheesemaker) on a granary bread; egg cress on a thinly sliced pillowy white bread; cucumber and mint vegan cream cheese on a beetroot bread. This last was also served on the vegan option, along with 'salmon' made from marinated tomatoes, seaweed and chipotle on the dark pumpernickel bread; a creamy tofu filling that resembled egg on the thinly sliced pillowy white bread; avocado, tomato and vegan mozzarella on a sun-dried tomato bread; and a roasted vegetable and hummus wrap.

Ruben, the tea sommelier, arrived at their table and, on introducing himself, enquired if they had questions or needed help in choosing their tea. They didn't. The detailed description in the menu of each brew had enabled them to make their decision, and as Benny said, this is a great place to try something new – after wondering who knew there were so many different types of tea.

Taking their orders which ranged from different blends of Earl Grey to Assam to Darjeeling to Lapsang Souchong, to Jasmine, to Moroccan Mint tea. Ruben weighed and infused their selected brews on the silver table he had wheeled up, which served as his dedicated tea station.

"Does one pour the tea or milk first?" asked Benny.

"Oh, most definitely the milk," responded Maggie.

“I prefer to pour the tea first,” said Saoirse. “I like to see its colour before I pour in the milk, and I hate it too milky. Actually, I started drinking black tea because when I would ask for a drop of milk, which was to colour the tea, it was always inevitably too milky for my liking. People tend to be very heavy-handed when it comes to pouring milk, I’ve found.”

“Ah, the age-old, much-debated question,” Ruben said. “Which comes first, the milk or the tea.”

“And is there a proper way?” asked Pascal. “I feel there may be a British etiquette around this.”

“The royal butler has said the royal family are firmly on the ‘TIF’ side, tea in first,” Ruben laughed. “However, it remains a much-disputed topic by ‘etiquette experts’. Here we are on the side of whatever our guest’s preference is.”

As Ruben served them their individually prepared silver pots of tea, he briefly described them, saying:

“Assam is named after its region of production in north-eastern India. It is known for its body and has a distinctive malty flavour and intense, bright colour.

“Earl Grey is a blend of black teas treated with the oil of bergamot which gives the tea a scented aroma and taste. It is named after Charles, 2nd Earl Grey, who was Prime Minister from 1830 to 1834.

“Darjeeling is a black tea from a province in Northern India. It is an aromatic and astringent tea with a hint of almonds and wild flowers.

“Lapsang Souchong is a Chinese tea dried over smoking pine needles, which produces a striking smoky odour and flavour, including notes of wood smoke, pine resin and smoked paprika.

“Moroccan Mint tea, also known as Maghrebi, is a green tea prepared with spearmint leaves. It is traditional to the regions of the northwestern countries of Africa. The mint brings a strong flavour, delicate sweetness, and mild aroma.

“Jasmine tea is a Chinese green tea that has been flavoured by adding petals of the jasmine plant, which is grown at high elevations in the mountains. It has delicate, sweet and smooth flavours.”

Before pouring their tea, Charlotte enquired of each of them if they would like milk and, if so, their preference of which came first and poured accordingly.

"Ruben, your knowledge of tea is really interesting," Saorise said. "Where does your passion come from?"

Ruben replied saying that he had worked in tea all his life, starting out as a young lad in a tea shop in the East End, then going on the road as a sales rep. A few years ago, he had taken early retirement. But after a while, he became bored and realised he wasn't ready to stop working. He was just tired of being on the road. 'Tea sommelier' was on his radar because of his work, but he'd never given it much thought before as a job. Then he started looking into it, and discovered he could get his qualifications at the UK Tea Academy here in London. Once he had those, then this job came up, and everything just fell into place. He went on to say that it's given him a renewed passion for tea, which he thought he'd lost. He loved working here, making tea for people, watching them enjoy this long-held British tradition. He laughed and said it's given him a new tea leaf of life.

The group all laughed, and Saoirse thanked him for sharing his story. Checking they had everything they needed, Ruben and Charlotte left them to enjoy their tea.

Annie: When we stepped through the curtain, it felt as though we were stepping back in time, and yet this tea room also seems to exist outside of time. Ruben's story somehow added to that. It's quite magical, really.

They all agreed as they took the first bite of their sandwiches, followed by a sip of tea – which, according to Maggie, was definitely the 'proper etiquette', though she admitted her 'proper etiquette' knowledge didn't go as far as knowing whether they were required to stick out their pinkies. But she sensed that was a 'posh' myth.

Benny: Does the Tea Building in Shoreditch have a history in tea? I know now it's a hub of creative activity, but does it have origins in tea?

Florian laughed.

Florian: That's the very question I asked in search of an interesting

snippet of Shoreditch history to share this evening. The answer is no, but yes.

It was initially built as a bacon factory for the Lipton brand. The Lipton brand is synonymous with tea, so I researched the brand and found a story on their website about Thomas Lipton, who opened his first grocery shops in Glasgow in 1871, where he sold tea to his customers. He saw the potential in this delicious aromatic beverage and bought a number of tea fields in Ceylon – now Sri Lanka. He was the creator of Lipton iced tea and was also said to have democratised tea. Believing it should be enjoyed by everyone and not just the wealthy. He found cheaper ways of packaging and transporting tea and make it available to the man on the street.

And there's a further connection to tea, which I gleaned from London tea history. While the Tea Building was built as a bacon factory, it was joined internally to the Biscuit Building next door, a warehouse which was principally used as a tea-packing warehouse.

In the Second World War, an air raid shelter was added to the building, and miraculously the Tea Building survived the blitz with little damage. In 1947 part of the building was converted to a self-service canteen, catering for over five hundred staff. I like to think tea would have been served, or self-served – not afternoon tea perhaps, more like a builder's brew, I suspect.

Benny: Builder's brew?

Florian: A British English colloquial term for a strong cup of tea. And so, while the Tea Building may not have pure tea origins, it has strong connections to the brew for sure. And now, as you say, it's a hub of creative activity and is full of original features that make it a unique place to work.

Benny: That's true. I've worked from there.

Pascal: Me too

Annie: And me, how strange. I wonder if we passed each other at any time.

Maggie: Like tea ships passing in the night.

Annie smiled and opened her copy of the book in which she had highlighted some passages.

Annie: To take us from the Tea Building's backstory to Arnold's backstory, which I liked. I mean I liked learning about his backstory, the difficulty he overcame following his bad summer internship experience, and how learning to say No to what didn't work for him and Yes to what did. I thought it was a good lead into his current situation of having to deliver bad news. And I liked the early passage from the book, which helped me understand the Nos and Yeses talked about.

When Ury said he needed to say No a lot in his WorkLife but that his Nos needed to be nice, I think that's key. I liked that he said he and his wife needed to learn to pause before responding in order to make sure their No was not only powerful but respectful – the first scenario he spoke about needed to be powerful as well as respectful because it was in relation to their daughter's health. I liked that he introduced the concept of a positive No – that their Nos were intended to be not negative but positive Nos, in that they served to protect their daughter, and that they were in service of a higher Yes to their daughter's health and wellbeing.

Benny: I liked that we got to that early too, because it immediately helped me to connect to Arnold's story of how he needed to deliver a positive No in service of a higher Yes, which in the Case was the way in which he could help both Dom and Rob move forward in their WorkLife after their job loss.

I really like when writers share personal stories at the outset; it helps to make a book more relatable from the off. That's important because Ury is much respected in his work, and so we get that he's qualified to write on the matter. But as he said, "the book is about the crucial part of delivering a positive No in every area of life," and so I think it's important that he shares stories from both his personal and professional life.

Maggie: I liked the early insight we got into why and how his WorkLife journey began. How, going to school in Europe, only fifteen years after the end of the Second World War, he grew up in a generation that lived under the threat of a Third World War. How he felt there had to be a better way of protecting our societies and ourselves. And how in pursuit of answers to this dilemma, he became a professional student of human conflict. And how he sought to apply what he was learning by becoming a negotiator and mediator.

Actually, I more than liked that. It blew me away. I think this may be particularly poignant to me in the work I do and the work I aspire to do. The last few months have gotten me thinking a lot about my learning, growth and development, and so I think this resonated with me on both a personal and professional level because of that.

Pascal: I connected with the book on both a personal and professional level, too. He said, by profession he's a negotiator specialist, a teacher, consultant and mediator, and he is by passion a seeker of peace. I'm that too. I don't mean peace in terms of world peace, but peaceful transitions in mergers and takeovers. I actually think many people are. Arnold was – his role and the situation his company was in demanded that.

When he said, "Even when agreements are reached, they are often unstable or unsatisfying because the real underlying issues have been avoided or smoothed over, the problem only deferred", I think that helped Arnold to avoid falling into that trap, as did the sage wisdom he received from Tom, to understand each individual's perspective.

That was also really fundamental because it allowed him to deliver the bad news to Dom and Rob, in effect saying No to them keeping their jobs without destroying their relationships. That was important to Arnold.

It's also true that "No is of equal importance to Yes, and indeed is the precondition to saying Yes effectively. You cannot truly say Yes to one request if you cannot say No to others. No, in that sense, comes before Yes." I had never thought about it like that before, but it has been so true for me many times, and it was true for Arnold.

I've fallen foul of all of 'The Three-A Trap':

1. I've said Yes when I wanted to say No;
2. I've said No poorly;
3. I've avoided saying No by saying nothing at all.

And the times I've done this have never ended well.

I 'accommodated' with the first No. At work, I accommodated someone else's needs and demands over my own, which negatively impacted my personal relationships.

"Speak when you are angry, and you will make the best speech you will ever regret" (Ambrose Bierce). That was one of my very 'poor' second Nos.

And my third No, I 'avoided' because I didn't want to offend others. I pretended nothing was bothering me, when in fact, I was really annoyed by a colleague's behaviour – he really wasn't pulling his weight.

That actually led to my poor No, because I'd suppressed the resentment I'd been feeling for so long, so that when he asked, yet again, for me to cover for him, at the expense of time with Philippe, I lost it, and I said everything that had been bubbling up inside of me, and more. It wasn't pretty.

It happened early in my WorkLife, and I'm thankful for that because it made me determined not to fall into that trap again. It hasn't been easy, and I haven't always succeeded in all three areas. It's still a work in progress, but I have gotten better. So, I can really relate to Arnold's bad summer internship experience.

It's so true that the key to a positive No is respect. Because instead of accommodating as I had been doing, when I learnt to say No to unnecessary demands on my time, I gave respect to myself and what was important to me. In doing so, my Nos weren't or didn't become an attack or a poor No, and I didn't procrastinate over it, so there were no avoidance strategies on my part.

Saoirse: That's so true, Pascal. The book helped me in that way too. When Ury said he believed readers will obtain more value from the book if they keep in mind one challenging situation in their life in which they would like to say No. Encouraging readers to apply the process to their situation and use it to help develop an effective strategy. I did that. I said No to some of my personal writing.

Over the last year, my personal writing in my journal allowed me to work through things, and that was really important in being able to move forward in my WorkLife. But at some point, it started to become self-indulgent – a pity party for one – and that wasn't helping me to move forward. It was holding me back. So, I had to say No to self-indulgent writing that I kept to myself, and say Yes to putting my story out into the world, my life with Patrick, how alone and lonely I felt in my first year without him by my side, how I'm beginning to move on in my WorkLife.

I'm writing a book to tell my story because I believe it will help other people who have experienced loss, and it will also allow me to share Patrick's story because our stories as so intertwined. Keeping Patrick's memory alive is so important to me, and the book showed me a way to respect that, and in so doing, to give respect to myself.

Pascal: That's so lovely, Saoirse.

Through their heartfelt smiles, the rest of their group silently echoed Pascal's words.

Charlotte and her fellow wait staff arrived with their next tea stands. The second act was fruity and plain: buttery scones infused with Earl Grey tea, kept warm under a cloche, ready to be topped with lashings of Dorset clotted cream, and locally made raspberry, strawberry and wild blueberry jams.

"Does one put cream or jam first?" Benny asked.

"Always cream first," responded Maggie.

"Oh no, always jam first," Saoirse exclaimed. "Otherwise how are you going to spread it?"

Smiling, Charlotte said that unlike tea, scones are decided primarily by region. The Cornish way is jam first, then cream. The Devon way is cream first, then jam: "As you're having Dorset clotted cream and locally made jams, the choice is yours."

"Maggie, it seems we'll have to agree to disagree on the finer details of the 'proper etiquette' when it comes to our scones," Saoirse said.

Maggie, having already spread her scone with cream and was adding the jam, said, "It seems we do."

"These are rather moreish," commented Annie.

"Indeed, and these jams are rather delicious," said Benny, as he scraped the jar.

Charlotte, who had been attentive in a non-intrusive way, stopped to pour their tea and said second helpings were encouraged.

The look on their faces communicated what they were all thinking: we should say No, but if you insist, we'll say Yes; and Charlotte happily obliged.

A momentarily focussed jam- and cream-spreading silence followed as the group gave their afternoon tea experience the attention it deserved.

Maggie: My No to get to my higher Yes, is to myself. I feel I get in my own way, in that I'm closed to seeing opportunities. Even if they're presented to me on a plate, I don't see them, or I'm suspicious of them. I've always been self-reliant and independent. My parents said from a young age, I never wanted help. I always wanted to do things for myself. And I think that's good, but I also think I've blocked good people, good ideas, good opportunities because I always felt I had to create my own opportunities; and I still do, but I don't want to be so closed, I want to be more open. So, my No is to being closed, and my Yes is to being open. Because I think that will allow me to learn, grow and develop in my WorkLife, which is my higher Yes.

Florian: Do you know what your first Yes is going to be?

Maggie: It's a little abstract, which is totally taking me out of my comfort zone because I'm very detailed. Detail is important in my work, and I'm good at detail, and I think that's good. Although my family and friends would probably beg to differ because they think I obsess too much about detail outside of work. Anyway, I want to develop my soft skills because I think I can be too intense or pedantic, as I've been told on more than one occasion, and I think there's a power in soft skills that will help me to be able to lighten up, too. My mum says the arts are soft power, so I'm going to dabble a little in the soft power of the dramatic arts. There's a course I can do, which uses techniques from the performing arts in negotiation scenarios, and so my first Yes is to that.

Florian: That's really interesting, Maggie.

Benny: Yes, I like the sound of that. Is this course specifically designed for the Met police, or can anyone do it?

Maggie: We're bringing in a company that does this. I think they also run open programmes that individuals can attend. I can get details for you if you would like.

Benny: Yes, that would be great.

Annie: I'd like to find out more about the open programmes too.

Maggie: Sure.

Florian: Pascal, to pick up on your point about how Arnold said No to Dom and Rob keeping their jobs without destroying their relationships. I think this is also connected to what Ury says: "The single biggest mistake we make when we say No is to start from No. We derive our No from what we are against – the other's demand or behaviour. A positive No calls on us to do the exact opposite and base our No on what we are for. Instead of starting from No, start from Yes. Root your No in a deeper Yes – a Yes to your core interests and to what truly matters."

Arnold didn't make this mistake because on knowing he had to say No to them keeping their jobs, he was open to what he could do to help them. He didn't know what that was going to be, what he would be saying Yes to, but he had a sense that he could do something and a desire to do whatever that was. I suppose for me, that shows how the process in the book works. When we know we have to say No, but we don't know what our higher Yes is. A trust-it-and-it-will-come scenario, if you like.

Pascal: That's true, and it's true in many WorkLife negotiations. You say No to something because you know that's the right thing to do, but you don't know where or what that will lead to, or when it will lead to something, but somehow it usually leads to a higher Yes.

Maggie: I didn't understand the metaphor "going to the balcony". I got that the balcony is a detached state of mind anytime you choose. But when he said, "imagine yourself for a moment as an actor on a stage about to speak your lines – your No. Now picture yourself up on a balcony overlooking the stage, a place where you can see the scene clearly from afar. The balcony is a place of perspective, calm and clarity. From a balcony perspective, it is much easier to uncover the Yes behind your No." What I didn't get was why was speaking lines being the No. Surely for an actor, that would have been a Yes.

Saoirse: The actor's No wasn't clear to me either, but I understood the message to be about the importance of taking time out.

Pascal: Yes, and "these days the scarcest resource is time to think. Look for opportunities to go to the balcony whenever possible so that you can reflect on your Yes." Even though I also didn't get the actor's No, that served as a good reminder for me to not say a quick Yes, that I could come to regret.

Maggie: That's exactly what I mean – a teaching moment or what! I got so hung up on not understanding the actor's No, that I didn't see the bigger picture as you all have. Well, I did, but not as quickly as you did. I was being so pedantic in feeling the need to tie up all loose ends, I obsessed on that detail, so it took me longer to move beyond that to see the bigger picture.

Pascal smiled at Maggie.

Pascal: Detail is important too. In my work I've had to learn to adapt in how I communicate to people's preferred way of taking in information – detail or big picture. For me, it began from a place of awareness of knowing people have preferred ways of learning, because that's what taking in information is, which is what you've identified too. Once you have this awareness, then it becomes more of a natural process, or a way of thinking about things.

I liked how the book had served Arnold well in different Work-Life situations over the years: the lessons from his bad summer internship experience; the learning he needed to build from that and to rebuild his trust in himself and his leadership abilities; the wisdom of how to say No in support of a higher Yes in delivering the bad news. I think the prospect of having to say No triggered anxiety for him, and the book helped him to go out onto the balcony if you will.

Florian: Ury talked about "crystallising your Yes" and the practice of "distilling a single intention", which comes from your wants, needs and values. He said: "What can give real power to your No is to distil all your varied motivations into a single, concentrated intention – your YES." I think Arnold's Yes was to finding a way to support a way forward for both Dom and Rob in their WorkLives. It's true, going into the meetings, he didn't know how he would achieve his intention; but whether knowingly or not, he trusted the process, and it worked. Reading Arnold's story and the book, it sounds easy and straightforward – to believe and trust in the process, having blind faith if you like. Even if it is driven by your wants, needs and values, it's not always that easy to follow through, to say No to what you don't want in support of your higher Yes of what you do want.

Reading the book, the situation I applied the process to in order to help develop an effective strategy was around wanting to move with Elena to spend more time at our winery and vineyard with our children. I came to realise that it's never going to happen if I keep saying Yes to all of the great ideas and initiatives I'm involved in within my industry – mostly here in London, but some further afield too. These Yeses are aligned with my wants, needs and values, so they've always been an easy Yes and a higher Yes. And yet, they're also holding me back from saying my highest Yes of all: time with my family.

It's a realisation that has caused me conflict. I've realised I need to begin to say No to things that honour my wants, needs and values, to be able to say my highest Yes. And I feel conflicted about that, and so I don't think it's always as easy and straightforward to follow through. I talked it through with Elena, and we both feel we need to honour our highest Yes.

Being an artist, I think it will be easier for Elena; she has always been able to paint from wherever she's lived, and she already has a studio at our home in Spain. She's already thought about how she can continue her teaching work, and her work supporting her fellow artists, which is important to her; while I've always worked to give autonomy to the people who work with me, through the various initiatives I'm involved with helping people to be self-reliant. I think I could have done even more on those fronts. I think perhaps I liked an element of people relying on me, but that's the thing that has delayed my higher. Yes – and not just mine, but Elena's too.

I hadn't thought about it before, but my quick Yes to ideas and initiatives that aligned with my wants, needs and values, were selfish Yeses because they held Elena's highest Yes back. That realisation upset me. Elena has never said anything or pushed me on it, and that actually makes it even more upsetting because she has always supported my Yeses, at the cost of her higher Yes.

That was the realisation for me to know it's now time for me to respect and honour Elena's higher Yes – which of course, is also respecting my higher Yes. At the moment we spend 75 percent of our time in London and 25 percent in Spain. Our intention over the next year is to spend 50 percent in each place. The following year 75 percent of our time in Spain and 25 percent in London. Neither of us wants to sever ties completely with London. We may reduce our time here further, or we may find 25 percent of our time here works. We'll figure that out.

Saoirse: That will be a significant WorkLife change, Florian, and a positive one for you and Elena.

Florian: Thanks, and yes, I agree. Actually, Saoirse, you may be able to help me with something. Or a couple of things actually. The first is an initiative I've just become involved in to help out in getting it started. It's a one-month paid sabbatical programme where each year ten people will get to live their dream or give a dream and be given £10,000 to pursue whatever that is. The idea is to empower people within our industry to flourish in and out of the workplace by providing personal and professional growth opportunities. We want to elevate people to new perspectives to cultivate diverse and inclusive environments and to create great workplaces that work for all. We want to create a bright future for hospitality and let people know, now is the time to join. Perhaps you could help in raising awareness to this initiative and in time to tell the stories of each person who lives a dream or gives a dream.

The second is an initiative to help tell the stories of our street food vendors here in Shoreditch. At Spitalfields Market, at weekend markets – Columbia Road Flower Market, Brick Lane Market, Sunday Upmarket, Backyard Market, and new markets that are popping up all the time. We want to celebrate cultural diversity through the stories of each vendor. Our idea is to feature their signature recipe and to pair that with a portrait and a personal narrative.

Perhaps, Saoirse, you could help with interviews in helping them to tell their stories.

Benny, I'd really appreciate any wisdom you could share from the brand-strategy work you do.

Pascal, I'd also really appreciate any wisdom you could share, not to say No to these wonderful initiatives, but to take them on in a way, that perhaps I can consult on them. In a way that I can work to empowering others to do what is needed, and once that's achieved I can hand off on the project. Saying Yes to letting go and No to staying involved beyond that.

Annie, I'd appreciate your help with technical or social media support, to help share this idea/initiative.

Maggie, I'd appreciate your help with interviewing people.

Saoirse: What wonderful initiatives, Florian, that's an easy high Yes from me.

Pascal: These initiatives are so in line with your values and the values of your industry, Florian. The strong focus on serving your customers and also serving your workforce. I really like that, and it's an easy high Yes from me too.

Benny: That's an easy high Yes from me too.

When I was in New York, we ran a campaign that celebrated the cultural diversity of our city through our street-food vendors and their stories. We helped them to share their personal stories and also the stories of their cuisines. The stories of American immigrants and the role they played in the business of food in New York.

We also spoke to their customers, who are part of the constantly unfolding street theatre of street food. They sit or sometimes stand, but they always mingle and talk. We observed lots of people, lots of cultural interaction, lots of stories. Because everybody's got something interesting to say, and food is a great way to engage. Because you've got to put something in your mouth, and when you do, your ears are open to listening.

Food has always tied communities together. I can talk from my experience as a New Yorker, but I think the history of immigration defines a very open culture throughout cities of the world.

New Yorkers, by definition, are an optimistic lot. Because the fact is that the vast majority of New Yorkers have emigrated from somewhere else, whether from another country or from another part of the United States. When you think about the act of immigration, it's an act of optimism and resilience. New Yorkers are tough because of that. That's why New Yorkers always bounce back, whether after 9/11 or after the financial crisis. If people were to write New York's obituary after those events, it would say that New York always bounces back because of its optimism and resilience.

I believe it's the same for London. Immigrants who come here are also optimistic and resilient. The noise and the buzz, and the energy of the city is what attracts people to cities like New York and London. And that's also what defines the great cities of the world, and that's what keep people coming. These are the stories that need to be told. These are the stories that will be valuable not only to future historians but also to anyone curious to listen to today.

Annie: It's a high Yes from me too. I can also be a runner and do anything else that's needed.

Maggie: And a high Yes from me. I'm also happy to be a runner, and do anything else that's needed.

Florian: Thank you so much everyone. Your support will help me get to my high Yes with confidence that I'm honouring all of my Yeses.

Oh, and it goes without saying you're all invited to come and stay when we do get to Spain, Our restaurant can be our destination for our first international WorkLife Book Club chapter.

They all raised their cups to the next chapter of Florian's Worklife and a new international chapter to their Book Club.

The third act was perhaps the most spectacular, as Charlotte arrived with the silver glided cake carriage, on which they all feasted their eyes. The sumptuous cakes included gooey apricot and pistachio cakes, Victoria sponges, salted caramel éclairs, lavender coconut macaroons, tiny red velvet cupcakes filled with hundreds and thousands, sunflower salt tea cakes, slices of chocolate and raspberry filled Swiss roll, and more. The miniature puddings included baked apple cheesecakes, fruit trifles, fluffy Eton messes, sticky date puddings, seasonal fruit and bite-sized pavlovas, and more.

This huge display of sweets, that were as brilliantly retro as they were modern, was wheeled around so that guests could make their own selection, or indeed choose to indulge in them all.

Appreciating the beauty of the cakes and deciding which one to taste first, Florian said:

Florian: There is a very skilled art in creating such an iconic experience as afternoon tea, and the skill in keeping its authenticity lies with the staff who create the experience, keeping it a treat while also keeping it real.

Saoirse: Yes, and there is an art to feeling looked after, and here that art has been perfected.

Pascal: The attention to detail is excellent. There's a charismatic charm resonating through all the little touches, from the interiors that create the ambience to the exquisite flavours of these cakes. It's all these combined details that will hold the memory for people.

Benny: Afternoon tea has captured the imagination of people everywhere in the world. There is a theatre to it, and right now, this trolley is the stage.

Annie: It feels special to go out for afternoon tea. And these vegan cakes and puddings are an impressive feat without butter, eggs or milk.

Maggie: It's so good you'll find your head goes on autopilot to nod Yes in agreement to the offer of a second helping, while the voice inside your head is screaming NO. I don't think I've ever experienced that phenomenon before.

They all smiled through cake-filled mouths.

Pascal: Your change will be a positive change for sure, Florian. Family is so important. Speaking of which, Philippe and I have said Yes to starting a family together.

Maggie: Whaaaaaat! That's super news.

The group turned their gaze of excited anticipation towards Pascal, eagerly awaiting what else he was going to share. Pascal laughed at their somewhat intense focus on him.

Pascal: Philippe and I read the book with a combined focus on the situation we wanted to apply the process to in helping develop an effective strategy. We have a wonderful life together, and we love our life, but over the last year or perhaps two, we've felt there was something missing. We both love children, but despite us being together for so long, we never discussed having children of our own.

My company introduced an adoption programme a couple of years ago. Helping people who wanted to become parents through adoption to make it happen. This was mostly taken up by couples but didn't exclude single people. The wonderful thing for me was that it is as much for same-sex couples as it is for opposite-sex couples. I shared what my company was doing with Philippe, and he thought it was wonderful too. But not in a way that either of us said we wanted to do it, just that it was a wonderful thing. However, I think it planted a seed for both of us, which has grown over the last year. Last summer, when we holidayed with our families, our siblings and their children, we knew we also wanted our own little family.

Working through the book, we learnt we need to say No to just being us and Yes to being a family. I think we held off because the adoption process was daunting to us. So we kept saying Yes to things that were wonderful, experiences that kept us busy and occupied but kept our minds off what we really wanted: saying Yes to welcoming a child into our lives.

The great thing about the adoption programme is that it helps with the application and courts process. It covers all costs, as well as offering one-year parental leave. Philippe and I are going to share the parental leave, and his company are fully on board with that. We don't know how long it will take as we're only beginning the process. But once we welcome our child, after the first year, we're considering moving back to France to be close to our families, and we're figuring out how each of us can adapt our WorkLife, so that one of us can be home with our child, and hopefully in time children. There's no limit on the number of children for the adoption programme.

Annie: Wow, that's just amazing Pascal, congratulations to you both.

They all clinked their cups to Pascal, Philippe and their hopefully soon new arrival.

Pascal: It makes me proud to be part of my company. The adoption support alone is wonderful, but it's a lot more than that. It's their willingness to help Philippe and me to achieve a dream we want so much.

Maggie: So much good news tonight. This is all so wonderful and so exciting.

Pascal: Ah yes, but we digress in delivering our good news. We seem to be talking around the case and book this evening, or it seems it's bringing up a lot for each of us personally – which is rather nice, actually.

Annie: Yes, I like that too. But I do have a question about the case. I think how Arnold delivered the news and then followed through on what would happen next – how he could help both Dom and Rob – was really good. Was there anything he needed to have done differently? I ask because I've never had to deliver bad news, nor have I ever been on the receiving end of bad news.

Pascal: Yes, Annie, it was really good; and because Arnold did a good job in delivering bad news, Dom and Rob accepted his No. That doesn't always happen, which is why as Ury says, it's important to have a backup plan. Especially in negotiations, and that's true of companies and individuals within companies. The example in the book where there was a feeling of demoralisation and hopelessness in the company in being able to stand up for their rights, when they were tied into a contract with their one and only supplier, who were behaving badly, is not at all uncommon.

And as in the book, no matter how dire things are, coming up with a backup plan helps give confidence. The backup plan may not be great, but once it's good enough, it's well, good enough to help transform negatively charged emotions of fear and resignation into resolve and determination.

For a workforce, knowing they have a backup plan is empowering. And it's the same for individuals, even if that backup plan is to quit their job if their No to the situation or behaviour unacceptable to them is not heard. That's pretty big, but when enough is enough, when people have taken all they can take when they know they've made a decision that's right for them if their No isn't heard, that gives them confidence in knowing they now have a choice.

Maggie: Actually, the story in that chapter of the book, about one of the first passenger planes to fly after the horrifying attacks of 9/11. When the pilot announced to the fearful passengers: "If anyone stands up and is trying to take over the plane, stand up together, take whatever you have and throw it at their heads. You have to aim for their faces, so they have to defend themselves. We the people will not be defeated." If, in that situation, at that time, people can come together to avoid defeat, then in most situations, people can.

Benny: Yes, but sometimes it takes something so bad, so terrifying, to remember that. There was also a line from a story in that chapter that said, "We all too often forget that there are others in the room, too." The story was about students, which related to Arnold's story. He could have said, "Help me, friends." And cried out to his fellow students. "Although the master with the stick may be more powerful than the student, he is not more powerful than all the students put together."

Annie: The question Ury proposed to ask ourselves: "Who shares my interests or might be persuaded to work with me to make sure my needs are respected?" The book gives the example of how if you're faced with an abusive boss, it helps to gather support so that collectively you can confront the boss about his behaviour. It's helpful to remember we're not alone, but I agree we can forget that. I think for Arnold, he felt the responsibility lay with him as the chosen leader, but over time he's come to ask for help and support, as he did with his colleague Tom. It's a good reminder for sure, both in and out of the workplace, whether with colleagues or friends and family.

Benny: I also think the "Consider the Worst Case Scenario" Ury suggests to be good. Thinking in advance by asking yourself: "What is the worst thing the other can do if you say No to them?" As he says: "If they're not going to literally kill me, then I'm probably going to survive. I'll be OK."

Annie: True, but what Frank Barron said is also true: "Never take a person's dignity: it is worth everything to them, and nothing to you." That was true for Arnold in his summer internship experience.

Benny: Yes, that's true too. I think in learning that respect was his greatest motivation, Arnold also learnt that "You give respect to the other not so much because of who they are but because of who you are. Respect is an expression of yourself and your values."

Which brings me in a roundabout way to the challenging situation in my life that I would like to say No to, and develop an effective strategy to say Yes to what I want.

When I was going through the twelve steps, I threw myself into my work. I said Yes to everything that came my way, and I said No to social engagements, both at work and outside of work. I didn't want to put myself in a situation where I would be tempted to drink and fall off the wagon. It was my way to protect my sobriety. Our meetings have been the most sociable thing I have done for a long, long time. And they've helped me realise that I can do it, I can have a good time socially and not need a drink. I haven't felt I've been missing out by not drinking, and the dry drinking scene is actually pretty exciting.

My No is to taking on the workload I have been taking on in

support of my higher Yes to a social life. I love social events, and my inner social animal is ready to come out to party.

I joke, but actually, it's more than that. I'd like to meet someone. I've been on my own for a long time now. But I'm an old romantic at heart, and I like to believe there's someone special out there for me.

In the first year of recovery, beginning romantic relationships is discouraged. This is because the priority needs to be staying sober. There's so much going on. It's an emotional rollercoaster. And after that, I felt I needed to get to know myself better, and I needed to do that before I got to know someone else. But now, I feel ready to rebuild my life and get back some of the things I have lost. Through you all, I've built new friendships that are so important to me. It's also important to me that I have been able to bring new friends into my life and build good friendships from that. I doubted I could do that because I had destroyed so many good friendships. Now I want to, hopefully, bring romance and love into my life and build that relationship too.

Annie: That's so lovely, Benny, and I believe there is someone very special out there for you, who will be very lucky to have you in their life. Here's to romance and love.

They all raised their cups to romance and love.

Charlotte and her fellow wait staff arrived with more plates and glasses of bubbly.

Charlotte said, "Florian let us know that you're celebrating Benny's birthday, and in honour of that, we've prepared our special carrot cake spiced with cinnamon and smooth rhubarb compote, which is best served with a glass of fizz."

"Oh, wow, this is so amazing," Benny said. "Thank you so much."

Charlotte smiled as the group once again raised their glasses in wishing Benny a happy birthday.

"This is definitely the final act because it's going to finish me off," said Maggie.

"Where do all the ideas for the wonderful food we've experienced this evening come from?" asked Saoirse.

Charlotte said the team are from different parts of the world, and when they each go home or on holiday to somewhere different they're asked to bring something back so they can try it. There might be something that they grew up eating or something they discover as their tastes evolve. She went on to say that she's Austrian, and the first thing she does when she goes home is to go to her local café for a plate of apple strudel, which she loves, but she's now also appreciating all of their other wonderful pastries with more refined tastebuds.

She said their philosophy is that food and travel are the best ways to experience different cultures. In bringing those experiences to their menu, they're enriching the experience of afternoon tea while honouring the British tradition and an ever-evolving culture. They all share a purpose to be ever-evolving and to be a place where they pour their collective creative energy to collaborate on what they're passionate about. This is so as to provide a memorable experience for all their guests that will remain with them long after their last sip of tea as they step out into the afternoon or evening air, oftentimes taking a leisurely stroll through the streets of Shoreditch to walk off that last slice of cake, "Which," said Charlotte, "almost 'did them in'".

Charlotte smiled at Maggie on those last words before walking away.

Maggie (laughing): I'm not sure if Charlotte realised, but she just paraphrased what I said in cockney slang. Is that an evolution or a merging of cultures?

Annie: Talking about a merging of cultures and secondments too, my family is a merging of cultures. My mum is Scottish, and my dad is Canadian. They were quite free spirits. When they first met, they had an old VW camper van and travelled throughout Europe before they settled in Scotland, and I came along. My dad had an accident when I was very young, which left him in a wheelchair. He's quite able and has lived a full life, but their camper van days ended when he had the accident. My mum could have driven but didn't; I'm not sure why. I think maybe it would have been too painful for my dad. I know my dad always wanted to show me the countryside he grew up in, which brings me to my secondment.

We can take one month's secondment at work, over and above our annual leave. I plan to rent a wheelchair-accessible RV to take my parents through Canada, to experience all the places my dad wanted to show me. It's unpaid leave, and so I need to come up with the money to pay for it – which brings me to my higher Yes, which is to develop a side hustle idea I have. I'm a bit of a geek when it comes to things like spreadsheets and databases, and when I was at uni I made extra money by designing software to help streamline different processes for different companies. Mostly small and medium-sized companies as they began to grow. I plan to say Yes to opportunities to do this and No to anything that will take my time and energy away from it. It means a lot for me to do this trip with my parents, and I hope I can do it next year. I need to generate interest in my proposed side hustle, so it's all a little uncertain. I just know I was able to do it before, and I'm hoping I can replicate that somehow.

Pascal: That's such a lovely thing you want to do with your parents, and such a good idea for your side hustle too. I'd like to understand it more because I'm sure I will be able to connect you with people who would benefit from streamlining their processes.

Florian: I think I could too, and I would like to understand it better.

Benny: Me too.

Saoirse: I'm not sure I could connect you with anyone, but I'd like to understand it better, then if I come across someone who needs it, I can recommend it. Or I could write a story about how you've helped someone's business. I have a lot of followers on my blog, and it may be of interest to someone.

Maggie: I'm not sure how I can help, but I'd like to in whatever way I can.

Annie: Thank you all so much. I really appreciate and it will take up your offers of help and support.

EPILOGUE

Annie: That's what I'm taking from this evening. Whatever situation we're in – whether it's bad, or we have to deliver bad news, or it's good, or a potentially good situation – we don't have to do it all on our own. It's OK to ask for help.

Pascal: What about everyone else? What did you take from this evening?

Maggie: Allow plenty of time. Afternoon tea is a wonderfully drawn-out affair, and there's so much food, you'll need to pace yourself and wear an elasticated skirt or trousers. Oh, did you mean the case, Pascal?

Pascal laughed.

Maggie: My take away from the case is, sometimes it's the villains of a story – in Arnold's case, the people at the school of his summer internship – that start people on a path to something better. For Arnold, that was initially to know what he didn't want – his No to working for a company or with people who didn't respect him, and his Yes to a company and people who did. But actually, it was more than that. The growth he gained from that bad experience which took him so far out of his comfort zone, was invaluable. That's important because we can all be crushed by people or situations, and it's good to know we can recover and build ourselves and our WorkLives back stronger. And in so doing, we can do the same for the people we work with, which is what Arnold went on to do throughout his WorkLife. We can be heroes in our own stories and in other people's stories.

Benny: My takeaway is that things that happen in our WorkLife can come close to destroying us, but that there is always a way to rebuild ourselves and come back stronger.

When bad things go down, good things can happen because it forces us to do something else. And before we grab onto the future, we need to let go of the past.

Florian: Sharing bad news is not easy. Learn to be straightforward in saying the toughest stuff. Listen and work through people's responses and say what you're going to do next. And remember both personally and professionally to be ever mindful of our higher Yes, put it at the forefront of every decision and trust in the process.

Pascal: Every worthwhile chapter in our WorkLives will have its challenges. In difficult times, it can be easy to get fixated on how bad things are and forget why we said Yes to the job in the first place. If we can go home at the end of the day feeling good about the decisions we've made at work, then that's a sign that the challenge is something we need to weather. And if we can't, then that's a sign that it's time to consider a move and say No to what is no longer working and Yes to the next chapter of our WorkLife.

Saoirse: The past is still everywhere, and that's good. It's made us who we are, today, in this present moment. The future, which hasn't been written yet, is looking good too.

Saoirse's words were the perfect summation of their evening's discussion, and they raised their glasses in a toast to the past, present and a good looking future.

Afterword

From their respective streets of Shoreditch Annie, Benny, Florian, Maggie, Pascal and Saorise bid you adieu and leave you with a final assignment to ponder over your accompaniment of choice as they close the first six cases of the Shoreditch Chapter of the WorkLife Book Club.

Getting to your Higher Yes Assignment

What is your higher Yes?

What do you need to learn to say No to in order to create space for the higher Yes in your WorkLife?

Let's Keep Reading and Talking ...

My hope is that this book will be the beginning of many more WorkLife Book Club stories to come. I want to continue the stories of the characters you met in the Shoreditch Chapter of the WorkLife Book Club. And I want to begin to tell you the stories of new characters in newly launched WorkLife Book Club Chapters from whatever part of the world they take place.

I'm working to create resources to help you start and continue your own WorkLife Book Club Chapter should you wish to. These will be in the form of a *Learning Through Reading* series – stories inspired by real WorkLife struggles and successes, presented as case studies for group discussion. The case and the accompanying recommended book will be required reading for each meeting, and will help to frame the subsequent discussion. These resources will be available from my website.

If you do start your own WorkLife Book Club Chapter, I would love to hear about it. You can contact me through my website: https://schoolofworklife.com/contact/

Guidelines for Starting and Running your WorkLife Book Club

The WorkLife Book Club is designed for people who work for the same company, for people who work at different companies, for people who are flying solo (self-employed freelancers, contractors, consultants, side-hustlers, business owners), people who are not working (people who are taking time out), and people who are retired (who although no longer part of the workforce, have curious minds, and a desire to maintain mental stimulation through discussing case studies of WorkLife struggles and successes, and the wisdom that can be gleaned from books). The connecting factor is that members have a love of reading and enjoy learning through reading.

Whether your WorkLife Book Club is going to take place in person at your workplace, remotely via an online meeting platform or in a more social setting, the following guidelines will help you establish your WorkLife Book Club Chapter:

- Decide on a regular meeting time – as a suggestion, monthly is good – but meetings can be closer together or further apart as appropriate to the group's WorkLife needs and demands, while allowing time to read the case study and accompanying book (the prerequisite reading for the School Of WorkLife book club meetings);
- The optimum length of the meeting needs to fit in with the group's needs – i.e. if it needs to fit in around a lunch hour, allow time to get from and back to work. If there are no time restraints, longer meetings may work better for members;
- The optimum number of members can vary. As a suggestion, if numbers go above ten, consider setting up two or more groups. Also, a group can be as small as two people;
- Meet over food and drink (this applies for remote meetings too)

– it can be anything from coffee or tea and cake, to slices of pizza and beer or wine, to a potluck supper, to canapés and cocktails, to recipes from a specific cookbook, to cuisine from a particular culture;

- At the first meeting (or before), to help people get to know each other in the context of reading, a good question to ask everyone is: *What do you enjoy about reading?*;
- Take turns to choose the WorkLife case study and featured book;
- When reading the case study and accompanying book, noting particular areas of interest is good practice – simply highlighting them on the page or making brief bullet point notes is sufficient;
- Begin the meeting by having the person who chose the case study read it aloud;
- At the end of the meeting, each person summarises the WorkLife lesson they took from the experience – the case study, the book, the discussion;
- It is good practice for the person choosing the WorkLife case study and featured book for the next meeting to let everyone know their choice before wrapping up the meeting.

Below are suggested questions for people to ponder while reading the case study and book. These can also help to structure the discussion and to keep the flow going – if needed. Feel free to add your own. And please note there are no hard and fast rules – dip in and out as and if you see fit.

QUESTIONS TO PONDER

What are the main themes of the story?

What are the underlying themes of the story?

Can I connect to aspects of the story through my WorkLife story? (my experiences)

Do I have thoughts and emotions that are consistent with the storyline?

Am I having emotional responses and insights into the character's emotions?

Are there valid and competing viewpoints that I find interesting?

Was there anything that caused me to look at things differently?

Has anything brought about thoughts or ideas for change?

Has anything brought about thoughts or ideas for remaining constant?

Does the reading apply to my WorkLife? If so, how?

Does the reading apply to my organisation/network? If so, how?

What did I enjoy about the book?

What did I enjoy about the case study?

What was my impression of the protagonist of the story? (sometimes, there can be more than one protagonist)

What was my impression of the antagonist of the story? (sometimes, there can be more than one antagonist)

What were the struggles and successes for the protagonist?

How did the book wisdom help the protagonist?

Were there support characters? If so, what was my impression of them?

Who were the heroes in the story? (heroes can sometimes be abstract, e.g. circumstances)

Who were the villains in the story? (villains can sometimes be abstract, e.g. circumstances)

What piqued my curiosity?

Where did the reading take my imagination?

These are generic questions to help enhance the learning-through-reading experiences (and the flow of conversation, if needed). They can help develop a rhythm and flow as a group. In the beginning, they may be helpful to guide different areas, but it's also OK to go with the flow and see where that takes you. A more structured or a more free-flowing approach is up to you individually and/or collectively as a group to figure out what works best for each and all of you.

It's important to remember that nothing is set in stone and that there will be meetings where people say more and other meetings where those same people say less. It doesn't have to be precisely measured – just fairly balanced. The important thing is that everyone has an opportunity to speak while not feeling forced to do so or to say more or to be shut down to say less. Mutual respect among members in listening and speaking will help get the balance right. This is not a place for hard and fast rules. This is a place for a relaxed and enjoyable discussion.

And finally: make it easy for people to participate.

Many companies have book programmes that people who enjoy learning through reading can tap into. It's quite simple: the company covers the cost of the books and, if relevant, accompanying case studies. This represents a meaningful investment by the company to support people who enjoy learning through reading to continuously learn, develop and grow personally and professionally in their WorkLife.

Happy Reading and Happy Learning.

Carmel

References

All of the gallery stories in Interlude 4 were adapted from their respective websites.

Information about the Art Pavilion and Mile End Park was adapted from Tower Hamlets website.

Alex Sainsbury's story was adapted from 'Close-up Alex Sainsbury' by Lena Corner, *The Independent,* 18th July 2013.

The story of Petticoat Lane was adapted from 'Petticoat Lane gets a makeover with its own festival – after 500 years' by Mike Brooke, *East London Advertiser*, 21st May 2021.

The Alternative London Bike Tour Experience was informed by their website, www.alternativeldn.co.uk.

Madame Clicquot and Yayoi Kusama's stories and the story of Veuve Clicquot La Grande Dame 2012 by Yayoi Kusama was informed by their respective brand websites.

Illustrations

Bibliography and Resources

Bibliography

- Anderson, Hamish. *Vino: Great Wine for Everyday Life* (Century, 2003)
- Arden, Paul. *It's Not How Good You Are, It's How Good You Want To Be* (Phaidon Press, 2003)
- Blanchard, Ken and McBride, Margaret. *The One Minute Apology* (HarperCollins, 2003)
- Carey, David and Clark Carey, Rebecca. *The Vocal Arts Workbook: A Practical Course for Developing the Expressive Range of Your Voice* (Methuen Drama, 2008)
- Galley, Timothy. *The Inner Game Of Work* (Villard Books, 1997)
- Sandberg, Sheryl. *Lean In* (W. H. Allen, 2013)
- Ury, William. *The Power Of A Positive No* (Bantam Dell, 2007)

Resources

I am also grateful to the following TV shows, podcasts, publications and learning platform from which I get so much inspiration.

TV SHOWS

Anthony Bourdain: *Parts Unknown*, *No Reservations* and *The Layover.*
BBC 2 Production: *Remarkable Places to Eat*, Presented by Fred Sirieix.

PODCASTS

Big Questions with Cal Fussman
Design Matters with Debbie Millman
Radical Candor The Podcast
Side Hustle School with Chris Guillebeau
The Growth Show by HubSpot
The Tim Ferriss Show
Work Life with Adam Grant

PUBLICATIONS & NEWSLETTERS

Derek Sivers
Fast Company
First Round Review
Forbes
Harvard Business Review
Hubspot Inc
Seth Godin
The Do Lectures
Wired

LEARNING PLATFORM

www.masterclass.com

INDEX

About the Author

Carmel O' Reilly is the founder of School Of WorkLife.

She was born and grew up in Ireland, and now lives in Shoreditch, London.

Her work and subsequently her first book, *Your WorkLife Your Way,* and its companion workbook, focus on helping people live their best WorkLives by managing their learning, development and growth, through effective self-feedback, insightful questions and the ability to shape and tell their unique story.

Her *School of WorkLife* book series tells WorkLife stories of the obstacles, failures and successes people encountered in their WorkLife. Each book includes the exercises that helped navigate these situations, which are presented as assignments for readers to work through and adapt to their challenging WorkLife situations.

Her books are designed to help you gain insight and inspiration in your chosen area of WorkLife, and then support you in achieving what is important to you in your WorkLife learning, development and growth. You will learn to recognise and take ownership of your strengths and potential, as well as assessing your challenges to determine where you are stuck, to then uncover solutions to move forward.

You can connect with Carmel through her website www.schoolofworklife.com, where you can sign up to receive stories that are grounded in the reality of real situations of the ups and downs people experience in their WorkLife. People's incredible stories designed to be helpful, insightful and inspiring.

Also by Carmel O' Reilly

Your WorkLife Your Way (book and workbook)
School Of WorkLife Book Series:

- How To Make Your Values Matter
- How To Use Your Purpose To Help Others
- How To Drive Your Vision and Motivated Abilities
- How To Live True To Who You Really Are
- How To Build Your True Personal Brand Identity
- How To Use Your Voice To Express and Protect Your Identity
- How To Pursue The Superpower of Happiness
- How To Embrace The Superpower of Self-Awareness
- How To Fine-Tune The Superpower of Observation
- How To Plan Effectively Professionally and Personally
- How To Be Autonomous In Your Development and Growth
- How To Self-Coach, Direct and Lead Effectively
- How To Use Turning Points To Start Something Different and Better
- How To Build Your Life Around What Engages and Inspires You
- How To Be Creative In Your Thinking
- How To Get To Self-Realisation and Self-Acceptance
- How To Overcome Self-Doubt Through Self-Appreciation
- How To Successfully Invent and Reinvent Yourself
- How To Recover From Rejection and Build Strong Resilience
- How To Apologise With Humility, Sincerity and Integrity
- How To Motivate Through Self-Respect and Trust
- How To Overcome Your Fear To Live Your Life With Courage
- How To Let Curiosity Be Your Driving Force
- How To Be Vulnerable and Courageous
- How To Overcome Self-Sabotage
- How To Start Something New In Difficult Times
- How To Turn Your Story Into a Powerful Presentation

School of WorkLife

The idea behind School of WorkLife is a simple one and follows a Guiding Statement that I wrote when I embarked on my journey as a WorkLife learning practitioner and writer.

MY GUIDING STATEMENT

To help people pursue their WorkLives with greater clarity, purpose, passion and pride, by creating continuous WorkLife learning programmes and resources that are accessible to everyone.

www.schoolofworklife.com

About the Artist

Ian Remedios is a learning and development professional with a love for graphic novels and pop culture. Through sketchnoting, he has managed to merge his two passions by designing sketchnotes on human resources, management, and learning and development topics, using pop culture references, creating a fun and accessible way to learn and retain information.

He also loves doing ink sketches of urban landscapes and experimenting with traditional inking techniques.

You can find his sketchnotes on his website, www.lndtips.com.

Also published by Amaurea Press

Anna Lidia Vega Serova, *Un Jardín en Miniatura (A Miniature Garden).* Poetry (Spanish original with English translation), accompanied by photography by Gonzalo Vidal

Anna Lidia Vega Serova, *Sideways Glance*. Short stories from Cuba

Jonathan Curry-Machado, *Cuba: Living Between Hurricanes.*

Amaurea is a London-based independent creative production company, specialising in publishing and film media. Amaurea Press undertakes all aspects of book editing, design and publication, working in creative partnership with our authors.

Contact us at publications@amaurea.co.uk

www.amaurea.co.uk

www.ingramcontent.com/pod-product-compliance
Ingram Content Group UK Ltd.
Pitfield, Milton Keynes, MK11 3LW, UK
UKHW041831200726
13854UKWH00002BA/980